World Faiths Today

Miss Timmins

CW01651647

World Faiths Today

teachers' handbook for
World Faiths Today Series
a religious education programme for
key stage two

Tania ap Siôn, Leslie J Francis and Diane Drayson
with illustrations by
Phillip Vernon

Canolfan Genedlaethol Addysg Grefyddol
Welsh National Centre for Religious Education

Welsh National Centre for Religious Education
Bangor University
Bangor
Gwynedd LL57 2PZ
Wales UK

First published 2009

Sponsored by the Welsh Assembly Government

British Library Cataloguing-in-Publication Data
A catalogue record for this book is available from the British Library.

ISBN 978-1-85357-192-3

Printed and bound in Wales by Gwasg Dwyfor

CONTENTS

PREFACE

The *World Faiths Today Series* has its origins in the Welsh language and bilingual classroom commissioning programme of the Qualifications, Curriculum and Assessment Authority for Wales (ACCAC), which is now the Department of Children, Education, Lifelong Learning and Skills (DCELLS). Set in this context, the series has been written with the explicit aim of supporting religious education at key stage two as reflected in the National Exemplar Framework for Religious Education for 3 to 19-year-olds in Wales. The breadth of coverage in the series and a focus on developing skills makes the series equally relevant to religious education in England and the non-statutory national framework for religious education.

The project has been overseen by a monitoring group appointed by the commissioning body, and has been trialled in both Welsh and English medium schools in Wales. We wish to record our gratitude to Denize Morris (RE Subject Officer, DCELLS) and the monitoring group for their advice and support, to the teachers and pupils who trialled the material, to the faith communities who helped us with our research, to Father Deiniol, Dr Nathan Abrams, Professor Gareth Lloyd Jones, and members of the Practical Theology Research Group who read and commented on the story book texts and pictures, to Nant Roberts and Tegid Roberts who worked with us on the Welsh language editions of the material, and to Phillip Vernon who visited the faith communities with us and who inspired us with his illustrations.

Tania ap Siôn, Leslie J Francis and Diane Drayson
St Mary's Centre
St Deiniol's Library
Church Lane
Hawarden
Flintshire CH5 3DF

Autumn 2008

WORLD FAITHS TODAY SERIES

A story-based programme for RE

In 2003 Leslie J Francis and Diane Drayson authored the *Exploring Christian Special Places Series* for key stage one pupils. The series follows two young children called Aled and Siân as they explore six very different churches and chapels in Wales and learn about the Christian year, Christian life, and Christian service. Through six story books and a teachers' handbook, Aled and Siân learn that the country in which they live has been heavily shaped by the Christian tradition, a tradition which is still significant in the twenty-first century.

Building on this foundation, the *World Faiths Today Series* for key stage two pupils broadens this exploration further. The series follows two young children called Rees and Sara as they celebrate the diversity of religious belief and practice in Wales with their friends from Buddhist, Christian, Jewish, Hindu, Muslim, and Sikh traditions. Through seven story books and a teachers' handbook, Rees and Sara learn how religious beliefs relate to practice and they begin to think about their own responses to the issues raised.

Developing skills in RE

The *World Faiths Today Series* has been written to support the *National Exemplar Framework for Religious Education for 3 to 19-year-olds in Wales*, a guidance document for local education authorities and agreed syllabus conferences. The exemplar framework for religious education has been welcomed by SACREs across Wales as a document which can be adopted or adapted by local agreed syllabus conferences when they produce their locally agreed syllabi for religious education.

In line with the other subjects in the revised curriculum for Wales, the defining characteristic of the exemplar framework for religious education is its skills-based approach to learning. A range of contexts is studied by pupils with the aim of developing three interrelated skills:

- engaging with fundamental questions
- exploring religious beliefs, teachings and practice(s)
- expressing personal responses.

The same skills-based approach is reflected in the *World Faiths Today Series*. The series begins with the exploration of 'religious beliefs, teachings and practice(s)', which raises 'fundamental questions', and stimulates pupils to express their 'personal responses'.

The exemplar framework for religious education also provides guidance on pupil assessment through the provision of level descriptions for religious education. With reference to the level descriptions, the *World Faiths Today Series* helps teachers to assess pupils' progress in religious education by providing opportunities to:

- discuss questions raised by life and aspects of religion;
- name and describe selected religious beliefs, teachings, and practices;
- explain through examples the relationship between religious beliefs and practice(s);
- discuss their own views and the views of others in relation to the themes and issues covered, and relate these to their own lives;
- relate symbol to meaning in religious contexts.

Rees and Sara

Rees and Sara have friends who are practising members of seven different faith communities. Many of the friends attend the same school as Rees and Sara, some live in the same street, while others are met on holiday. Rashid and Fatima are Sunni Muslims; Dan and Rebecca are Reform Jews; Anna and Michael are Orthodox Christians; Tomos and Bethan are Anglicans; Hana and James are Mahayana Buddhists; Sanjit and Yasmin are Sikhs, and Rajeev and Meena are Hindus. These friends introduce Rees and Sara to their places of worship, their religious festivals, their sources of religious authority, their understanding of care for others and the world, and their distinctive foods. They also make the important point that diversity in belief and practice occurs in each of the faith traditions.

As Rees and Sara learn more about what their friends believe and practice, they begin to know and understand them better. Rees and Sara are also challenged to think about the things that are important to them, and to start sharing these with their friends.

The World Faiths Today Series

The seven chapters of the teachers' handbook have been designed to support Rees and Sara's seven different adventures. Each chapter contains three types of material: background information for teachers; classroom activities, and a series of worksheets.

The background information for teachers includes:

- a summary of the story;
- aims and learning outcomes;
- basic introductory information about the religion;
- detailed information relating to each of the five themes (place of worship, festival, authority, caring for others and the world, and food);
- keywords.

Classroom activities and worksheets develop pupils' understanding and responses to specific aspects of each theme, and support the non-statutory *Skills framework for 3 to 19-year-olds in Wales* by developing thinking, communication, ICT, and number skills relevant for key stage two. In addition, the activities and worksheets have been devised to contribute to learners' spiritual, moral, cultural, mental, and physical development from a religious education perspective (Aspects of religious education), as defined by the *National Exemplar Framework for Religious Education for 3 to 19-year-olds in Wales*, pp10-11.

Using the series

The series offers a flexible resource which teachers can use in a variety of ways. Each story book and handbook chapter covers one faith tradition, clearly divided into five main themes relevant for religious education. This allows for a religion to be studied systematically, or for selected themes to be studied across the faith traditions.

Using the worksheets

Each handbook chapter contains 14 worksheets that can be used in a flexible way, depending on teachers' preferences. Worksheets could be photocopied for individual use, scanned for class planning on an interactive whiteboard, or photo-enlarged for use in small groups. Some sheets are referred to by name in the Activities section but in most cases the use is left to the teacher. In each handbook chapter you will find that the footnotes on the worksheets give guidance as to which chapter they relate to. 'Worship' relates to chapter 1; 'Celebration' relates to chapter 2; 'Authority' relates to chapter 3; 'Environment' relates to chapter 4; 'Food' relates to chapter 5; 'Vocabulary', 'ICT' and 'Miscellaneous' can be used at any time.

Supporting learning across the curriculum

As defined by the *National Exemplar Framework for Religious Education for 3 to 19-year-olds in Wales*, the *World Faiths Today Series* supports learning across the curriculum through promoting learners' 'knowledge and understanding of Wales, their personal and social development and well-being, and their awareness of the world of work'.

The series contributes fully to the Curriculum Cymreig from a religious education perspective by providing opportunities for learners to appreciate:

> the significance, value and impact of the rich Christian heritage and dynamic multi-faith composition of Wales past and present. By using a range of stimulating resources from the locality learners are challenged to ask fundamental questions about meaning and the purpose of life, and the significance and impact of religion and religious thinking on twenty-first century society. Such insight supports social cohesion, cultural/religious awareness and cooperation within society and individual communities. (*National Exemplar Framework*, p. 8)

The series contributes fully to personal and social education from a religious education perspective by providing opportunities for learners to explore:

> the spiritual, moral, social and cultural dimensions. Learners develop understanding of and respect for the various world religions and explore how religion impacts on decisions made, and lifestyles adopted by individuals and societies within various cultures around the world. Learners focus on the desire of many religions to foster values and aspirations such as equality, justice, responsibility, peace and morality through such things as social action, sustainability and global citizenship. Learners will also be to encouraged question the values and aspirations of their own lives, the lives of others and of society. (*National Exemplar Framework,* p. 9)

Opportunities are also provided for learners to develop an awareness of the world of work from a religious education perspective, focusing on 'how religion influences believers in their choice of career and the standards expected of them in their working lives', 'business ethics', and 'promoting sustainable green industrial processes and practices'. In addition, important foundations are being laid which will support 'community cohesion and understanding in the workplace ... through knowledge of essential religious, cultural and ethical beliefs and practices' (*National Exemplar Framework,* p. 9).

Exploring

Buddhism

Exploring Buddhism

The story

Rees and Sara have two Buddhist friends, James and Hana, who live next door. James and Hana introduce Rees and Sara to key beliefs and practices in Buddhism. The children explore a Buddhist Centre and learn about the Three Jewels which lie at the heart of Buddhism. They attend a Buddhist children's festival and learn about the significance of the life of Shakyamuni Buddha (Siddhartha Gautama) and the purpose of meditation. Rees and Sara are introduced to sources of authority in Buddhism in the form of a lineage of Buddhist teachers who pass on central beliefs and practices to others. They investigate Buddhist attitudes to the environment and caring for others through exploring the symbolism of the Tibetan Wheel of Life. Rees and Sara learn about ethical livelihood, informed by Buddhist beliefs, through visiting a coffee shop run by Buddhists and listening to a story about a Tibetan Buddhist monk.

Aims

Exploring Buddhism provides opportunities for pupils to:

- **engage** with fundamental questions;
- **explore** religious beliefs, teachings, and practices;
- **express** personal responses in relation to the material studied.

Learning outcomes

Pupils should be able to:

- discuss questions raised by life and aspects of Buddhism;
- name and describe selected beliefs, teachings, and practices of Buddhism;
- explain through examples the relationship between belief and practice in Buddhism;
- discuss their own views and the views of others in relation to some of the themes and issues covered, and relate these to their own lives;
- relate symbol to meaning in some Buddhist contexts.

The basics

Buddhism appeared in northern India around the sixth century BCE as a result of the life and teachings of Siddhartha Gautama, or the 'Buddha Shakyamuni', from whom Buddhism derives its name. Today, there are two main Buddhist traditions: the Theravada tradition and the Mahayana tradition. Theravada Buddhism claims to have preserved accurately the teachings of Siddhartha Gautama in its sacred text called the Pali Canon. Mahayana Buddhism includes many different Buddhist groups such as Zen, Pure Land, and Tibetan Buddhism, for example. Each group has its own special sacred texts or Mahayana sutras, which it traces back to Siddhartha Gautama, although Theravada Buddhists would dispute such claims.

In *Exploring Buddhism* Rees and Sara are introduced to the New Kadampa Tradition which is a popular branch of Tibetan Buddhism in the West and a part of Mahayana Buddhism.

Mahayana Buddhists believe in:

- Dharma (teaching or truth): the basis for belief and practice. The source of Dharma is the cosmological Buddha, which is the ideal that lies behind and within all things. Siddhartha Gautama (Buddha Shakyamuni) was one important physical manifestation of the cosmological Buddha;
- rebirth: all unenlightened beings are tied to and suffer in a continuous cycle of rebirth;
- karma: all thoughts and actions (karma) produce negative or positive consequences which affect a person's life and rebirths in negative or positive ways;
- tanha: grasping and craving for physical or non-physical things for oneself is negative karma and produces negative consequences. It is this grasping and craving which causes the suffering in the cycle of rebirth;
- universal Buddhahood: the ideal is that all living beings are capable of becoming full Buddhas through following the Path of the Bodhisattva (Bodhisattva = one who is working towards Buddhahood). The Path of the Bodhisattva teaches Mahayana Buddhists how to control suffering and rebirth in order to help other suffering beings.

Mahayana Buddhists practise:

- seeking refuge in the Three Jewels: Buddha; Dharma (Teaching); and Sangha (Community) to help them progress on the Buddhist path;
- invoking Buddhas and Bodhisattvas for assistance on the Buddhist path, often through rituals performed before the shrine;
- meditating to develop the skills of wisdom and compassion, which are central to following the Path of the Bodhisattva leading to Buddhahood.

Chapter 1 Visiting a Buddhist centre

James and Hana take Rees and Sara to the shrine room in their Buddhist Centre to see the Three Jewels which lie at the heart of Buddhism. The Three Jewels, like the ring the children found at the swimming pool, are old and precious, and have been passed down by Buddhists, from generation to generation. Buddhists regularly express their faith and confidence in the Three Jewels and their ability to help them on the Buddhist path, by reciting this statement of belief:

I take refuge in the Buddha.
I take refuge in the Dharma.
I take refuge in the Sangha.

The first Jewel: Buddha

The first Jewel is Buddha. Buddha is 'one who is fully awakened' to the truth, which is: everything suffers, there is a reason for this suffering, and there is a cure for this suffering.

In the story, Rees and Sara are shown a Tibetan shrine which has Buddha Shakyamuni (Siddhartha Gautama) in the centre and, on either side, Bodhisattvas (those on the path to becoming full Buddhas, committed to helping other suffering beings). Popular Tibetan bodhisattvas include:

- Bodhisattva Avalokiteshvara who represents Buddha's compassion. A popular story relates how Avalokiteshvara vowed to help all suffering beings, and because of the enormity of the task he had to grow extra arms and heads;
- Bodhisattva Manjushri who represents Buddha's wisdom. He is often portrayed holding a flaming sword which symbolises wisdom cutting through ignorance;
- Bodhisattva Vajrapani who represents Buddha's power. Depictions of Vajrapani are often ferocious and filled with battle-related imagery; he strikes warlike poses, holds weapons, and wears a skull around his neck. The power is directed to all that impedes correct thought and action;
- Bodhisattva Tara who represents Buddha's deeds or action. Tara is a female aspect of Avalokiteshvara, and is also linked with compassion. She is depicted in many different forms which symbolise her various qualities, for example, white Tara symbolises compassion and black Tara symbolises power.

Each image of a Buddha or Bodhisattva is carefully crafted according to specific rules, which vary among Buddhist traditions. The images hold their hands in a number of different positions which are called mudras. For example, in the story Buddha Shakyamuni is shown touching the earth because when he attained enlightenment, tradition records that he touched the earth to witness the event. Other mudras include hand symbols depicting: no fear, teaching, meditation, giving and generosity.

Practices associated with the First Jewel include:

- presenting offerings to Buddhas and Bodhisattvas on the shrine;
- bowing and prostrating before Buddhas and Bodhisattvas;
- chanting mantras associated with specific Buddhas and Bodhisattvas;
- creating and offering mandalas to Buddhas and Bodhisattvas.

Symbolic offerings to Buddhas and bodhisattvas on the shrine include:

- water and food: Buddhism originated in India and has inherited Indian practices such as the tradition of offering guests food and water (for drinking and bathing). Food offerings in the West may consist of various food jars and packets, including chocolate bars;
- cut flowers: the beautiful flowers will eventually wither and die. This reminds Buddhists of the important truth that everything is impermanent and that nothing lasts forever;
- light: this symbolises the Buddhist ideal of enlightenment, when the darkness of ignorance is replaced by the light of wisdom;
- incense.

During devotional worship before the shrine, Mahayana Buddhists invoke Buddhas and bodhisattvas for their guidance and help.

When Buddhists enter the shrine room, they remove their shoes, and bow and prostrate themselves before the figures on the shrine as a sign of respect. Mantras (words which are believed to have great sacred power) are recited and each Buddha and Bodhisattva has its own mantra. Mahayana Buddhists believe that these mantras help to focus the mind and generate merit (positive karma) for the person chanting them as well as for others. Often a string of beads (usually 108 beads) is used to keep count of the mantras recited. Mantras are translated and interpreted in many ways by different Buddhists. Examples of Tibetan mantras include:

- Om Mani Padme Hum for Bodhisattva Avalokiteshvara;
- Om Tare Tuttare Ture Svaha for Bodhisattva Tara;

- Om Ah Ra Pa Tsa Na Dhih for Bodhisattva Manjushri.

Mandalas are popular in Tibetan Buddhism. A mandala is a powerful tool in meditation, which includes the act of constructing it. A mandala is a geometric symbolic representation of the Buddhist universe; it may be a physical picture or model (painted or constructed from a variety of materials such as coloured rice or sand) or it may be a mental image. The focus of the mandala is its centre; everything else points towards it and emphasises it. In traditional Tibetan mandalas, a Buddha or Bodhisattva will be at the centre. Meditating using a mandala is particularly powerful because it focuses the mind on what it wants to achieve ultimately – enlightenment and Buddhahood via the path of the Bodhisattva.

Buddha's position as the first Jewel shows that Buddhism is unlike most other faiths which have God or gods at their centre. Buddhists believe that gods, like all other things, are also trapped and suffering within the cycle of rebirth. Gods, then, are of limited use on a Buddhist path which seeks control over the cycle of rebirth. The Buddhas and Bodhisattvas, however, know how to control the cycle of rebirth, and they use this knowledge to help others out of compassion for their suffering.

The second Jewel: Dharma

Dharma is the second Jewel. Dharma means 'teaching' or 'truth'. Buddhists believe that this teaching or truth was taught and practised by Buddha Shakyamuni (Siddhartha Gautama) and is taught and practised by all Buddhas and Bodhisattvas. Dharma explains why people are unhappy and suffer, and it shows them how to experience real happiness and end suffering. Dharma is presented in written form in the different sacred texts of the various Buddhist groups. In Mahayana Buddhism, Dharma is usually found in their sutras; however, on the Westernised Mahayana Tibetan shrine in the story, a collection of books written in English by the founder of the community represents the Dharma.

The third Jewel: Sangha

The third Jewel is Sangha which is the Buddhist community. Placing faith and trust in Buddha and Dharma alone is not enough to progress on the Buddhist path; Buddhists also need a supportive, like-minded community. As the story of the King's Elephant illustrates, a person's social context has a great effect on how that person thinks and acts. To progress more quickly and more effectively on the Buddhist path, Buddhists believe that it is important to spend time with those who have similar ideals and practices. At the Buddhist Centre in the story, some members of the community reside there full-time, and other members of the community live in their own homes and visit the Centre for various events, devotions, and classes.

Helping others

The Three Jewels provide Buddhists with the right kind of support necessary to develop spiritually and to follow the path of the Bodhisattva. In Mahayana Buddhism the motivation behind this aim is to be in a position to help suffering beings tied to the cycle of rebirth. An important part of Mahayana Buddhism's practice is creating and giving 'merit' (good karma) to others to make their lives better. Mahayana Buddhists do this in a number of ways, for example, through rituals and prayers offered before the shrine, the Tibetan prayer flags (see worksheet) and prayer wheel, and reading sacred texts.

Activities

Visiting a Buddhist place of worship

Visit a Buddhist place of worship and identify the places mentioned in the story. How does it differ from the places in the book and how is it the same?

Mix and match

Cut out the nine boxes on the 'Write a story' worksheet, and then cut each box into three sections: the heading, the information, and the picture. Mix up all the sections and place them in an envelope. Divide pupils into pairs or groups and give each pair or group an envelope. Pupils need to match heading, information, and picture correctly.

Pupils can then do the task on the 'Write a story' worksheet (the story can easily be adapted to another genre such as a diary entry or newspaper article, if needed).

Mudras: using our hands to talk

Hands are very important because they help us to communicate with one another. Discuss the different ways in which we use our hands, for example, when we are talking, police/traffic wardens directing traffic, diving language, semaphore flags. What advantages do hands have in these situations (instead of writing or talking, for example)?

Look at and try to copy the various mudras (hand symbols) depicted by pictures or statues of the Buddha. What advantages do hands have in these situations (instead of writing or talking, for example)?

Picturing the Three Jewels

Show pupils a picture depicting the Three Jewels – often they are represented as three flames. Why do you think that this is the case? In small groups, design your own picture for the Three Jewels. Share your design with the rest of the class, explaining the thinking behind your picture.

Living together

Discuss the importance of community for Buddhists, using the story of the King's Elephant as a focus. The story can be acted out. Explore how the children's school or home community affects them. Ask them about the behaviour of others around them that causes them to be helpful or irritable.

Chapter 2 A children's festival

In non-Buddhist countries like Britain where there are comparatively few Buddhists it can be difficult to gather together regularly for communal activities or to celebrate festivals. It is also more difficult to bring children up in a faith tradition without the support of a faith community. In the last chapter we learnt the importance of belonging to a community in Buddhist tradition. To address this problem the New Kadampa Tradition featured in the story holds an annual 'Buddhist festival' and a 'Kid's Festival' where New Kadampa Buddhists can meet up and engage in activities as a large community.

At the children's festival Rees and Sara learn more about Buddhism in the workshops. They are introduced to the life and teachings of the historical founder of Buddhism, Buddha Shakyamuni (Siddhartha Gautama). The story of Siddhartha Gautama is an excellent teaching tool because it outlines the main concerns of Buddhism in a simple way.

Siddhartha's life in more detail

- Siddhartha Gautama was born into a tribal group called the Shakyas. This explains the title given to him by Mahayana Buddhists - Buddha Shakyamuni, which means sage of the Shakyas. As a son of the tribal leader, he would have lived a privileged and luxurious life.
- His conception and birth were miraculous. Legend says that his mother, Maya, dreamt that a white elephant entered her womb, and after ten months she gave birth; he was born on a full moon in Lumbini Park and deities paid homage to him; immediately after his birth he took seven steps and proclaimed his mission. Siddhartha's mother died when he was seven days old and he was brought up by his mother's sister who was also his father's wife.
- Siddhartha's training to be a great ruler would have included learning academic skills such as how to read and write and do mathematics as well as the skills of war such as archery and sword fighting. He was a fast learner and excelled in all his lessons.
- At sixteen he married Yasodhara, the daughter of an elder from a neighbouring tribe, and they had a son called Rahula. Rahula means 'fetter'; a tie which would make it particularly difficult for Siddhartha to leave on his quest to find the cure for suffering. In spite of this, he left his sleeping wife and newborn son to join a group of wandering holy men; this is called the Great Renunciation, which is symbolic of the detachment needed for following the Buddhist path. After enlightenment Siddhartha returned to see his family, and his son, Rahula, became a Buddhist monk.
- Siddhartha had a number of respected teachers while he lived the life of a holy man. He learnt all that they knew, but they did not know the cure for suffering. Siddhartha tried all the traditional methods for attaining spiritual knowledge, such as practising different meditation techniques and depriving his body of food. This made him very ill but it did not help him to discover the cure for suffering, so he gave up this lifestyle. Statues of the Buddha exist where he is pictured as a starving, skeletal figure meditating, which recall his pre-enlightenment spiritual search.
- While he sat under the Banyan tree in Bodhgaya on the night of his enlightenment, he entered into higher and higher states of meditation. In these states he learnt why everything suffers and the solution to this suffering. This is what he taught to his first disciples in his first sermon in the Deer Park at Sarnath.
- When Siddhartha Gautama, now the Buddha, died at Kusinara, he was cremated and his remains were buried under monuments called stupas.

The places of the Buddha's birth (Lumbini), enlightenment (Bodhgaya), first sermon (Sarnath), and death (Kusinara) are now important places of Buddhist pilgrimage alongside the stupas.

Meditation

Practising meditation is very important in Buddhism. In the meditation workshop Rees and Sara learn that meditation helps to control the mind by stilling and calming it. When the mind has been quietened, it is easier to concentrate and focus on really important things like the truth of the impermanence of everything around us. Buddhists believe that learning how to use the mind effectively is the key to enlightenment and following the Path of the Bodhisattva.

Buddhists can use a number of different techniques for meditation, for example:

- sitting in the lotus position;
- walking meditations;
- chanting mantras;
- undertaking everyday tasks like peeling potatoes, washing up, or gardening;
- focusing on an image or statue of a Buddha or Bodhisattva;
- focusing on their breathing;
- practising on their own or in groups.

Activities

What are my ties?

Make a list of the ties or 'fetters' that would have been difficult for Siddhartha to leave behind as he set out on his spiritual journey (for example, beautiful house, clothes, servants, friends, wife, child, food).

All of us have ties of some sort, even in our everyday lives. Imagine that your mother has asked you to tidy your room (or do your homework or some other task). You have promised to do it before tea. It is a beautiful, sunny afternoon and your best friend arrives with a new bike which has to be tested in the park. What ties or 'fetters' might stop you from tidying your room? Try to explain carefully why.

Learning to recognise and let go of fetters and ties in all parts of a person's life is central to the Buddhist path.

Special places

What makes a place special to us? A special place is often associated with people who are special to us or events which are special in some way. Draw a picture/diagram illustrating the special places of Buddhist pilgrimage linked to the life and death of the Buddha. Draw another picture/diagram to illustrate the special places in your life and write a sentence about each to explain why. And/or, ask adult members of your family to identify four special places in their lives, and to explain why they are special. Have they ever been back to those places? If they have, how did they feel?

Amazing birth and childhood stories

Compare the birth and childhood stories of Siddhartha Gautama with the birth and childhood stories of Jesus, noting all the clues which show that they are very special and different from those around them. Do you think that it is important for great religious teachers to have amazing stories about their birth and childhood? What do you think these amazing stories about birth and childhood are trying to teach those who hear them?

Does your family have any favourite stories about when you were a baby or a very young child? Why do you think that they remember them?

Mind over body

Practise a simple meditation using breathing. Sit pupils comfortably cross-legged on the floor with their eyes closed or, if this is not possible, at their desks. Ask them to inhale and exhale, not too quickly or too slowly, and try to concentrate on their breathing. Every time the mind wanders to anything else, they should gently bring it back to their breathing. After a few minutes, ask the children to stop and quietly reflect on the experience:

- How do they feel now?
- Was it difficult to focus on their breathing?
- What things distracted them?

Practise a focused meditation in groups concentrating on an everyday picture or an object which is not religious. Ask pupils to look carefully and silently at the picture or object: its shape, colours, and tiny details, for a few minutes. Remove the picture/object from each group, and ask one pupil from each group to describe in detail what s/he noticed. Can the other members of the group add any more details? Does anything surprise them about what they noticed? How easy was it for them to concentrate on the picture/object?

Celebrating festivals in Buddhism

There are other more traditional types of Buddhist festival which you can also study. A very useful and important festival is Wesak which celebrates the birth, life, and death of Buddha Shakyamuni.

Festivals across religious traditions

Work on a calendar or book of festivals from all religions. This would need to be a loose-leaf folder, or pages joined together with treasury tags so that pages can be added as needed in chronological order.

Talk about the importance of organising material well so that people can quickly find the information they need. With the pupils, decide on a useful structure for the book, for example, section headings could include stories, how the festival is celebrated today, recipes, and so on.

Chapter 3 Teachers

Although all teachers are different, in the story Hana observes that 'a good teacher is anyone who knows how to help people learn things'. Teachers have a central role to play in many Mahayana Buddhist groups. A good Buddhist teacher knows that people are different from one another and that individuals need to be taught in different ways if they are to progress on the Buddhist path. In Tibetan Buddhism (and the New Kadampa Tradition), a good teacher will know exactly which spiritual exercises will be most useful to individual pupils, and will make sure that the pace of education is not too fast or too slow. This appreciation of difference may be linked to the appreciation of different learning styles for different children which is part of good educational practice in schools today.

Teaching as skilful means

Mahayana Buddhism uses the term 'skilful means' when referring to this flexible and individualised kind of teaching. 'Skilful means' is using your wisdom and compassion for the benefit of others in the most appropriate way. In the Lotus Sutra there is a famous story which illustrates skilful means.

> A father returned home to see his house in flames. He could hear his children playing inside. He called to them to get out, but the children were too interested in their game to leave and they did not realise the danger that they were in. The father knew that the only way to save his children was to offer them something they wanted which would grab their attention, so he promised them the best toys that they could imagine, if they came out of the house immediately. His children came out of the house and were saved.

The father gave his children the greatest gift of all – life, although through indirect means because the children were not mature enough to understand their real needs. The message of the story is that teaching needs to be presented in a way that people can understand, and this will be different for each individual.

A long line of teachers

Like all Buddhists, the New Kadampa Tradition traces its teachings back to Buddha Shakyamuni (Siddhartha Gautama), and like all Mahayana Buddhist groups, it has a line of recognised and famous teachers who have passed on the teachings. This is a way of proving that the teachings are authentic as well as protecting them from being corrupted and distorted.

The New Kadampa Tradition recognises an Indian Buddhist called Atisha as the most important founding father of Kadampa Buddhism in Tibet (982-1054 CE). The next most significant Kadampa Buddhist teacher in Tibet was Je Tsongkhapa who lived in the fourteenth century. According to the New Kadampa Buddhist Tradition, Buddha Shakyamuni predicted that Bodhisattva Manjushri would appear in the form of Je Tsongkhapa. Je Tsongkhapa modernised the tradition and founded New Kadampa Buddhism. A Tibetan called Geshe Kelsang Gyatso wanted those who lived in the West to benefit from New Kadampa Buddhism as well, and so he made it his mission to present the teachings in a way which Westerners would understand. He founded the very successful New Kadampa Tradition, the International Kadampa Buddhist Union which contains over 1,000 Buddhist centres from around the world.

If religious traditions are to be meaningful, they need to adapt appropriately to changing times and cultures without losing that which lies at the heart of the tradition. Gyatso may be said to have done this for the New Kadampa Tradition in the West.

Biography of Geshe Kelsang Gyatso

- He studied Buddhism in Tibet.
- He spent 18 years meditating in a Himalayan retreat supported by his spiritual teacher.
- In 1977 he came to England to teach and introduce New Kadampa Buddhism to the West, and settled at the Manjushri Centre in the Lake District.
- He established the New Kadampa Tradition, the International Kadampa Buddhist Union, which consists of over 1,000 Buddhist centres from around the world.

Activities

The Middle Way

Buddha Shakyamuni (Siddhartha Gautama) recommended the middle way between a life of luxury and a life of asceticism. He compared it with a stringed instrument: if the string is too tight it breaks (asceticism); if it is too loose then it does not play (luxury). The instrument needs the middle way of balance to play best. Put the pupils into three discussion groups.

- Group 1: identify the signs of being very rich (for example, expensive car etc.).
- Group 2: identify the signs of being very poor (for example, little money to buy food etc.).
- Group 3: identify the basic things that we need to keep us alive.

Each group chooses one person to speak to the class on their behalf, presenting their ideas. Put the pupils back into their groups for the following discussions:

- Group 1: if you were very rich, what would be good and bad about it?
- Group 2: if you were very poor, what would be good and bad about it?
- Group 3: if you had enough to keep yourself alive, but no more or less, what would be good and bad about it?

It is interesting to note that research surveys suggest that after certain basic needs have been met, people's happiness levels do not appear to grow with increased wealth.

Creating a tableau

Prepare a tableau depicting the line of teachers in the New Kadampa Tradition (Buddha Shakyamuni, Atisha, Je Tsongkhapa, and Geshe Kelsang Gyatso) or in another Buddhist tradition such as Zen Buddhism, for example.

Tradition is important in Buddhism (and other religions), and correct belief and practice is passed on through reliable and respected people or groups. These reliable and respected people or groups adapt belief and practice sometimes to make the traditions relevant and meaningful to different countries and times. For example, India over two thousand years ago was very different from Britain today (you can discuss these differences with pupils). However, some important basic things remain the same (human suffering, illness, death, the desire to be happy, for example). Throughout their history, Buddhists have tried to present Buddhist teaching about suffering and its cure in ways that make sense to different people in different places at different times. The figures in the tableau are examples of this.

Lessons in life

There are many important lessons in life which people pass on from generation to generation. Ask pupils to interview an older family member or neighbour. Possible questions include:

- If you had to pass on only **one** piece of advice to others, what would it be?
- How did you learn that piece of advice?

The pupils can also ask themselves the same questions, and feed back to the class.

Before he died, Buddha Shakyamuni said, 'When I am gone, do not say that you have no teacher. Whatever I have taught, let that be your teacher when I am gone.' Ever since then the Buddha's teachings have been passed on from teacher to pupil, providing guidance for Buddhists on how to live their lives.

Chapter 4 Caring for the world and others

In this chapter Rees and Sara plant trees and look at a picture of the Tibetan Wheel of Life. They learn that Buddhists believe every action a person does (both good and bad) has an effect on others, the world, and ourselves. Many environmental organisations and charities also make a similar basic connection.

An important question is asked: why do people do things which damage others, the world, and themselves? It does not make sense. James and Hana explain the Buddhist answer to this question through looking at the symbolism in the Wheel of Life.

The Wheel of Life in more detail

The centre

The three symbolic animals in the centre fuel the wheel of life and keep it turning. Ignorance (pig), greed (cockerel), and hatred (snake) are shown either biting one another or throwing one another up. This symbolises that they feed on one another and are connected to one another. For example, if people are ignorant of how the world works, they become greedy and strive to possess things for themselves, and this often leads to hatred towards anything which stands in the way. By replacing ignorance with knowledge (practising the Buddha's teaching or Dharma) a person becomes 'enlightened'; an enlightened person is without greed and hatred, and the wheel stops turning because it runs out of fuel. In the picture, the figure of the Buddha sits in meditation outside the Wheel of Life, which represents the potential in everyone to free themselves from the cycle of rebirth through following Buddhist practice.

The inner circle

This shows what happens if people's lives are dominated by ignorance, greed, and hatred. They are trapped in an endless cycle of rebirth which is marked by pain and suffering. Rees and Sara learn that Tibetan Buddhists believe that there are many different realms of existence which co-exist and, depending on a person's actions (karma), that person will be reborn into one of these realms. Although Buddhist scriptures sometimes say what actions would lead to rebirth in a particular realm (for example, rebirth in the hell realm for killing a Buddha), the whole process is very complicated and simple connections like this are best avoided.

Tibetan Buddhists also believe that skilled Buddhists can choose where they want to be reborn, and they will choose the best rebirth for helping those still suffering in the cycle of rebirth. This is part of following the Path of the Bodhisattva.

The outer circle

This takes one human life and shows the cycle of birth, death, and rebirth. In a more detailed picture of the wheel of life, it is possible to see how all actions are connected to one another and how they contribute to the endless cycle of rebirth and suffering. Although these connections are too complicated for pupils in this age group to understand, it is useful for teachers to see how they work in more detail:

- blind man: failure to 'see' the truth;
- potter: creates pots (actions) based on ignorance of the truth;
- monkey: unruly, uncontrollable, and restless, swinging from tree to tree, like actions based on ignorance;
- three men in a boat: the boat (body) takes a person across a stream (a life journey), and the route taken is affected by a person's past actions (karma);
- house: actions are determined by sensory information passing through sense entrances into the mind (windows and doors of the house);
- lovers: the link between sense organs and the sense information entering the mind produces sense-based feelings;
- man with arrow in his eye: the strength of the sense-based feelings damages a person's ability to see things properly;
- an intoxicated man, drinking: damaged sight turns sense-based feelings into desire, and a need to have more than a person requires;
- monkey eating fruit in a tree: the monkey is symbolic of a person clinging to a desired thing despite the fact that the uncontrolled clinging makes that person unhappy;
- pregnant woman: the uncontrolled clinging produces the seeds for a new life;
- woman giving birth: a new life begins;
- an old man weighed down by a heavy bag: the life is weighed down by all its 'history', and so the cycle continues.

The Wheel of Life is held in the jaws of Yama, the Lord of Death.

A diagram of the wheel of life is provided in the worksheet for pupils to discuss, label, and colour.

Activities

Practising mindfulness

How often do we really think about what we say and do, and the effect that it has on ourselves and those around us? Arrange a break time when pupils can practise 'mindfulness' to understand better an important skill that practising Buddhists try to develop. They will need some practical pointers.

- Think before you say or do anything. How will what you say or do help or harm other people or yourself?
- Look around you. Is there anything that you can do to help others or the environment?

It is important that pupils are given an opportunity to feed back to the class directly after the break time, focusing on their experiences in response to the practical pointers.

Caring for the environment

Buddhists believe that everything they do should be helpful to themselves and others. Planting trees is helpful for the environment. However, you need to make sure that the trees are planted in the right place (for example, not near pipes or overhead wires) and cared for properly. There are several organisations that will work with groups to ensure trees are planted sensitively, such as the Forestry Commission of Wales Education Team, the Tree Council (which runs a National Tree Week around November), and the Woodland Trust. Create a research project based on one or more of these organisations.

What can I do?

Sit in a circle and allow each child in turn to complete the sentence, 'I can care for the world by ...' (If children do not wish to say anything, allow them to pass.) These ideas can be displayed in the classroom to act as a reminder.

The domino effect

Set up a line of dominoes or cards, and demonstrate the domino effect. This is similar to an important belief in Buddhism. Buddhists believe that all things are connected to one another, and that every action has a knock-on effect.

Make a list of 'actions', for example, planting trees, buying fairtrade bananas, and supporting a chosen charity. Divide the class into groups, and give each group an 'action' to research further. Then, on a large sheet of paper, create a spider diagram which shows the effects of that action on other people and the world as well as us. Remember that knock-on effects can occur in all directions, so try to make the diagrams as complicated as possible.

Chapter 5 It is better not to kill

Right livelihood

Choosing the right livelihood (job or work) is important for many Buddhists, where a choice is available. Ideally, a job should support and not hinder one's progression along the Buddhist path, so a job should require actions which are good karma rather than require actions which are bad karma. By working in the organic coffee shop, James and Hana's mother believes she is producing good karma and showing compassion for the world and living beings within it. In Theravada Buddhism right livelihood is part of its Eightfold Path which guides a person on the path to enlightenment. One of the accompanying worksheets describes the Eightfold Path and suggests an activity. In Mahayana Buddhism the idea of right livelihood is understood in the context of the Path of the Bodhisattva, which guides Mahayana Buddhists to enlightenment. The Path of the Bodhisattva focuses on practising Six Perfections: giving; moral discipline; patience; effort; concentration; and wisdom.

Practising compassion

In Buddhism it is important to show care and compassion towards all living beings, and not just human beings. Buddhism is traditionally less human-being focused than religions like Christianity, Judaism, and Islam. This is because of its beliefs about rebirth and the interconnectedness of all living things. Like other religions which emerged from India such as Hinduism, Sikhism, and Jainism, the principle of ahimsa (non-violence) is often central to Buddhist practice. The Tibetan tale of the meditating Buddhist monk illustrates this.

However, Buddhist beliefs about non-violence do not mean that all Buddhists are vegetarian or that they treat the natural world in exactly the same way. In the story two reasons are given which explain why. The first reason is that different Buddhists and Buddhist groups live in different cultures and environments. In Theravada Buddhism (and Theravadin Buddhist countries such as Thailand and Sri Lanka) the laity see it as their duty to provide monks with food and other means of support, and monks are not expected to 'work' in a traditional sense. The laity accepts the Theravadin rule that monks should not till the soil because it would produce bad karma for them to kill living creatures. However, Theravadin monks are allowed to eat meat if an animal has not been killed to feed them. By providing food and other support for the monks, lay Buddhists believe that they are making good karma which will help to produce a good rebirth in their next lives.

Mahayana Buddhist groups were established in places where it was unrealistic for the laity to provide them with food, for example, in China and Japan. Also, Mahayana Buddhism is more flexible in the way that it approaches scripture, and tends to adapt to its environment to a greater extent than Theravada Buddhism. As a result, Zen monks are able to do work which would not be acceptable to Theravadin monks.

The second reason given for difference in practice among Buddhists is that people are at different stages on the Buddhist path, so you should not expect the same standard of practice from someone just beginning as you would a Buddhist monk, whose life revolves around the path. Everyone should do what they reasonably can by putting in the right effort (not too much or too little); this is called the Middle Way. Everyone should do what is appropriate in their particular life situation and stage of spiritual development.

Activities

Difference in Buddhism map

Display a map of the world and mark the countries where there is a large population of Buddhists (for example, Thailand, Cambodia, Myanmar, Bhutan, Sri Lanka, Tibet, Laos, Vietnam, Japan, Macau, Taiwan, China, Japan, South Korea, and India). Illustrate the map with pictures from the internet of famous Buddhist buildings, locations, and statues. You could also show the different styles of dress for Buddhist monks and nuns (for example, black for Zen in Japan, purple for Tibetan in Tibet or one of the New Kadampa Tradition centres, saffron for Theravada in Thailand and Sri Lanka).

Make a graph

Some Buddhists may prefer to use organic food because they believe it is better for the environment and the body. Do your parents use organic food? Ask at home how often (if ever) your parents usually include organic food in cooking, selecting one of these five descriptions of frequency: never, a few times a week or more, at least once a week, at least once a month, less often.

If your parents do use organic food, find out the reasons why. If your family does not use organic food, find out the reasons why.

Construct a block graph to display the results for the class, using the five frequency categories. This could be further developed by asking different questions based on the graph. For example: How many families use organic food in their cooking? How many families use organic food at least once a week or more? Also, the selected information could be presented in a different way, for example as a pie-chart, or table.

Difficult decisions

There are many difficult choices to make in life and making the right choice can be a complicated business. Also, people often disagree about what the right choice is. Gather together or prepare information about one or more of the following for the pupils:

- organic farming and organic food/conventional farming;
- food available in the UK/food from around the world;
- free-range animals and battery-farmed animals;
- fish farms/open-water fishing.

It would be useful to include a comparative price list in this information, and you could include air miles, where relevant.

Working in groups or pairs, ask pupils to use the gathered information to answer the following question, which can be adapted according to the topic selected.

Do you agree or disagree with the following statement? Give reasons for your answer.

- Organic farming is better than conventional farming.

Groups should feed back their answers to the class. Did every group have the same answer and reasons?

Buddhists have to make difficult choices too. They may decide what to do by weighing up the effects of certain actions on others, the world, and themselves. As it shows in the story, there is often more than one answer, and different Buddhist groups can make different choices.

Keywords

ahimsa non-violence

Bodhisattva *one who has taken the Bodhisattva oath, and is on the path to becoming a full Buddha*

Dharma *teaching or truth*

enlightenment *waking up and seeing things as they really are*

Geshe Kelsang Gyatso *the founder of the New Kadampa Tradition*

karma *action: there is positive action (karma) and negative action (karma)*

Mahayana Buddhism *one of the main Buddhist traditions; many Buddhist groups fall in the category of Mahayana Buddhism, including the New Kadampa Tradition*

mandala *a tool used in meditation*

mantra *words which are believed to have great sacred power*

meditation *the practice of calming and focusing the mind*

Middle Way *not doing or having too much or too little of anything, it provides the ideal context for Buddhist practice.*

mudra *hand symbol present in Hindu, Buddhist, and Sikh iconography*

New Kadampa Tradition *a tradition within Tibetan Buddhism*

Pali Canon *the scriptures of Theravada Buddhism*

rebirth *the belief that all things are subject to a continuous cycle of birth and death*

Sangha *the Buddhist community; often used more specifically for the monastic community*

Shakyamuni Buddha *another name for the historical Buddha*

Siddhartha Gautama *the Buddha from whom Buddhism derives its name*

skilful means *the use of wisdom and compassion to help suffering beings in the most appropriate way*

sutra *a sacred scripture in Mahayana Buddhism*

tanha *grasping and craving for the self; the cause of suffering*

Theravada Buddhism *one of the main Buddhist traditions*

Three Jewels *Buddha, Dharma, and Sangha*

Wheel of Life *a Tibetan picture which depicts the universe, the cycle of rebirth, and the Buddhist ideal of enlightenment*

Write a story

Imagine you have visited a Buddhist Centre with a Buddhist friend. Write a story about it, giving details of all the places you visited and the things you saw there. The pictures and descriptions below will help you.

shoe rack

As a sign of respect, dirty shoes are left outside the shrine room. This also keeps the floor clean so people can sit down.

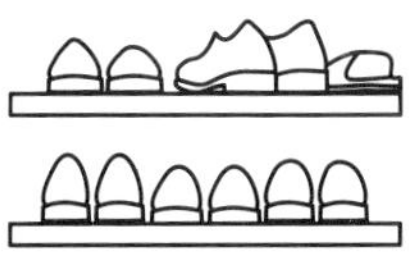

Buddha

A large statue of Buddha Shakyamuni sits on the shrine. People may greet the statue by putting their hands together in front of their chests and bowing slightly.

candles

People may light candles on the shrine as a gift of light and as a symbol of the light of Buddhist teaching.

shrine room

There are no seats here so people sit cross-legged on the floor to listen to the teaching and to meditate.

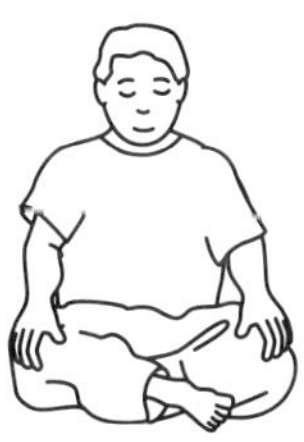

Dharma

The teachings of Bhuddhism have been passed down for hundreds of years. These special books sit on the shrine as a sign of how important they are.

flowers

The shrine may have several beautiful flower arrangements. Buddhists like to be surrounded by peace and beauty.

shrine

Buddhist shrines are beautifully decorated. The shrine is considered to be a special place and is treated with respect.

incense

Sometimes Buddhists burn incense (a strong-smelling spice) on the shrine.

meeting room

The community is very important to Buddhists, so they may stay and drink tea together after their meeting time.

Make a prayer flag

Some Buddhists write prayers on brightly coloured flags and place them outside. They believe that as the wind blows across the flags, the prayer is repeated over and over as the wind carries it into the world.

You will need

- scrap paper
- scissors
- brightly-coloured paper or fabric
- pens or felt-tipped pens
- string

What to do

1. Write a prayer for the world. What is it that you most wish for our world and for all the people on it? Share your ideas with your friends and then write down what is most important to you.
2. Write your prayer on brightly coloured paper or fabric. (Use felt-tipped pens to write on fabric.) Cut it into your chosen shape for a flag.
3. Punch holes in corners of the flag and thread string through the holes.
4. Tie your flag outside where you will see it and be reminded of your own wish for the world. Each time you see it, think of what you can do to help fulfil your hopes.

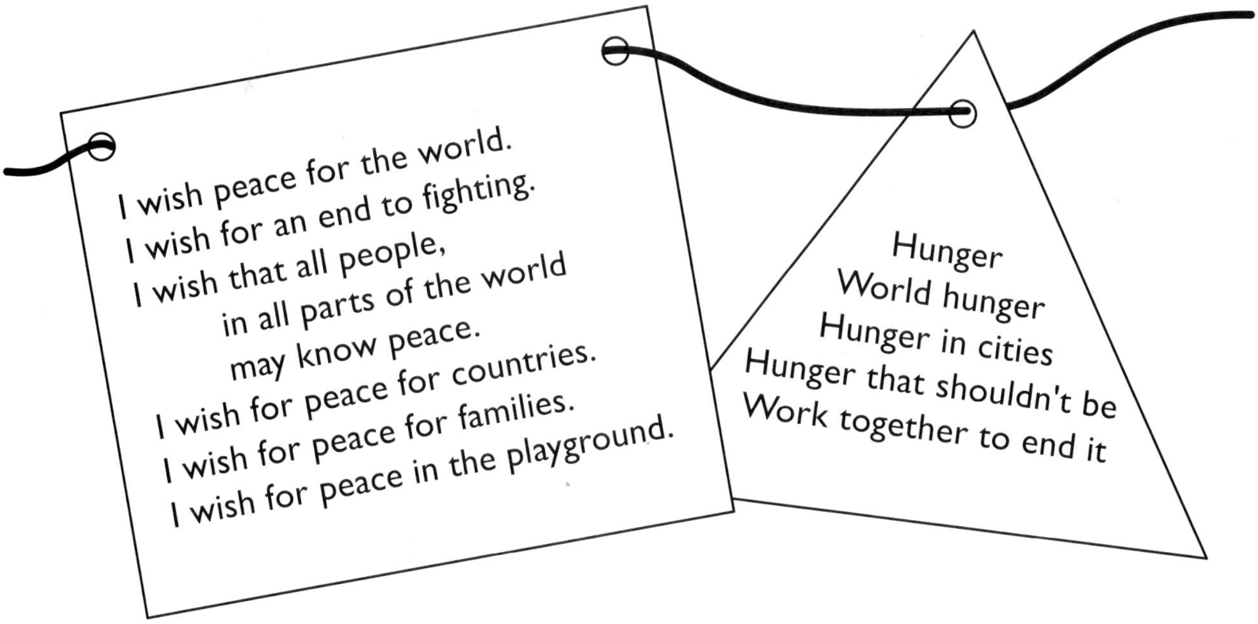

Design a mandala

Some Buddhists use mandalas to help them meditate. A mandala is a circular design with geometric patterns made from circles, triangles, squares and diamonds. Some mandalas include pictures of Buddha Shakyamuni.

What to do

1. **Research:** Find pictures of traditional mandalas for ideas. Look in books about Buddhism or search the internet using keywords like 'mandala' and 'pictures'.
2. **Discuss:** Look at the pictures with your friends. Talk about how the elements of the mandalas would help Buddhists to meditate. Why do some include pictures of Buddha Shakyamuni? Why are some geometric patterns?
3. **Reflect:** Buddhists meditate on the teachings that are important to them. What is important to you? What do you need to work at in your life?
4. **Design:** Plan a mandala that will help you think about the things that are important to you.
5. **Make:** Make your mandala. Mandalas can be drawn or painted, stitched on cloth or made out of coloured sand that is then blown away by the wind. (You can make coloured sand by putting clean, washed sand in a plastic bag, adding food colouring and shaking it until the colour mixes. For brighter colours, use sugar and food colouring.)

Make a cut-away card

There are many Buddhists with many different traditions. In Buddhist countries, Wesak is an important festival. It is a time to remember the life of Buddha Shakyamuni. It is celebrated on the day of the full moon in April or May.

Generosity is important to Buddhists. At Wesak (sometimes known as Buddha Day) they make offerings and give gifts to the monks. Some people send cards or give small gifts to family and friends.

You will need

- ½ sheet of A4 card
- ruler
- pencils
- cutting knife and scissors

What to do

1. Rule a faint line down the centre of the card where the fold will be.

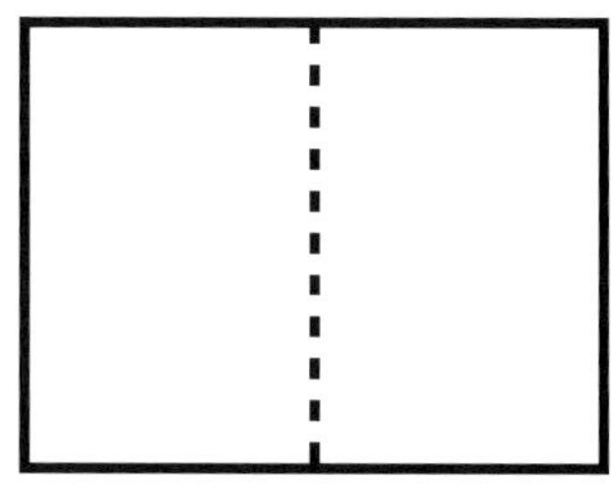

2. With a cutting knife, cut out the three sides of the rectangle as shown. (The fourth side is the ruled line.)

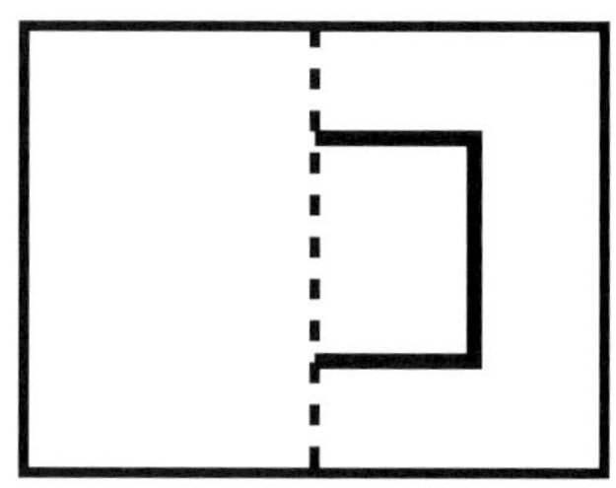

3. Make a mountain crease pointing up along the outsides of the ruled line so that your cut-out section stands up. Do not crease this part.

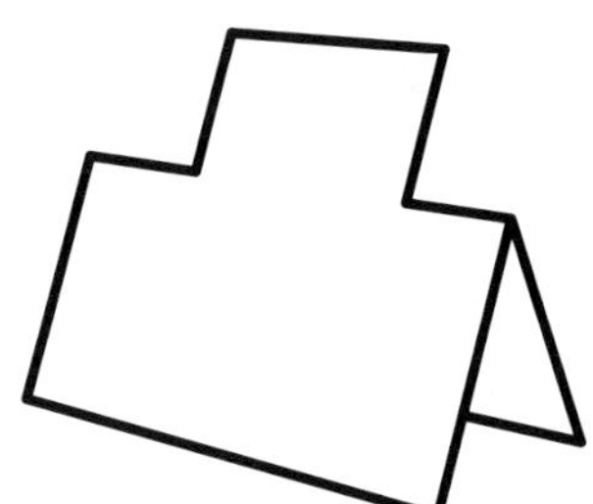

4. Choose a suitable design for your card, such as Buddha Shakyamuni, a lotus blossom or an eight-spoked wheel. Draw this on the card. Carefully shape the top of the card to fit the design. When you understand how to make these cards you can change them. You can make them smaller, fold them sideways or cut away part of the bottom of the design.

5. Write 'Happy Wesak' or 'Happy Buddha Day' on the card.

Discover the cycles of the moon

Many Buddhist festivals are held at the time of the new moon. This is because most important events in the life of Buddha Shakyamuni are believed to have happened then.

Fill in the details on the calendars below. Choose the next two months. Write the days at the top of the columns. Mark in the new moon days for each month. You could also fill in the dates of the full moon and the two half moons.

The month of ________________

___ day	___ day	___ day	___ day	___ day	___ day	___ day
1	2	3	4	5	6	7
8	9	10	11	12	13	14
15	16	17	18	19	20	21
22	23	24	25	26	27	28
29	30	31				

The month of ________________

___ day	___ day	___ day	___ day	___ day	___ day	___ day
1	2	3	4	5	6	7
8	9	10	11	12	13	14
15	16	17	18	19	20	21
22	23	24	25	26	27	28
29	30	31				

key

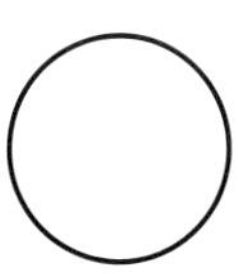 new moon 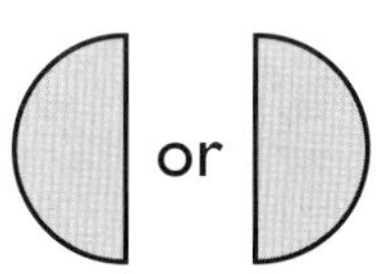 half moon 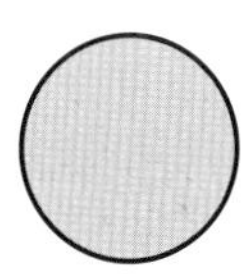 full moon

Make a wheel

The wheel is a symbol of the teaching of Buddha Shakyamuni. It has eight spokes to represent the Noble Eightfold Path, which Buddhists believe to be the way to end suffering.

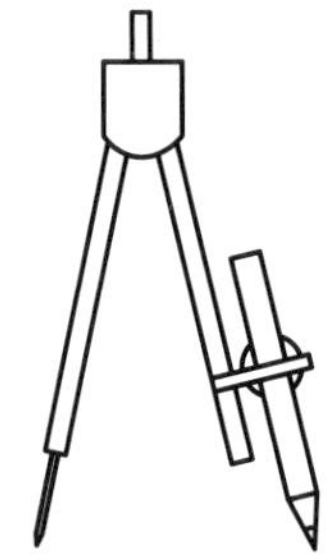

You will need

2 sheets of A4 card	compass	pencil
scissors	sticky tape or glue	pens

What to do

1. Use the compass to draw a circle about 18 cm across. (This means the compass point and the pencil need to be about 9 cm apart.) Draw a second circle 2cm inside this. Cut this out as the rim of the wheel.
2. Draw and cut out another circle about 3 cm across for the centre of the wheel.
3. Cut out 8 spokes, each about 7 cm long. Make them 2 cm wide where they meet the rim and 1 cm wide where they meet the centre.
4. Join the pieces of the wheel together with glue or tape on the back of the model.
5. Decorate the rim and centre.
6. On each spoke write one of the steps to right living:
   - right understanding
     (of Buddha Shakyamuni's teaching)
   - right thought
     (think kind thoughts)
   - right speech
     (do not tell lies or speak angrily)
   - right action
     (do not steal or harm others)
   - right livelihood
     (a job that does no harm)
   - right effort
     (work to do the right thing)

- right awareness
  (be alert and aware)
- right concentration
  (train your mind to be calm)

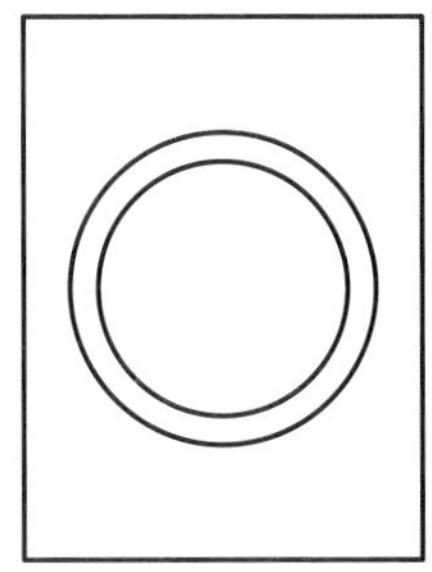

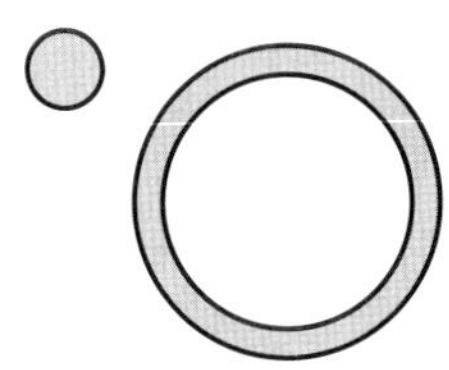

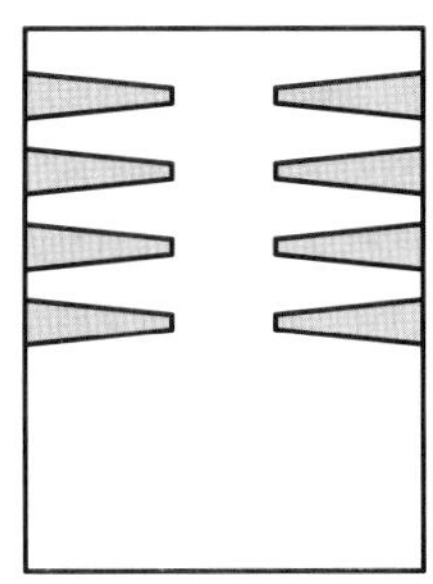

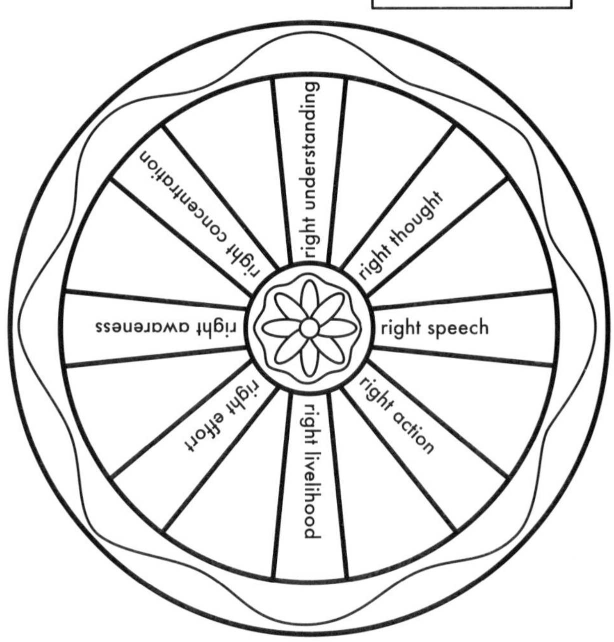

What is happiness?

This is the Metta Sutta, a famous talk given by Buddha Shakyamuni. Metta means 'loving kindness', which is very important to Buddhists. This talk shows the importance of happiness to Buddhists.

> May all beings be happy and secure.
> May their hearts be whole.
> Whatever living beings they are -
> Weak or strong, tall or short,
> Small or large,
> Those seen or unseen,
> Living near or far away,
> Those who are born
> And those yet to be born -
> May all beings, without exception,
> Be happy!

Buddhists believe that happiness is a state of mind. If our mind is pure and peaceful we will be happy, no matter what is happening around us. Fill in the acrostic with words and phrases about happiness.

H ________________________________

A ________________________________

P ________________________________

P ________________________________

I ________________________________

N ________________________________

E ________________________________

S ________________________________

S ________________________________

Make a lotus flower

The open lotus flower is important to Buddhists as a symbol of spiritual purity. They believe that Buddha Shakyamuni had a vision in which he saw people as being like a lake of lotus plants that had not yet opened.

- Some people are like buds still buried at the bottom of the lake.
- Some people are like buds that have grown a little taller but are still muddy and tightly closed.
- Some people are like buds that have reached the surface of the lake and just need a little help from the sunlight to open into beautiful flowers.

You will need

1 cup of salt	3 cups of flour
a dribble of cooking oil	1 cup of water
white paint	PVA glue

What to do

1. Make saltdough by mixing together the salt, flour, oil and water. If the dough is too dry, add more water.
2. Knead the dough for at least two minutes. Leave it to rest for half an hour before using it.
3. Shape the dough to make models of an eight-petalled lotus flower. (If you have any dough left over it will need to be used by the next day or else thrown out.)
4. Ask an adult to cook the models for you. Small models can be cooked for an hour at 150°C (300°F or gas mark 2). Large models need to be cooked for 3 hours at 135°C (275°F or gas mark 1). Cook the models until they are thoroughly dry. Test by tapping them on the bottom. If they sound hollow, then they are ready.
5. Paint the models white and varnish them with PVA glue.

Wheel of life

The way of life

Buddhists believe that unhappiness is caused by ignorance, hatred and greed. Write in some problems that are caused by these three things. Think of their opposites and a symbol for each. Write in some good deeds that are caused by these.

The pig is a symbol for ignorance.  Some problems caused by ignorance are	The _____ is my symbol for knowledge. Some good deeds caused by knowledge are
The snake is a symbol for hatred. 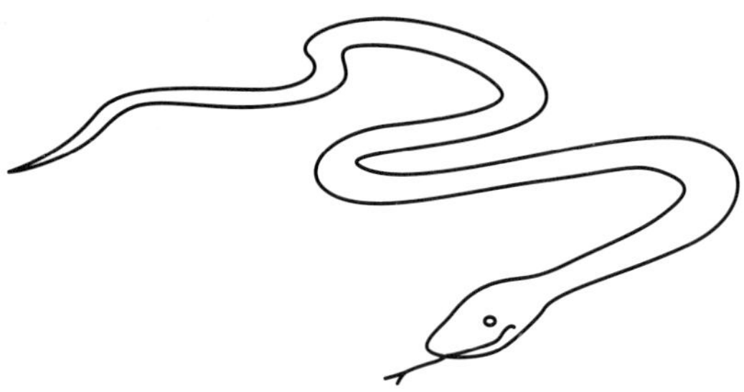 Some problems caused by hatred are	The _____ is my symbol for love. Some good deeds caused by love are
The cockerel is a symbol for greed.  Some problems caused by greed are	The _____ is my symbol for generosity. Some good deeds caused by generosity are

Think about occupations

Buddhists believe they should choose their jobs carefully. They should select jobs that do not harm themselves or other living things.

First, write a list of jobs down the first row. Next, think about whether these jobs help or harm the world and the creatures in it. In the second row put a tick for helping and a cross for hurting. As you do this, fill in your reasons in the third row.

job	x or √	reasons

Organic food

Buddhists prefer to eat food that does not harm the earth as it grows and does not harm their bodies when they eat it. Some Buddhists choose to do this by eating organic food. Is this easy? Could you prepare your favourite meals if you only bought organic food from the supermarket?

Check it out by logging on to an online supermarket. (You may need to ask someone to access an account for you to use.) In the search field, type in 'organic' to see the variety the supermarket offers. Fill in the food in the categories below.

dairy and eggs	**meat**
bread, cakes and biscuits	**fruit and vegetables**
ready meals	**general**

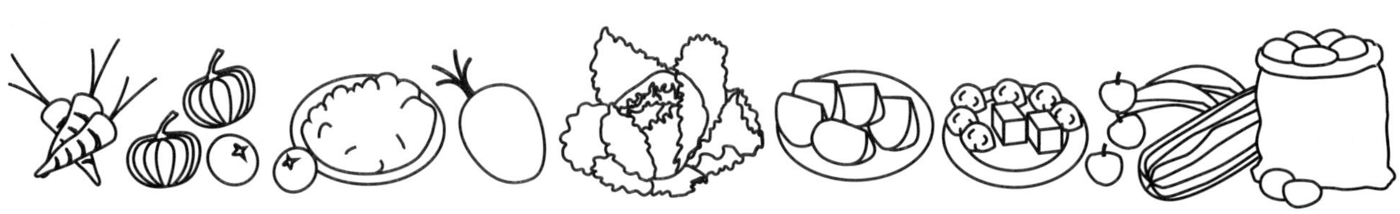

My dictionary

You will meet many new words in *Exploring Buddhism*. Some of these will be English words and some will be either Pali or Sanskrit words. Keep a record of them, along with their meanings.

meditation	training the mind, emptying it of all thoughts in order to focus on things that are important
Dharma	the teaching that has come from Buddha Shakyamuni
Sangha	the community of Buddhists
______	______________________
______	______________________
______	______________________
______	______________________
______	______________________
______	______________________
______	______________________
______	______________________
______	______________________
______	______________________
______	______________________
______	______________________
______	______________________

Compose music

Have you noticed the effect that different sounds have? Some sounds make us excited; some can scare us; some leave us feeling peaceful. Buddhists choose special words and sounds (known as mantras) to help them meditate. Sound is very important.

What to do

1. Choose a feeling that you would like to explore.

2. Experiment with musical instruments and everyday items in and around the classroom. Select some that produce the feeling you wish to evoke.

3. Try out your sounds in different combinations to produce the best effect.

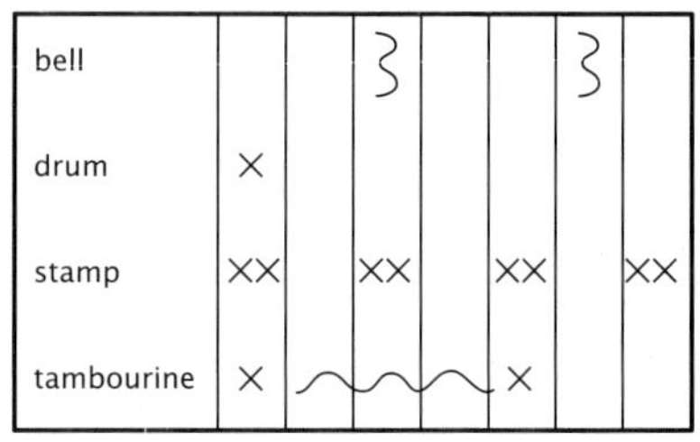

4. Write down the sequence in a way that helps you remember it.

5. Record your music on a tape recorder or computer.

6. Test your music on a friend to see if it creates the feeling you chose. If it does not, then work out how to change it and then re-record it.

An extra idea

If you record your music on computer as a sound file, you could import it to a programme such as 'PowerPoint' and find pictures from the internet or from Clip Art to accompany it for a presentation to the whole class.

Exploring
Hinduism

Exploring Hinduism

The story

Rees and Sara have two Hindu school friends called Rajeev and Meena who introduce them to key beliefs and practices in Hinduism. The children explore a mandir and learn about God in Hinduism and how their friends worship God. They celebrate the festival of Diwali and learn about the story behind the festival. Rees and Sara are introduced to special books in Hinduism through the Bhagavad Gita and the great myths, and they learn about how these affect the lives of Hindus. They investigate Hindu attitudes to the environment and caring for others through a story about tree huggers in India. They learn about Hindu attitudes towards food, including vegetarianism, and why cows are sacred in Hinduism.

Aims

Exploring Hinduism provides opportunities for pupils to:

- **engage** with fundamental questions;
- **explore** religious beliefs, teachings, and practices;
- **express** personal responses in relation to the material studied.

Learning outcomes

Pupils should be able to:

- discuss questions raised by life and aspects of Hinduism;
- name and describe selected beliefs, teachings, and practices of Hinduism;
- explain through examples the relationship between belief and practice in Hinduism;
- discuss their own views and the views of others in relation to some of the themes and issues covered, and relate these to their own lives;
- relate symbol to meaning in some Hindu contexts.

The basics

Hinduism is made up of a vast number of different traditions with various beliefs and practices. In the story book a popular example of Hinduism is presented which practises devotion (bhakti) to personal forms of God represented by different gods and goddesses.

Hinduism has its origins in India and is the oldest of the great Indian religious traditions. Some of the earliest roots of Hinduism are over 4,000 years old. Unlike many other religions, Hinduism does not have a founder, although there are many significant characters and teachers in its history. Today, the largest Hindu population is found in India where over 80% of the population is thought to be Hindu; other large populations exist in Fiji, Mauritius, Nepal, the Caribbean, and Guyana. Smaller populations and communities are now established in many countries throughout the world. Often, Hindus use the term Sanatana Dharma (Eternal Law) to describe their religious tradition.

The Hindu tradition represented in the story book believes in:

- God: Supreme Reality, and represented in many different forms;
- Dharma (law, duty, teaching or truth): the basis for belief and practice. In Hinduism, everything has specific duties and responsibilities (Dharma) which need to be fulfilled in order to create balance and harmony;
- rebirth: all unenlightened beings are tied to and suffer in a continuous cycle of rebirth;
- karma: all actions (karma) produce negative or positive consequences which affect a person's life and rebirths in negative or positive ways. In Hinduism, fulfilling or failing to fulfil one's Dharma (duties) produces either positive or negative karma;
- atman (soul): every living thing possesses a soul which passes from one body to the next during rebirth;
- Moksha: liberation from the cycle of suffering and rebirth, when the atman (soul) enjoys a perfect relationship with God.

The Hindu tradition represented in the story book practises:

- devotion to various gods and goddesses, often performed before a shrine;
- fulfilling one's Dharma (duties) in daily life;
- ahimsa (non-violence) towards living things.

Chapter 1 Visiting a mandir

Understanding God in Hinduism

In the story Rajeev and Meena explain to Rees and Sara how Hindus understand God. Although Rajeev and Meena believe in a Supreme Reality which is God, they believe that God takes many different forms. Some of these forms are illustrated in the statues of gods and goddesses in the mandir's shrine room. Each god or goddess has its own special characteristics, qualities, and myths associated with it.

Other Hindus might understand God in a slightly different way. For example, some Hindus believe that the Supreme Reality should be worshipped directly and do not include the various gods and goddesses in their worship. Some Hindus may give the name Brahman to the Supreme Reality. Other Hindus believe that the god or goddess they worship is the Supreme Reality and will focus devotion on that god or goddess (popular gods with large numbers of devotees include Shiva and Vishnu, and a popular goddess is Kali, for example).

However, like Rajeev and Meena, many Hindus worship a number of different gods and goddesses at different times, depending on the circumstances and their needs. Families often have favourite gods and goddesses who are passed down the generations and are included on their family shrines at home. Also, Hindus will pray to a specific god or goddess for particular needs (for example, Ganesh is believed to remove obstacles) and during a particular festival (for example, Lakshmi during the festival of Diwali). The deities featured in the story are Shiva, Ganesh, Durga, and Lakshmi.

Shiva

Shiva is portrayed in a number of ways in Hinduism. In the story and worksheet Shiva is presented as the Lord of the Dance. For the worksheet, it is important that pupils are allowed to think about possible symbolism and meaning first before being given 'right' answers (it is worth remembering that often there is more than one 'right' answer). The thinking process and an appreciation of the purpose of Hindu iconography are the main skills to develop.

Interesting features in the iconography of Shiva include:

- the third eye: this is a symbol for his inner, spiritual knowledge;
- long, unkempt hair: Shiva is seen as a great yogi and as such he has the matted hair of a yogi. Sometimes Shiva is depicted with the sacred river Ganges flowing through his hair;
- fire: symbol of his power to destroy;
- wild animal skin: many meanings have been suggested, for example, it may symbolise Shiva's spiritual attributes or it may be related to a myth about Shiva killing a wild animal;
- evil dwarf: the dwarf represents ignorance. Shiva is crushing the dwarf which symbolises his ability to crush and remove ignorance;
- hand pointing to foot: this is a common mudra (hand symbol) which shows that Shiva sustains those who devote themselves to him, worshipping at his feet;
- raised hand: another common mudra which means 'do not fear'; Shiva protects his devotees;
- four arms: Hindu gods and goddesses usually need a lot of arms to carry various objects and to perform mudras which symbolise their actions in the world;
- cobra: snakes are greatly feared and respected in Hinduism. They are deadly, symbolising destruction but also have healing properties, symbolising preservation;
- drum: the drum is part of the dance. The rhythm of the drum is linked to the creation of the universe. Shiva is seen as creator in this depiction;
- crescent moon: the moon can be associated with time and so symbolises that Shiva has control over time.

Shiva is often pictured with a bull and his consort Parvati, who is a beautiful, benign goddess.

Ganesh

Ganesh is the son of Shiva and Parvati. Many myths exist which explain why he has an elephant's head. One myth is that Shiva had been away for many years meditating and returned home to find a boy he did not recognise guarding Parvati, so he cut off the boy's head. On learning that Ganesh was really his son, he gave Ganesh the first head he could find – the head of an elephant. Ganesh is the god of obstacles and wisdom; he removes obstacles which are both physical and spiritual. Many Hindus pray to Ganesh when they begin a new project, get married, or take exams. Ganesh is a very popular god, portrayed with:

- one broken tusk;
- a big belly;
- three weapons – an axe, lasso, and hook;
- a rat.

Durga

Durga is a beautiful, fearsome goddess, who is associated with battle. She is depicted with many arms so that she can hold all her weapons (for example, a spear, sword, club, and bow). In the picture she is shown with the 'do not fear' mudra (hand symbol) and accompanied by a lion. Durga can also carry a thunderbolt, symbolising that she cuts through ignorance.

Lakshmi

Information about Lakshmi has been placed in the teachers' notes for the second chapter because of her importance during the festival of Diwali.

Puja service

In the story, devotion is shown to the deities in the puja service where they are presented with traditional offerings. In response, the deities give the devotees their blessings through the blessed fire and food.

Activities

Create an image of a god

Create your own image of a god or goddess. What qualities do you want it to have? What sort of activities would it do? In what ways would it help the world and people? Draw a picture of your god or goddess, thinking carefully about how you are going to show its character and activities. Pass your picture to the person sitting next to you. How well does that person understand your god or goddess?

Picturing God

Divide the class into groups of five. Give each group a large sheet of paper. In turn, take one member out of each group, and give them 20 seconds to study the picture of Shiva on the 'Learning about God' worksheet. Send them back to their groups where they are given 30 seconds to draw and/or label what they can remember. Pupils cannot draw or write anything unless it is their turn, although ideas may be offered at any time.

Do the task on the 'Learning about God' worksheet, which explores the symbolism behind the image.

Visiting a Hindu place of worship

Visit a Hindu place of worship and identify the places mentioned in the story. How does it differ from the places in the book and how is it the same?

Mix and match

Cut out the nine boxes on the 'Write a story' worksheet, and then cut each box into three sections: the heading; the information; and the picture. Mix up all the sections and place them in an envelope. Divide pupils into pairs or groups and give each pair or group an envelope. Pupils need to match heading, information, and picture correctly.

Do the task on the 'Write a story' worksheet (the story can easily be adapted to another genre such as a diary entry or newspaper article, if needed).

Make a shrine display

Using a table placed against a wall, construct a Hindu shrine display. Include on the display:

- incense holder and incense;
- five-wick arti lamp (this can be made by filling a heat proof small container with ghee and placing 5 string wicks in it. Ghee can be bought or made following the recipe in the activities for chapter 4);
- offerings of flowers, fruit, nuts, and rice;
- bell for alerting the deities that puja is to begin;
- pot of water and spoon which is used to give water to the devotees after it has been offered to the deities;
- gods and goddesses (try to include statues and pictures which can be pinned on the wall behind the shrine. Decide carefully which gods and goddesses to include and also add some pictures of living and dead famous Hindu teachers like Mohandas Gandhi. Respected teachers and reformers are often considered to be avatars or manifestations of God working in the world);
- Hindu symbols like OM (sacred symbol for God) and the swastika (symbol for good fortune).

Chapter 2 Celebrating Diwali

Most religious festivals have at least one foundation story which explains their origins and the reasons for the celebrations. For many adherents of a religion, celebrating a festival is one of the most important contexts for learning about their religion's beliefs and practices.

In the festival of Diwali, the foundation story is one of the great Hindu myths from the sacred text, the Ramayana. Rajeev and Meena's grandmother retells the story for Rees and Sara. Many different versions of the story exist. Rama is presented as the perfect man and Sita, the perfect woman. Both have traditionally acted as powerful role models depicting valued qualities such as loyalty, fulfilment of duty, devotion, honour, valour, perseverance, justice, and piety.

Diwali is a five-day festival which is celebrated by Hindus, Buddhists, and Sikhs. The way in which the festival is celebrated varies from region to region. In addition to the activities mentioned in the story, Hindus might also have an early morning bath, wear clean or new clothes, and conduct pujas for various gods including Lakshmi.

Rangoli patterns

In the story, Rajeev does not appear particularly bothered that the beautiful rangoli pattern he created with Meena could be destroyed in the rain. It is made with perishable materials deliberately to illustrate the impermanence of all things (apart from the atman or soul). If the impermanence of the rangoli pattern is understood and accepted, you cannot be attached to it. Non-attachment to physical and non-physical things is an important teaching in Hinduism (as well as in Buddhism and Sikhism). Also, the process of creating the pattern is an important spiritual exercise.

There is also an environmental aspect to rangoli patterns. If they are made from edible products, they provide food for other living creatures.

Lakshmi

Lakshmi is the goddess of wealth and good fortune. Hindus clean and paint their houses in the hope that she will visit during Diwali and bless them with wealth and good fortune for the coming year. A special puja is made to Lakshmi during this festival. Lakshmi is the consort of the god Vishnu. Rama and Sita are believed to be avatars (incarnations) of Lakshmi and Vishnu, respectively.

Lakshmi is often depicted standing on a lotus flower in water which refers to the myth about her origins. As the gods were churning the ocean to gain the nectar of immortality, Lakshmi emerged out of the ocean. The lotus flower is a symbol of spiritual purity and power; like the pure soul, it is unsullied by its muddy origins because the flower bud does not open until it is above the water. The coins flowing from her outstretched hand symbolise her gifts of good fortune to her devotees.

Activities

Art for the moment

Most artists create art which they hope will last a long time. Also, galleries and museums make a big effort to preserve artists' work so that people can see and appreciate it for many years. Look at some pictures of older art by famous artists (perhaps artists that pupils have been studying at school, like van Gogh or Picasso). The paintings are being preserved in different galleries around the world. Explore how these galleries preserve them, for example, ensuring that temperature, light, and humidity levels are right and that they are transported appropriately when moved. Also, when they do start to decay, galleries use the right materials and techniques to repair them.

Some artists, though, deliberately create art which only lasts for a short time, for example, snow and sand sculptors. Show some pictures of snow and sand sculptures. Amazing examples can be accessed on the internet by searching for words like 'snow art', 'sand art', or 'snow art competitions'. Also, there are artists who explore impermanent art as well as more enduring art, such as Dieter Roth who created the Chocolate Lion and a chocolate self-portrait. For these artists being able to experience the erosion and change in their art is an essential part of their 'art'.

- What is the point of this type of art? Can we learn anything from it?
- Create your own piece of impermanent art. It could be made of sand and water, or any other material which displays its impermanence relatively quickly. Put it to one side and check it over a period of time, noting how it changes and is gradually destroyed.
- Link this work to Hindu rangoli pictures, offering a Hindu understanding (see teachers' notes). Complete the worksheet 'Make a tri-tetraflexagon of rangoli patterns' or 'Draw rangoli patterns'.

What do I value?

Do the 'Write character profiles' worksheet which explores the qualities/values held by the characters in the story of Rama and Sita.

Make a list of the qualities/values identified in the activity, and place it so that it can be easily read by all pupils. On a sheet of paper, ask pupils to draw (or provide) a large circle, with a smaller circle within it, and a smaller circle within that. Working individually, pupils need to select and place the qualities/values in order of importance to them in the circles. They should choose ONE most important quality/value and place it in the smallest circle at the centre. Then, moving outwards in order of importance, place ONE quality/value in each of the other two circles. Encourage them to use their own words.

In pairs, pupils can discuss their choices with their partner. If they wish to 'rethink' and change any ideas as a result of their discussion, they are allowed to do so.

Festivals across religious traditions

Work on a calendar or book of festivals from all religions. This would need to be a loose-leaf folder, or pages joined together with treasury tags so that pages can be added as needed in chronological order.

Talk about the importance of organising material well so that people can find quickly the information they need. With the pupils, decide on a useful structure for the book, for example, section headings could include stories, how the festival is celebrated today, recipes, and so on.

Linking story and practice

Make links between the events in the story of Rama and Sita and how Diwali is celebrated today. This can be approached in different ways, for example, write relevant parts of the story of Rama and Sita on small cards and do the same with relevant parts of the celebrations today. Ask pupils to match up the story cards with the celebration cards. Suggested content for the cards:

story	**celebration**
villagers lighting path home for Rama and Sita	lighting divas
Sita (avatar of goddess Lakshmi)	cleaning and painting house puja for Lakshmi rangoli design by door
Rama (avatar of god Vishnu)	puja for Vishnu
the battle with the evil Ravana	fireworks, fire crackers
villagers celebrate return of Rama and Sita	eating special food with family and friends

Chapter 3 Some special books

In this chapter Rees and Sara are introduced to Hindu sacred texts through the Bhagavad Gita and classical Indian dance which retells some of the great Hindu myths. They learn the importance of duty for many Hindus and some more ways in which Rajeev and Meena show their love and devotion to God.

Bhagavad Gita

There are many sacred texts in Hinduism and these texts are all part of the Vedas, which means 'knowledge', and they are written in Sanskrit. Hinduism is a broad and flexible religious tradition, accepting many different beliefs and practices within it. However, acceptance or rejection of the Vedas determines whether or not a person or group is Hindu. This fact illustrates how central the Vedas are in Hinduism.

In the story, a Vedic text called the Bhagavad Gita is Rajeev and Meena's sacred book. Bhagavad Gita means 'Song of God'. The Bhagavad Gita has been chosen because it is popular with many Hindus from all traditions. It also presents clearly some major beliefs held by Hindus, such as the importance of doing one's duty (Dharma). Performing one's duties in relation to the world and other people is more important than personal concerns, and these duties should take priority.

Like other religious sacred texts, it is easy to access free readings of the Bhagavad Gita on-line in Sanskrit and in English.

Duty and the Caste System

A central concept in Hinduism is Dharma, which can mean law, duty, teaching or truth; Dharma underpins all life. Everything which exists (people, animals, plants, and the natural world) has its own laws and duties to follow. Fulfilling the laws and duties produces positive karmic consequences, while failing to fulfil the laws and duties produces negative karmic consequences. The Hindu world should be an ordered place, and this order is based on everything in the world fulfilling its Dharma. In chapter 4, Dharma is explored in relation to the environment and human beings.

In the story, Krishna tries to persuade Arjuna to go to battle because it is the Dharma (duty) of a warrior to fight. In order to understand this argument properly, it has to be placed within traditional Hindu beliefs about the structure of Indian society. In the Vedas, four main social groupings called Varnas (Castes) are identified, which relate to the types of work people perform:

- Brahmin (priests and teachers);
- Kshatriya (warriors and rulers);
- Vaishya (artisans, farmers, and traders);
- Shudra (labourers).

According to the Vedas, the Varnas can be traced back to the creation of the world and were not a human invention. One of the Hindu creation myths tells of the sacrifice of the Great Man, Purusha, who created the world from his body. Brahmins came from his mouth, Kshatriyas from his arms, Vaishyas from his thighs, and Shudras from his feet. The Vedas also describe the duties (Dharmas) that each Varna should perform. Arjuna belonged to the Kshatriya Varna, and this means that he was expected to fight and display all the skills of a good warrior.

Traditionally, social interaction between the different Castes is regulated, for example, it is common to marry someone from your own Caste and eat with members of your own Caste. A person is born into a Caste and remains in that Caste until rebirth into a new body. Each Caste is further sub-divided into different jatis, which relate more specifically to the type of work a person does. For example, there are jatis of potters, bakers, gardeners, and barbers. There are several thousand jatis in India today, and each jati in each Indian village is regulated by its own council of elders.

A social group outside the Caste system exists called the Dalits ('oppressed'), who are also known as 'the Untouchables'. Traditionally, Dalits perform jobs that Caste Hindus are reluctant to do because they are believed to make people ritually impure, for example, working with dead animals. The injustices committed against Dalits have been well-recorded alongside the work of prominent Hindu reformers such as Dr Ambedkar and Mohandas Gandhi, who raised the profile of Dalits and helped to effect legal reforms in India which banned discrimination on the basis of Caste. In India equality laws can be difficult to enforce, especially in rural communities which tend to be more conservative and traditional than cosmopolitan urban communities.

Hindu dance

Rees and Sara are introduced to other sacred texts in Hinduism through the medium of dance. The Vedas contain many great myths about the gods and goddesses which are re-enacted or expressed through dance. There are a number of classical styles of dance in India. The style of dance depicted in the story is called Bharatnatyam and originates in South India. A lot of its techniques come from a text called the Natya Shastra which is believed to be over two thousand years old. The Natya Shastra includes directions on music, stage design, and makeup as well as dance.

Activities

Special lessons

The Bhagavad Gita is a very special book for many Hindus because it contains some important lessons about how people should behave and their relationship with God. One important lesson is that everyone has duties and they must try to perform them. They should perform these duties because it is right to perform them, and not for any rewards. They should offer what they do as a gift to God. Explain, simply, the background to the story, placing Arjuna as a warrior in the Caste System.

Ask pupils to write out lists of duties for some or all of the following people:

- teacher;
- doctor;
- policeman/woman;
- parents.

Ask pupils to identify their own duties. Is it easy for them to do these duties? In the story, Arjuna found it hard to do his duty as a warrior until he understood Krishna's lessons.

What kind of book?

There are many different kinds of books which have been written for different purposes. Place pupils in groups and give each group a wide selection of books taken from the school or class library (include different genres and subjects such as story books, history books, reference books like the encyclopaedia/dictionary, science books, art books, poetry books, text books, Bible, Bhagavad Gita, and so on). Ask each group to sort the books physically into different piles in a way which makes sense to them. They need to be able to explain to the teacher or class how the books have been sorted. Note: There is no right answer to the task because it is possible to sort books in different ways (genre, subject, paperback/hardback, years of publication, reading age, for example). Pupils need to be given time to think for themselves and debate a logical way of categorising the books in front of them.

This task can be extended by asking the groups to identify the purposes of each group of books. Why were they written? What are they trying to do?

Link this to the story. Different books have different purposes. For many Hindus the Bhagavad Gita is a special book because it teaches important lessons about how to live and how to have a good relationship with God. Pupils can then do the 'Write about books' worksheet.

Showing devotion to God

Discuss with pupils the different ways that Hindus show love and devotion to God. Some of these ways have been illustrated in the story:

- puja;
- singing;
- prayer;
- correct behaviour (list examples from the story);
- dance.

Some devotion takes place before a shrine (either in a temple or at home) but a lot of devotion is shown in Hindus' everyday lives. For a Hindu (as in other religions), devotion to God is a way of life and not just something that you do in a specific religious place.

Dance is one popular way of showing love and devotion to God. It uses the whole of the body and focuses the mind on God. Do the 'Create a dance' activity on the worksheet. It is important that pupils are encouraged to use the whole of their bodies creatively to express the story.

Chapter 4 Caring for others and the world

In the story, two reasons are given to explain why Hindus respect all life forms. These are:

- every living creature has an atman (soul) which deserves acknowledgement and respect;
- the world is governed by rules (duties or Dharmas) which provide order and harmony if they are kept. Not respecting life breaks one of these rules.

Rees and Sara learn that it can be serious when people break the rules of nature because they can cause a great deal of harm. This is illustrated by a true story about the Chipko Movement ('tree huggers') in India.

Rebirth

Hindus believe that everything is subject to change, decay, and death apart from the atman (soul) which resides in every living being. This makes the atman very special and sacred. The atman, though, is tied to a cycle of rebirth, and it enters a new body with each rebirth. The type of rebirth experienced is determined by one's past actions (karma) both positively and negatively. The ultimate ideal is the release of the atman from this cycle of rebirth permanently so that it can experience an eternal relationship with the Supreme Reality or God. This is called Moksha.

Hindus hold different views about the precise nature of the atman. Some Hindus believe that the atman is the same as the Supreme Reality (the idea that God is present within everything). Other Hindus believe that the atman and the Supreme Reality are different from one another, although they share the same basic qualities, such as permanence, which set them apart from everything else.

Many of these concepts (rebirth, karma, and impermanence) are shared with Buddhism, although Buddhists do not accept the Hindu belief in the atman or understanding of God.

The Chipko Movement

In the Himalayas in Northern India deforestation caused by commercial interests has had a major environmental impact. Local village life is often seriously affected because villages rely on the forests to provide:

- fuel;
- building materials;
- food;
- medicine;
- and fodder.

As a result, women in the villages affected have had to travel further for fodder and fuel, and the villages are less self-subsistent and more reliant on importing products from outside the villages.

The exact origins of the Chipko Movement are unknown, although the trade-mark tree hugging tactic to prevent the logging of trees first emerged in the early 1970s. It is interesting to note that the Movement consists mainly of women and children, who have become environmental activists to protect their communities and livelihoods. They practise satyagraha (peaceful protest), which was also the method of protest adopted by Mohandas Gandhi who worked on behalf of the Dalits ('Untouchables'). Satyagraha supports the Indian principle of ahimsa (non-violence). As a result of the actions of the Chipko Movement, it is estimated that over 100,000 trees may have been saved, and now more respect is given to local communities by the timber companies concerned.

Activities

Peaceful protests

A number of Hindus believe that if people do 'violent' things to you, it is best to protest and fight back in a non-violent, peaceful way. This kind of peaceful protest is called satyagraha. The story about the Chipko Movement shows satyagrapha in practice. Another Hindu called Mohandas Gandhi also protested against injustice towards the Dalits or 'Untouchables' through using peaceful means (satyagraha), and with pressure from other reformers, he succeeded in implementing laws in India to improve the lives of Dalits.

Explore with pupils how they deal with things that they think are unfair, for example, with hurtful behaviour in the playground or bullying. What are the different ways they could deal with these situations practically? (For school-related issues, you need to listen to the pupils but make sure that they are aware of the relevant policies set up to deal with relevant issues.)

Our local environment

Look closely at one small part of your environment to find all the living things in it. You can mark the area with a hoop or with string. Choose an area which is likely to have some life in it (grassy or wooded area, for example). Draw a plan of the area which includes the living things in it, both plants, insects, etc. Selecting the living things in your marked area, complete the 'Make a collage' worksheet.

There are many living things in our environment which often go unnoticed unless we look very carefully. As the story explains, many Hindus believe that it is wrong to deliberately harm life in the natural world for two reasons:

- all life is special because it has an atman (soul) within it which is holy;
- breaking the rules and destroying things has an effect on more than the thing you destroy.

You can also explore other Indian religions which believe in ahimsa (non-violence) such as Buddhism and Jainism. Jainism is particularly interesting because its monks and nuns take this belief extremely seriously. They watch carefully where they tread and gently brush the ground before they walk to avoid killing any small creatures. They also wear material tied over their mouths and sieve water in order to avoid swallowing living things. Lay Jains are not so strict and support monks and nuns with food.

Cause and effect

In the story, Rees and Sara learn that Hindus believe that everything has rules to follow which give each living thing a specific role to play in the world. These are the rules of nature. Do the worksheet 'Write rules for the world', which asks pupils to identify rules for people generally and rules for another living creature.

Animals and other things in the natural world do not consciously choose to follow rules, but human beings do have more of a choice. This means that when human beings break rules they can potentially have a great effect on themselves and the world around them. This is illustrated by the events which created the Chipko Movement in the story. This can be explored further by looking at other environmental problems created by human beings.

Chapter 5 Food

For human beings food does more than simply feed the body and keep a person alive. In both the religious and secular world food is used creatively for many purposes. Some examples of this include using food for:

- strengthening social bonds within the family or community through sharing food together;
- marking special times such as festivals and rites of passage;
- communicating through symbols, beliefs, ideas, and feelings.

In addition, as Rees and Sara discover in the story, we are able to experience food from around the world and appreciate its rich cultural diversity.

Indian food

Today, Hindu communities exist in many countries in the world, far beyond the borders of India. However, for many Hindus in Britain part of their cultural heritage includes Indian cuisine, which is especially prominent at times of celebration such as festivals or weddings. Much of Indian cuisine is traditionally vegetarian, although it can contain meat if it has culinary influences from the few Indian states where meat-eating is popular or where it has been tailored to appeal to the Western palate.

The sacred cow

Most Hindus believe that the cow is a sacred animal. Cows and bulls are respected because historically they have provided Hindus in India with the basic resources they need to live, for example:

- dairy products to eat;
- dung for fuel and fertilisers;
- strength to pull carts and plough fields;
- ghee candles for light.

In India, cows are often seen wandering freely, and it is illegal in most Indian states to kill healthy cows or to harm cows. Any mistreatment of cows or bulls is a very sensitive issue in India, and Hindu animal rights activists are regularly in the news drawing attention to breaches in the law. Also, the sacredness of cows is linked to Krishna's strong association with them. How far the tradition of the sacred cow extends back into Hindu history is debated among Indian academics.

Krishna

Krishna is an avatar (incarnation) of the god Vishnu, and in the story he is pictured with one of his gopi (cow herder) devotees, Radha. Earlier in the story, Rajeev and Meena practised devotion to the gods and goddesses in the puja service and also through the medium of dance. Here, we continue to explore devotion by learning about the relationship between Krishna and Radha which exemplifies the ideal relationship between God and a devotee. The devotee offers God unconditional love and devotion and God loves the devotee.

Krishna can be depicted in many forms, for example, as a loveable and mischievous child, the wise charioteer in the Bhagavad Gita (chapter 3), or the adored cow-herder boy, playing a flute.

Activities

Hindus on the world map

In the story, Rees and Sara learn that Hinduism originally came from India, although today Hindus can be found in many countries of the world including Britain. Display a map of the world and mark the countries where there is a large population of Hindus (for example, India, Nepal, Bangladesh, Indonesia, Sri Lanka, Pakistan, Malaysia, USA, South Africa, Myanmar, Fiji, Mauritius, Nepal, the Caribbean, and Guyana).

Also display a map of Britain and mark some places which have fairly large Hindu communities – usually in the Midlands and South East of England (for example, London, Birmingham, Leicester, Preston). Two of the largest Hindu temples in Europe are found in Britian (Swaminarayan Temple in Neasdon, London and Bhaktivedanta Manor, near Watford). In Wales most Hindu communities exist in South Wales (for example, Swansea, Cardiff, and Newport) although Wrexham also has a Hindu community. Display some pictures of some of the larger Hindu temples from the internet.

Spices

Ask pupils to keep a three-day diary of the food they eat (see the 'Reflect on your food' worksheet). Where do these foods and dishes come from? Why do they enjoy them?

There are many different and exciting flavours and recipes to try from around the world. In the story, Rees and Sara's friends are vegetarian Hindus and Rees and Sara discover that many things can be done with vegetables to make them tasty and interesting.

Gather together a selection of spices and ingredients often used in Indian cooking. Examples of possible ingredients include: turmeric, coriander seeds, cumin, black pepper, mustard seeds, cardamom pods, fennel seeds, garlic, ginger, and chillies. Present these foods to pupils labelled only with a number and give them a list of the food names. Allow pupils to smell each item and try to match it up with the list. They should know a few and be able to guess some others.

Use some of the ingredients to make a very simple Indian vegetarian dish such as a potato curry. Whatever you choose, also prepare the potato or main vegetable used by simply boiling it and allow the pupils to compare the tastes.

As well as flavouring food, many of these spices and ingredients are believed by some nutritionists to provide health-giving benefits. For example, ginger and fennel could be good for the digestion, garlic could support the immune system, and most recently some scientists believe that turmeric may slow down the development of Alzheimer's disease. Pupils can look at their diet from the 'Reflect on your food' worksheet and identify what may be healthy about it and what may be unhealthy about it.

Link this back to the story, and reflect on the reasons given in chapter 5 for Rajeev and Meena's diet. There are many reasons why we eat certain types of food, and it is important to remember that, for some people, there are also religious reasons behind their choice of food.

Make your own ghee

It is easy to see why cows have been traditionally revered in Hinduism, looking at the list of gifts they provide for Hindus in India (see teachers' notes). One of these gifts is ghee which was a commonly-used source of light, and remains important in Hindu worship at home and in the temple today. For example, the five-wicked arti lamp is fuelled by ghee and so is the diva lamp lit during the festival of Diwali. Also, the statues of Hindu gods and goddesses on the shrines at home and in the temple will be regularly washed with ghee as part of Hindu devotion. Making your own ghee gives you a better idea of what it is.

Ghee is unsalted butter which has had the water and solid milk particles removed from it. Melt a block of unsalted butter in a pan and bring to the boil. Reduce heat. When foam appears on the top continue boiling until the foam disappears. The ghee is ready when a second foam appears and the butter is a golden colour. Pour through a fine strainer into a jar. You should be able to see the milk solids which have accumulated at the bottom of the pan. Discard these.

Use the ghee to make your own lamps using heat-proof containers and inserting string wicks. Ask pupils to complete the 'Write a poem' worksheet.

Keywords

ahimsa	non-violence
atman	eternal soul residing in every living being
avatar	a god or a goddess taking physical form (incarnation)
Bharatnatyam	a style of classical Indian dance
bhakti	devotion (to God)
Bhagavad Gita	a popular sacred book for many Hindus which is part of the Vedas
Brahman	the name some Hindus use for the Supreme Reality
Chipko Movement	the environmental movement protecting trees in India
Dalit	a social group outside the Caste System
Dharma	law, duty, teaching, truth
Diwali	the popular Hindu festival of light, celebrating the victory of good over evil
Durga	Hindu goddess associated with battle
Ganesh	Hindu god who removes physical and spiritual obstacles; son of Parvati and Shiva
gopi	cow herder
incarnation	the embodiment of God in a physical form
Kali	Hindu goddess associated with death and cremation grounds
karma	action: there is positive action (karma) and negative action (karma)
Krishna	a popular avatar of the god Vishnu
Lakshmi	Hindu goddess associated with wealth and prosperity; popular during the festival of Diwali
mandir	Hindu temple or place of worship
Moksha	ultimate aim for Hindus which is release from the cycle of suffering and rebirth
mudra	hand symbol present in Hindu, Buddhist, and Sikh iconography
Natya Shastra	an ancient Indian handbook of dance and drama
Parvati	Hindu goddess who is consort to the god Shiva and mother of the god Ganesh
puja	symbolic offerings made to deities before the shrine
Purusha	the Great Man in one Hindu creation myth from whom the world was created
Radha	Krishna's consort
Ramayana	a Hindu sacred text which relates the famous story of Rama and Sita retold at Diwali
rebirth	Hindus believe in an eternal cycle of rebirth for everything which exists; the ideal is liberation from this cycle
satyagraha	peaceful protest
Shiva	one of the main Hindu gods
Supreme Reality	God in an ultimate and abstract sense
Vedas	Hindu sacred texts
Vishnu	one of the main Hindu gods: he has ten avatars (incarnations); two of them, Rama and Krishna, are depicted in the story book

Write a story

Imagine you have visited a Hindu mandir with a friend who worships there. Write a story about it, giving details of all the places you visited and the things you saw. The pictures and descriptions below will help you.

OM

You may see the sacred symbol for God, written in Sanskrit, outside or inside the mandir.

shoe rack

As a sign of respect, shoes are left on a rack near the entrance to the mandir. This keeps the mandir clean as a place to worship God.

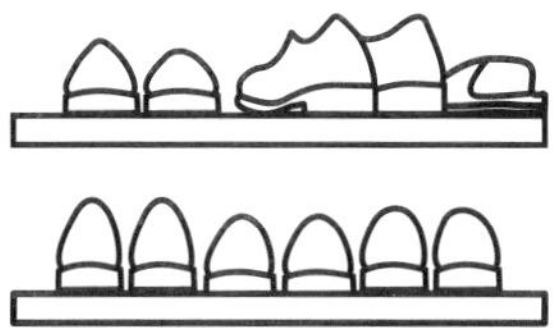

washing area

Clean hands before worship are a sign of respect.

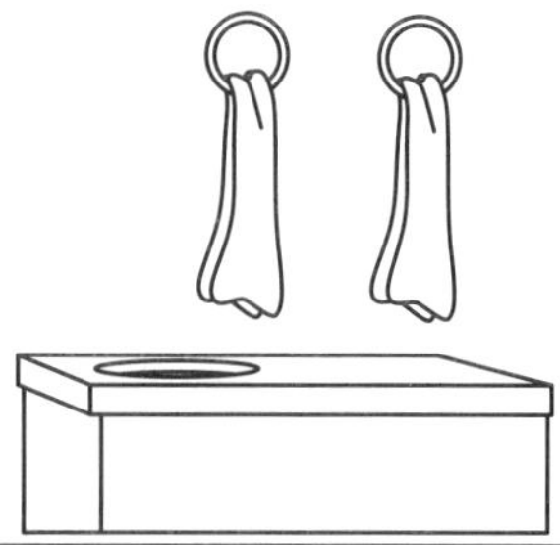

shrines

There are many different shrines in a mandir, each with different statues of gods and goddesses. These represent God, the Supreme Reality.

offerings

When people pray at a shrine they may leave offerings of money, rice, fruit or flowers.

arti lamp

During a puja ceremony, fire is offered to God. The fire is then offered to all the people present.

bhajans

Songs of worship (bhajans) are sung during the arti ceremony, accompanied by tablas (drums), hand cymbals and harmoniums.

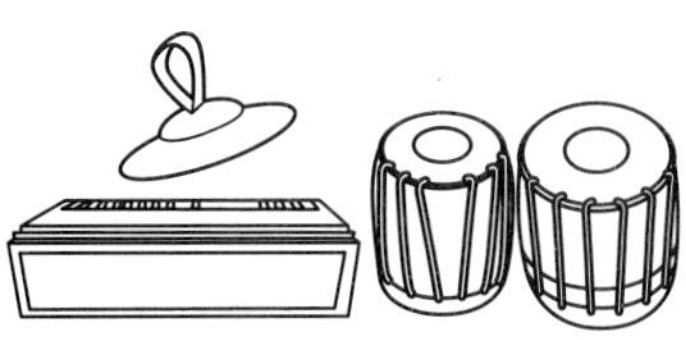

prashad

People eat the food that has been offered to God, as a sign that they accept God's love and blessing.

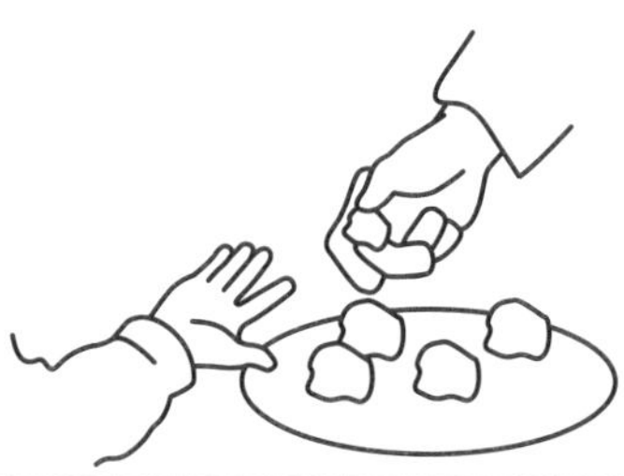

meeting rooms

The mandir is a meeting place for entertainment and a place to help people in need. It may have rooms for meeting and teaching.

Learning about God

Statues and pictures of gods and goddesses remind Hindus of God's character and God's actions in the world. For example, a god or a goddess may look kind, powerful, or fierce. A god or a goddess is always carrying, wearing, and doing something which shows Hindus some of the things that God does in the world.

This is a picture of the god Shiva as Lord of the Dance. What do you think this picture teaches Hindus about God's character and God's actions in the world?

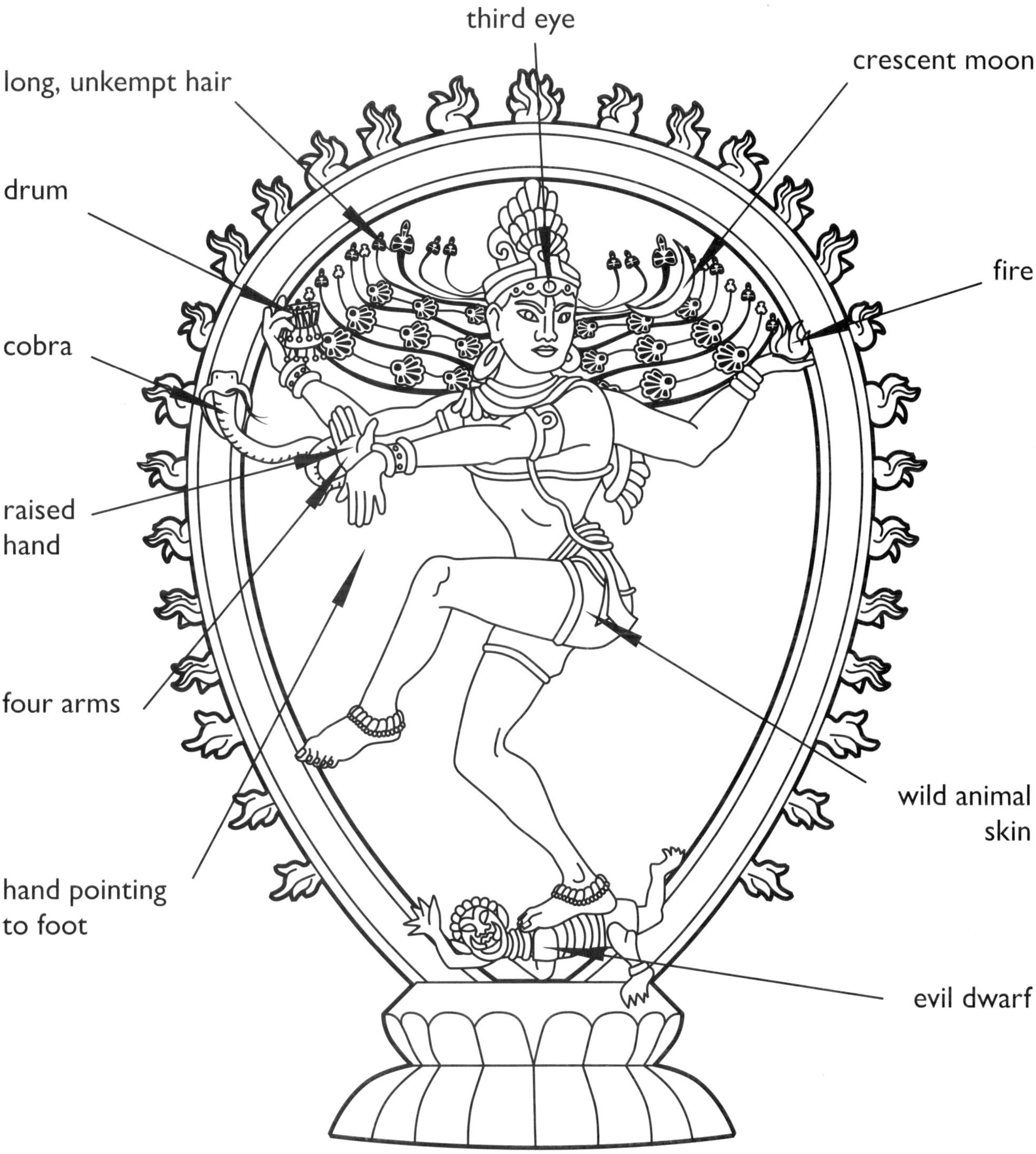

Make a diva

During Diwali, Hindus light divas and fill their homes with light. Years ago the divas were small lamps made of clay and filled with ghee with one or more cotton wicks to burn brightly. Nowadays candles are often used.

You will need

modelling clay
nightlight candles
clay tools
PVA glue

What to do

1. Roll a ball of clay to make it pliable.

2. Shape the clay into a dish that will hold a nightlight. (Test it to be sure the nightlight fits.) Make sure the clay is not too thin in any spot or it will crumble as it dries.

3. Decorate the clay with a simple rangoli pattern.

4. Leave the diva until it is completely dry.

5. Paint the diva with PVA glue to protect it and to give it a glossy sheen.

6. Put the nightlight inside the diva and plan where and when you will light it in remembrance of the Diwali story. (Ask an adult to light the diva for you.)

Make a tri-tetraflexagon of rangoli patterns

Rangoli patterns are made for Diwali. Often they are made on the ground using flour, rice grains or coloured chalk. It is a sign of welcome to visitors during Diwali.

Make a tri-tetraflexagon with three different rangoli patterns to display.

You will need

- paper or card
- pencils
- transparent tape
- ruler
- scissors

1.

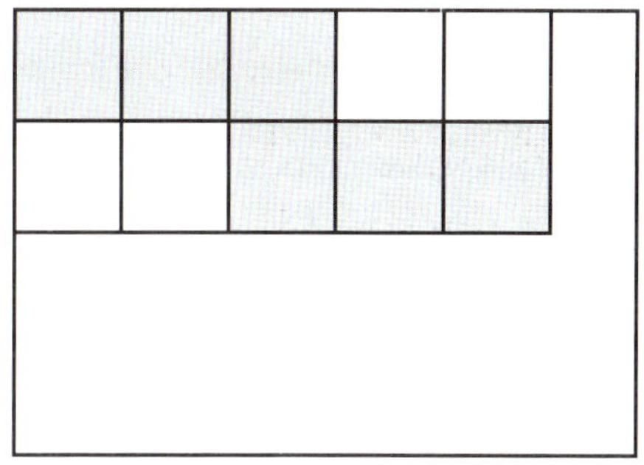

What to do

1. Rule a piece of A4 paper or card into two rows of 5 cm squares.
2. Cut out the squares as shown. Very lightly number them front and back. (You will need to be able to rub out these numbers when you draw your pattern.)

2.

3. Design three very simple rangoli patterns, each to fit into one of your 5cm squares. Choose patterns that touch on the edges of your squares.

4. Draw these patterns onto your shape, making sure that the designs go in the correct squares. (You will have two squares with pattern 1 on the front, and two squares with pattern 1 on the back, and so on.)

4.

5. With side A facing you, fold the last right hand square over, to show pattern 2. Fold the top two left hand squares under to show pattern 2. Put a piece of tape where shown to hold the squares in place.

5.

6. You can now see the four matching pattern 2 pictures on one side, and pattern 1 on the other side. To find pattern 3, fold or flex the square vertically, then open it up from your fold.

6.

Write character profiles

1. Read the story of Rama and Sita. (You might like to read a longer version with details of all their adventures.)
2. Think of the people mentioned in the story:
   - the king
   - the king's wife
   - Rama
   - Sita
   - Bharata
   - Laksmana
   - Ravana
   - Hanuman
3. Choose two of these and write a character profile on them. Think about their actions and what this shows us of their character.

Person: ______________________

Person: ______________________

Create a dance

Hindus think about dancing as being a gift from God. It is more than entertainment. It teaches the stories of the gods and goddesses, but more importantly it is a way to worship God. Hindu dancing has many special rules and hand movements, and it takes years to learn. Sometimes the dancers wear special masks and costumes to show who they are in the story.

In a group, create your own dance to tell a story.

1. Select a story

First choose the story you would like to show.

2. Choose characters

List the characters you will need to tell the story. These may be people or animals or other important elements such as plants or the wind. Decide which person will dance each character.

3. Plan the story

Work out the 'storyline' of your dance. Divide it into separate scenes to make this easier.

4. Experiment with movements and music

Try different movements to find the best way of presenting the story. Listen to different music and find some that works well with your storyline. Do you need soft, flowing music or loud abrupt rhythms?

5. Make costumes

Costumes can be simple. You might only need a piece of fabric as a cape over your gym clothes, or a scarf wrapped around your head.

Our dance

Story: ____________________

Characters: ____________________

Storyline: ____________________

____

____

Write about books

Rajeev and Meena took the Bhagavad Gita to class as their special book. It is special to them because it teaches them about worshipping God.

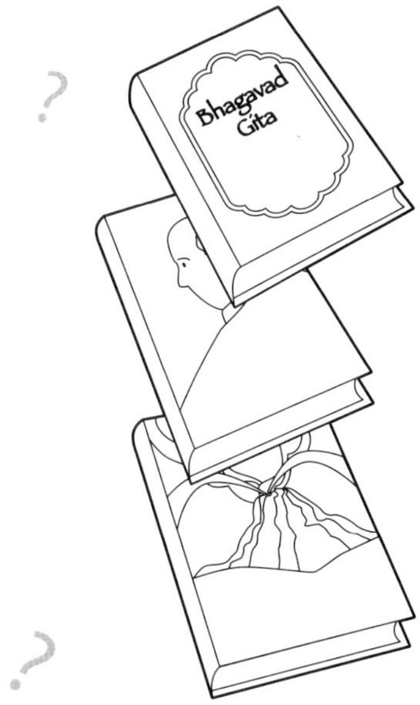

1. Choose a book

Name the book that was special to Rajeev and Meena.

___

2. Write about the book

Name the main characters and write briefly about the contents.

___

___

___

3. Write one thing that this book taught Rajeev and Meena.

___

___

___

___

4. Choose a book

Name one book that is special to you.

___

5. Write about the book

Name the main characters and write briefly about the contents.

___

6. Think of something you learnt from the book

Write one thing that this book taught you. (If your book is fiction, you might have learnt something from the way the characters acted.)

___

___

___

___

Draw a cartoon strip

Save the trees

Many trees grew wild in the Himalayan Mountains. The trees were important to the local people. They burnt the dead branches to cook their food and to keep themselves warm in the cold winters. They trapped and ate birds and animals that lived in the trees. They relied on plants growing in the forests for their food.

Over thirty years ago large companies went to the forests and began to cut down the trees. They sold the timber and grew richer and richer. They did not worry about the local people or about the damage to the environment.

In 1973 a group of local women planned to stop the timber companies. They travelled to where the trees were being cut down. Each woman chose a tree and hugged it. They refused to move. The contractors would have to cut down the women before they could cut down any more trees. The tree cutting was stopped. The forests were safe once more.

Draw a cartoon strip based on the story above.

Use the space below to plan the cartoon. Decide what you need to show in each box of the cartoon. Plan the pictures and the words. When you know how many boxes you will need, start work on a clean sheet of paper.

Make a collage

Hindus have great respect for the world. Many Hindus believe that it is wrong to harm or kill living creatures. Often in our world we kill insects without even thinking about it. Study an insect and celebrate the beauty of its creation. Learn to respect it.

You will need

library books
large sheet of paper
coloured paper or fabrics
glue
computer
pencil
scissors

What to do

1. Choose an insect to study. Learn all you can about it from library books or from the internet. Look at its shape and colouring. Find the beauty in it.

2. Draw a large outline shape of your chosen insect. Select fabric and paper to match its colouring. (If you cannot find the correct colours you could mix the colours and paint paper to match.)

3. Cut or tear the fabric or paper and glue it to the outline shape.

4. Display the picture, perhaps with a poem about its beauty or a description of its importance in our environment.

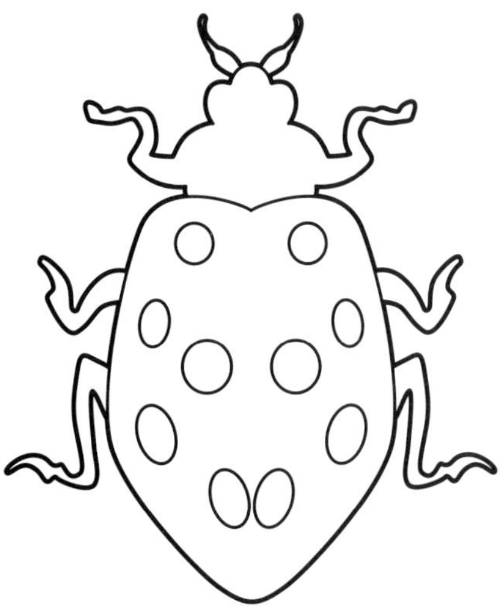

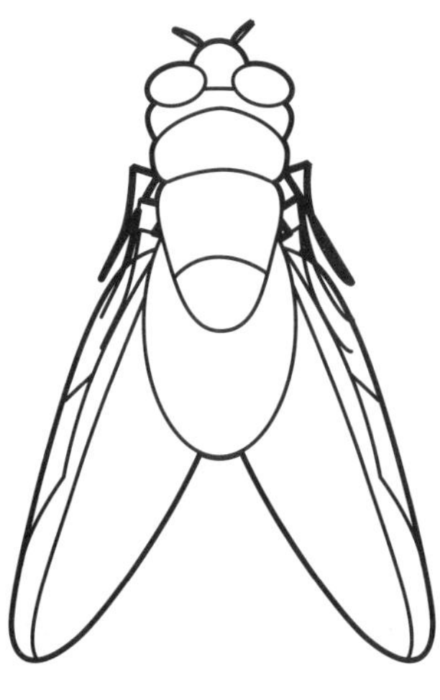

Write rules for the world

Hindus believe that God created the universe and everything in it. For them, everything has specific rules to follow so that the world works properly. Hindus believe that without these rules of nature, the world would be in chaos.

Read some rules for rivers and then write two sets of rules of your own. One set could be for people and one set could be for another living creature. Illustrate your rules.

Rules for rivers

- flow downhill
- combine with other water (for example, rain)
- provide water for drinking and watering crops
- end at the sea

Rules for people

Rules for

Discuss your rules with a friend

Write a poem

Cows are important and special to Hindus. They are important for worship, food, farming and transport. The milk from cows provides ghee for the arti lamps used on shrines, plus food. Bulls plough fields and pull carts.

Write a poem in praise of cows. Choose from these three suggestions or make up your own.

1. Pretend to be a cow or a bull and write a poem about your gifts to people.
2. Compose an acrostic. Write words such as 'COWS AND BULLS' down the page and select a word or a phrase to fit each letter of these words.
3. Think of words and phrases about cows and write them in a triangular shape. Use one word on the first line, two words on the second line, three words on the third line and so on.

My poem

Reflect on your food

Many Hindus believe that the food we eat affects our bodies and minds. Some food makes us feel dull and sluggish and lacking in energy. Some food makes us feel over-excited and full of action and makes it hard for us to concentrate. Other food makes us feel happy and healthy and gives us a long life.

Keep a record of all the food you eat for three days. At the end of that time, discuss it with a friend. How healthy is your diet? Is it helping you in your daily life?

Day 1

Day 2

Day 3

My dictionary

You will meet many new words in *Exploring Hinduism*. Some of these will be English words and some will be Sanskrit words. Keep a record of them, along with their meanings.

mandir	an Indian word for temple, a special place where Hindus go to worship God
OM	the sacred symbol for God, the Supreme Reality, written in Sanskrit
puja	giving gifts, or making offerings to an image of the gods and goddesses
____________	____
____________	____
____________	____
____________	____
____________	____
____________	____
____________	____
____________	____
____________	____
____________	____
____________	____
____________	____
____________	____

Draw rangoli patterns

Rangoli patterns are an important part of Hindu celebrations of the new year. They are often drawn outside the house as a welcome to visitors and to the goddess Lakshmi who is believed to visit each house during Divali.

Research

Use the internet to find out about rangoli patterns. Conduct a search using keywords such as "rangoli pattern" and "picture". Look at several designs to see how varied they can be.

Design

Draft some simple ideas for rangoli patterns, using only straight lines.

Draw

Use a CAD programme (Computer Assisted Design) on your computer to draw the rangoli pattern. You may find you need to change it from your draft design. Experiment, using the symmetry tool as you draw, in order to get a more complex design.

Make

Make your pattern on the ground outside with rice or flour, or draw it on a paved area with chalk.

Exploring
Islam

Exploring Islam

The story

Rees and Sara have two Muslim school friends called Rashid and Fatima who introduce them to key beliefs and practices in Islam. The children explore a mosque and learn about salah (ritual prayer) and what happens in the madrassah (mosque school). They celebrate the festival of Eid-ul-Fitr and learn about the significance of Ramadan (the Muslim month of fasting). Rees and Sara meet two sources of authority in Islam in the form of the Qur'an and the Prophet Muhammad, and they learn about how these affect the lives of Muslims. They investigate Muslim attitudes to the environment and caring for others through the story about the Prophet Muhammad and the camel and the practice of zakah (almsgiving). They learn about what is halal (permitted by Allah) and haram (forbidden by Allah) in Islam through a visit to a halal food shop and Muslim dress codes, and these make Rees and Sara aware of the diversity in belief and practice in Islam.

Aims

Exploring Islam provides opportunities for pupils to:

- **engage** with fundamental questions;
- **explore** religious beliefs, teachings, and practices;
- **express** personal responses in relation to the material studied.

Learning outcomes

Pupils should be able to:

- discuss questions raised by life and aspects of Islam;
- name and describe selected beliefs, teachings, and practices of Islam;
- explain through examples the relationship between belief and practice in Islam;
- discuss their own views and the views of others in relation to some of the themes and issues covered, and relate these to their own lives;
- relate symbol to meaning in some Islamic contexts.

The basics

'Islam' means 'submission' to the will of Allah (God), and a Muslim is a person who submits to the will of Allah. In *Exploring Islam* Rees and Sara are introduced to Sunni Islam, the tradition practised by around 85% of Muslims in the world today. Although there are different expressions of Sunni Islam, it is possible to identify a number of central beliefs and practices which provide a starting point for teachers and pupils exploring Islam.

Sunni Muslims believe in:

- the absolute oneness and unity of Allah, who is the creator and the sustainer of the universe;
- the Muslim duty to submit to Allah's will which brings unity, peace, and harmony in this world and Paradise in the afterlife;
- the centrality of the Qur'an as the fullest, most accurate, and final revelation of Allah's will in human history;
- the value of traditions concerning the Prophet Muhammad's speech and actions which provide a source of guidance for Muslims.

Sunni Muslims practise the Five Pillars:

- Shahadah: the Muslim statement of faith which is recited. It professes that there is no Allah but Allah and that Muhammad is the prophet of Allah;
- Salah: the obligatory set ritual prayer which is performed five times every day;
- Zakah: the obligatory almsgiving;
- Sawn: the obligatory fast during the month of Ramadan;
- Hajj: a single pilgrimage to Makkah which is obligatory if certain conditions are met.

Chapter 1 Visiting a mosque

The mosque

The mosque is a place where Muslims:

- practise congregational prayer (salah);
- receive Islamic education;
- gather together as a community.

Mosque means 'place of prostration', and its main purpose is to provide a clean, quiet place for Muslims to prostrate themselves in prayer before Allah. Many of the features, inside and outside a mosque, point to prayer.

Rees and Sara visit a purpose-built mosque with a minaret (tower) and a dome. From the minaret, a mosque official traditionally calls Muslims to prayer in Arabic five times a day. The adhan (call to prayer) contains the most important beliefs in Islam:

God alone is great [*Allahu Akbar*] – 4 times
I testify that there is no god but God – 2 times
Come to prayer – 2 times
Come to success – 2 times
God alone is great [*Allahu Akbar*] – 2 times
There is no god but God – once

Prayer does not have to take place in a mosque; any clean and quiet space is acceptable. The only requirement is for men to attend the mosque for Friday noon prayer (Jumah prayer).

Rees and Sara prepare themselves before entering the mosque by:

- removing their shoes;
- washing;
- covering their heads.

Removing shoes keeps the prayer areas clean. Ritual washing and covering the head are required before prayer and reciting the Qur'an. These preparations are not carried out because the mosque is especially sacred but because of the nature of the rituals themselves. While praying and reciting the Qur'an, Muslims are in the presence of Allah and they must prepare themselves appropriately. The same preparations are made wherever these rituals take place.

Prayer (salah)

Salah is the second Pillar of Islam. Rees and Sara are taken to the main prayer hall where they watch a group of men praying. All Muslim adolescents and adults, both male and female, are required to perform salah five times every day: at dawn, after midday, late afternoon, after sunset, and at night.

Sara and Fatima stand outside the doors because females pray separately from males, either on a balcony overlooking the main prayer hall or in a separate room. This avoids distractions during prayer. While praying, Muslims recite Arabic words which are accompanied by prescribed movements. Some movements are illustrated by the men in the story although, in real life, Muslims would perform the movements in unison. The movements symbolise submission to the will of Allah, and the accompanying words speak of the oneness, the glory, and the greatness of Allah. Muslims pray side-by-side regardless of social status or race; there are no places of honour. This illustrates the central Muslim belief that everyone is equal before Allah.

Salah helps Muslims learn how to:

- submit to the will of Allah through developing discipline and correct attitudes;
- centre one's life on Allah;
- praise and worship Allah;
- strengthen and unite the Muslim community, both locally and worldwide.

The mosque school (madrassah)

In a madrassah Muslims may learn:

- Arabic, and how to recite the Qur'an in Arabic;
- more about the beliefs and practices of Islam.

Rees and Sara observe a lesson in the mosque school (madrassah) where girls are being taught how to read the Qur'an in Arabic. Arabic is a Semitic language, and the girls are reading the text from right to left, and moving from the 'back' to the 'front' of the book.

Muslims learn how to recite the Qur'an in Arabic because they believe that it is Allah's will that it should be recited aloud for all to hear in the language in which it was revealed to the Prophet Muhammad. The word 'Qur'an' means 'recitation', and Muhammad was asked to recite the revelations which comprise the Qur'an as they were revealed to him. The recitation of the Qur'an is often described as the purest form of music in Islam because it focuses on and glorifies Allah. In the Islamic world there are recitation concerts and competitions where renowned reciters perform, and CDs are sold of their music.

In non-Muslim countries such as Britain, mosques help to keep Muslims in touch with their religious and cultural traditions as well as with one another.

Activities

Mix and match

Cut out the nine boxes on the 'Write a story' worksheet, and then cut each box into three sections: the heading, the information, and the picture. Mix up all the sections and place them in an envelope. Divide pupils into pairs or groups and give each pair or group an envelope. Pupils need to match heading, information, and picture correctly.

Do the task on the 'Write a story' worksheet (the story can easily be adapted to another genre such as a diary entry or newspaper article, if needed).

Another activity for pupils based on the 'Write a story' worksheet: cut out the nine boxes and ask pupils to divide the boxes into three groups:

- cleanliness (being clean);
- praying to Allah;
- learning about Islam.

In groups ask pupils to reflect on the following question.

- Which of these three activities do you think is the most important, and why?

There is no right answer to this question; the emphasis is on the ideas and quality of argument. Pupils' learning will be enhanced if they have opportunity to see a copy of the Qur'an and its stand, headscarves and prayer caps, and to listen to a CD of the Qur'an being recited.

Why do Muslims pray?

Complete the worksheet 'Practise Muslim prayer positions' and then do the following task.

Muslims believe that Allah is the creator of everything and nothing happens unless Allah wants it to. Allah is so great that Muslims try to put Allah and what Allah wants at the centre of their lives. Praying like this five times a day reminds Muslims of Allah and their duty to follow Allah's will.

Ask pupils to respond to the following questions.

- Why do you think that Muslims wash themselves so well before praying?
- Which prayer actions show that Muslims believe that Allah is very important?
- Imagine that you had to pray like this 5 times a day. What are some challenges that you would have at school?
- How does praying 5 times a day remind Muslims of their duty to follow Allah's will?

Visiting a mosque

Visit a mosque and identify the places mentioned in the story. How does it differ from the places in the book and how is it the same?

Flags

Look at flags for the different countries of Britain and explore their symbolism (or focus on your national flag). Provide a selection of pictures of flags from around the world, including flags which have obvious Muslim symbols such as the crescent moon. Can pupils identify the flags of Muslim countries? Muslim countries often include the crescent moon in their flags because Islam is seen as being important for that country.

Flags show what is believed to represent a country. Often the designs are quite old. In groups ask pupils to design their own modern flag for their country. They need to consider carefully what they think may represent their country today and explain why.

Chapter 2 Celebrating Eid–ul-Fitr

The festival of Eid-ul-Fitr

The festival of Eid-ul-Fitr celebrates the end of the fast of Ramadan. Muslims thank Allah for the benefits that they have gained from the fast. Eid-ul-Fitr is celebrated by:

- congregational prayer in the mosque;
- giving cards and presents to friends and family;
- sharing a special family meal (often at midday);
- wearing new or best clothes;
- giving zakah (alms) to provide for the poor.

Rees and Sara make an Eid card for their friends, Rashid and Fatima. Eid cards could have a number of different illustrations, for example:

- a mosque;
- a flower or floral pattern;
- a geometric pattern;
- an Islamic symbol such as crescent moon and star;
- calligraphy.

Flowers and floral patterns reflect Paradise, which traditionally is represented by a garden.

Geometric patterns portray central Islamic beliefs concerning the origins, nature, and purpose of the universe. A pattern starts from a dot which represents Allah. From this dot, complex geometric patterns are created which represent Allah's creation. Allah is the starting point and nothing happens without Allah willing it. The patterns represent the ideal universe, which reflects the qualities of its creator: oneness, balance, harmony, and peace. However, human beings break and destroy parts of the pattern through acting in ways which do not conform to Allah's will. Often a deliberate mistake will be included in a pattern to remind human beings that only Allah is perfect.

Beautiful Arabic calligraphy, with wishes for a happy festival, often features prominently on the card. Arabic is written from the right to the left side and an Arabic card opens from the 'back' to the 'front'.

Many of Rashid and Fatima's extended family are present for the Eid celebrations. In Islam the family has special significance because it forms a solid foundation for a strong Muslim community. There is less focus on the nuclear family.

The Ramadan fast

Sawn (the fast during the month of Ramadan) is the fourth Pillar of Islam. From dawn to dusk, nothing should enter a person's body – this includes food, drink, smoking, and non-vital medications and vaccinations. Each night of the fast, after sunset, there is a family fast-breaking meal. Each morning of the fast, before sunrise, there is a light breakfast.

Some of Rashid and Fatima's family have not been fasting. The Qur'an says that certain categories of people are exempt, such as the very young or the very old, women who are pregnant or breast-feeding, the sick, and travellers.

Muslims follow a lunar calendar which means that Ramadan is a moveable fast. This means that the number of hours per day spent fasting often varies according to the time of year. For example, a fast in Britain in June is more difficult than a fast in December, and Muslims living in extreme northern and southern locations are acutely affected by the number of daylight hours. Often, in uncertain or extreme situations, Muslims follow the times for the fast in Makkah.

The fast during the month of Ramadan provides Muslims with the opportunity to:

- submit to the will of Allah;
- empathise with the poor, providing the motivation to give alms;
- offer thanksgiving to Allah for the Qur'an;
- recite and meditate on the Qur'an;
- practise exercising self-control of the body;
- achieve spiritual purification;
- strengthen and unite the Muslim community, both locally and worldwide.

Muslims believe that Allah is the source and provider of all things including wealth. Allah's gift of wealth carries with it responsibility: wealth needs to be used wisely for the benefit of the whole community. The fast reminds Muslims of their duty towards less fortunate members of society.

Muslims around the world fast together, and this unites and strengthens the world-wide Muslim community. Ramadan is a time to focus on Allah and submit to Allah's will. Fatima's comment that Muslims should try not to be angry, argue, or tell lies is significant because negative emotions disrupt this focus, both for the person concerned and for those associating with that person.

Rashid and Fatima's grandfather introduces Rees and Sara to one of the most significant events in Muslim history, the Night of Power which marks Allah's revelation of the first part of the Qur'an to the Prophet Muhammad via the intermediary figure of the Angel Gabriel. Muhammad received subsequent revelations of the Qur'an over 22 years. Muslims believe that the Qur'an is Allah's greatest gift to human beings. This explains why there is a special focus on reading, meditating on, and thanking Allah for the Qur'an.

Activities

Festivals across religious traditions

Work on a calendar or book of festivals from all religions. This would need to be a loose-leaf folder, or pages joined together with treasury tags so that pages can be added as needed in chronological order.

Talk about the importance of organising material well so that people can quickly find the information they need. With the pupils, decide on a useful structure for the book, for example, section headings could include stories, how the festival is celebrated today, recipes, and so on.

A card for every occasion

Collect together different types of cards for different occasions. Ask pupils to divide the cards into different piles using the following category headings:

birthday	bereavement	birth of a baby
general	engagement/wedding	
good luck	congratulations	
Christmas	retirement	

Then, for each card category pupils need to identify some of the things in the cards' pictures which link them to the occasion for which they are intended. Pupils can also consider two further questions.

- Why do you think people send cards?
- How do you think people feel when they receive cards?

Cards are sent for different reasons. Do the worksheet 'Make an Eid card'. On the worksheet it suggests that the card is decorated with an Islamic-style pattern. Explore with pupils other possible decorations for the card which they can use if they wish. Link this back to the previous work on cards – the Eid (festival) card celebrates the successful completion of the Muslim fast and all that has been learnt from it. How might Muslims feel when they receive these cards?

Design a pattern

Do the 'Scale drawing of a pattern' worksheet. After pupils have completed their pattern, introduce the idea that Muslims believe that only Allah is perfect. Muslims try to do what Allah wants but they make mistakes. People are not perfect. However, the Qur'an reminds Muslims at the beginning of every chapter (apart from one) that Allah is merciful and compassionate. Muslims make a deliberate mistake in a pattern to remind them that they are not perfect.

Ask pupils to return to their pattern and to introduce one mistake in it to illustrate this teaching.

Pupils can reflect further on this by relating it to their own lives and the mistakes that they make. For example, they can think about a time when they made a mistake. How did they feel when they realised that they had made the mistake? What did other people do when they found out about their mistake? How was the situation resolved? What did they learn from their mistake?

Chapter 3 Understanding the Qur'an and Muhammad

Understanding rules

In this chapter the sources of authority in Islam (the Qur'an and the Prophet Muhammad) are compared with sources of authority in a school (school rules and teachers). Rules are created to help people live together peaceably and constructively. However, understanding and living according to rules is difficult; competent interpreters are required. In school, teachers help children to understand and live according to school rules. In Islam, the Prophet Muhammad helps Muslims to understand and live according to Allah's rules in the Qur'an.

The Five Pillars are five important rules in Islam. A traditional Arabian house was supported by pillars, and without them, the house would collapse. Likewise, the house of Islam is supported by the Five Pillars, and without them, Islam would collapse. The first pillar is the shahadah, which is the Muslim statement of faith: there is no Allah but Allah and Muhammad is the prophet of Allah. This belief is the motivation behind all human action, including the four practical pillars: prayer, almsgiving, fasting, and pilgrimage.

The Qur'an: the source book for rules

Rashid and Fatima treat the Arabic Qur'an with great respect because Muslims believe that it is the word of Allah, and the primary source of Allah's will.

Respect is shown by:

- storing the Qur'an in a place where no other book is higher than it;
- covering the Qur'an with protective material when not in use;
- performing ritual washing (wudu or ghusl) before touching the Qur'an or reciting the Qur'an;
- covering the head before touching the Qur'an or reciting the Qur'an;
- using a stand called a kursi on which the Qur'an sits while it is read;
- ensuring that the Qur'an is never left open, if it is not being read.

The Prophet Muhammad: an ideal interpreter and role model

Rees and Sara consider one of the main problems with rules in the Qur'an: how can you be sure that they have been understood correctly and applied appropriately to people's lives? Muslims believe that the Prophet Muhammad could understand and apply Allah's rules in the Qur'an because Allah revealed the Qur'an to Muhammad. Muhammad is seen as the perfect Muslim and role model.

Muslims believe that throughout human history Allah repeatedly sent prophets to make his will known to human beings. The first prophet was Adam, the first man, and other prophets include well-known figures shared with Judaism and Christianity such as Ibrahim (Abraham), Isma'il (Ishmael), Musa (Moses), Dawud (David), and Isa (Jesus). Some of these prophets were given a book containing Allah's will. For example, Musa (Moses) was given the Taurat (Torah) and Isa (Jesus) was given the Injil (Gospels). All of these prophets are highly respected in Islam, although it is thought that the books that they received (apart from the Qur'an given to Muhammad) have been distorted and changed by the communities to which they were given.

The Prophet Muhammad has a special place in Islam because he is believed to be the final prophet sent by Allah, and he was given the fullest and final revelation of Allah's will – the Qur'an. Muslims believe that unlike the books given to the other prophets, the Qur'an has been preserved accurately. This means that no other revelations and no other prophets are needed.

Following the example of the Prophet Muhammad

Fatima introduces Rees and Sara to the stories about the Prophet Muhammad. These stories are called hadith and they record the speech and actions of the Prophet Muhammad when he was alive. As Muhammad is a perfect role model for Muslims, knowing how he understood and lived out Allah's will is very important. Therefore, the hadith are used by many Muslims to explain things which are unclear in the Qur'an. It is in this sense that the Prophet Muhammad acts as an interpreter of Allah's rules in the Qur'an.

Sara cannot find any pictures of Muhammad in the book that she is reading, and she learns that Muslims do not usually show images of human beings or animals. This is to prevent people from mistakenly committing the most serious sin called shirk – the placing of someone or something on the same level as Allah. This partly explains the distinctiveness of Islamic art, with its focus on patterns and calligraphy centred on Allah.

It is important to remember that the Prophet Muhammad is greatly respected in Islam but never worshipped. Allah alone is worshipped and everything else points towards Allah and depends on Allah.

Activities

Role models

Do the 'Find out about Muhammad' worksheet.

Muslims believe that Muhammad lived like a perfect Muslim, in the way that Allah wants Muslims to live. This means that Muslims believe that Muhammad is a perfect example for Muslims to follow. This is called being a role model. Rees and Sara learn in the story that Muslims have tried to collect all the stories about Muhammad's life to help them follow his example.

Explore with pupils who their role models are (people they look up to and want to be like). What do they learn from their role models? How will this help them in their lives? (It is important that pupils are allowed to choose any type of person and they do not feel that they should give a particular type of answer.)

Exploring rules

Collate different rules for different contexts, for example, a library, airport, beach, and school, and explore them with pupils. In each case, why are they there? What is the point of them? Each context has a different set of rules which is appropriate and meaningful for that context. Religious communities have rules to follow too which are appropriate and meaningful for that religion.

The Five Pillars are rules which are important in Islam. The first Pillar is the most important – the belief in only one God and that Muhammad is the Prophet of God (shahadah). Muslims believe that the other four practical Pillars help them to learn how to live in a way which Allah wants. In groups, pupils could research the four practical pillars of salah (prayer), sawm (fasting), zakah (almsgiving), and hajj (pilgrimage), with the aim of completing the following task.

For your Pillar, write down the things which would help Muslims do the following (remember that the list is for all the four practical Pillars and some may not be relevant to your Pillar):

- think about the needs of other less fortunate Muslims;
- feel part of a large Muslim family;
- feel in touch with their history and the great Muslim prophets of the past;
- remember that Allah is the source of everything and deserves worship;
- understand that Allah sees all Muslims as equal and no one is greater than anyone else.

Pupils could then complete the 'Write 5 rules' worksheet.

A documentary about Muhammad's life

Plan a short documentary programme about the life of Muhammad. To help with the research and planning, focus on the following areas.

- Make a timeline of his life.
- What were his main teachings?
- Find some interesting stories about Muhammad's life.
- Why is Muhammad important to Muslims today?
- Who would you want to interview about Muhammad's life and teaching? (You might want to include a Muslim.)
- Think about useful props which would make the programme interesting, for example, maps, pictures of Mount Hira and other places in Saudi Arabia, the Qur'an (with a recording of its recitation), stand and Qur'an cover.
- Remember that Muhammad should NOT be portrayed in any form.

Use a camcorder to record the documentary (in small sections). This can be shown to other classes in the school or placed in an assembly context.

Chapter 4 Caring for others and the world

The relationship between people and the natural world

Rees and Sara visit an aquarium with their friends, Rashid and Fatima, where they learn about the complexity and interdependency of aquatic life. These principles can be extended to include the rest of the natural world. Rees and Sara also learn about the capacity of human beings to affect the fragile relationships which exist between living things, often in a destructive way.

The natural world is a very important theme in Islam because the natural world is closely connected with its creator, Allah. The Qur'an repeatedly asks Muslims to reflect on the perfection and wonders of nature, which point towards Allah.

> It is He who sends down to you water from the sky: from which you have to drink, and from it are trees, for you to pasture your herds. And thereby He brings forth for you crops, and olives, and palms, and vines, and all manner of fruit. Surely in this is a sign for a people who reflect. And He subjected to you the night and the day, and the sun and the moon: and the stars are subjected by His command. Surely in this are signs for a people who understand.
>
> Qur'an 16:10ff

The most important Muslim beliefs about the relationship between nature, Allah, and human beings are:

- nature points to its creator, Allah;
- Allah has created everything necessary to sustain human life;
- the bounties of nature are a gift from Allah;
- human beings are totally dependent on Allah who provides for their needs;
- the natural world is Allah's;
- human beings are Allah's vice-regents in the world. This means that they act on behalf of Allah in the natural world to implement Allah's will.

In Islam the beauty, grandeur, and bounty of nature should invoke a sense of immense awe and gratitude, which should be expressed in the natural human response of worship and submission to Allah. The greatness of Allah is always contrasted with the total dependence of human beings on Him.

The story about Muhammad and the camel is an example of how Muslims use stories and traditions about the Prophet Muhammad for guidance. There are many stories about the Prophet Muhammad and animals which show the Prophet's respect and compassion for them. The story about Muhammad and the camel is particularly useful because it provides an example of human beings in an interdependent relationship with nature, and how respecting this relationship brings mutual benefits to both parties.

The relationship between people

Fatima tells Rees and Sara that it is the duty of Muslims to look after one another. Muslims who have the material means should help those in need. This action is based on the belief that wealth is a gift from Allah, and it should be used for the benefit of the whole community. With wealth comes great responsibility, and Muslims believe that they will be judged by Allah on how well they have responded to this responsibility.

The fourth Pillar of Islam, zakah (obligatory almsgiving), provides an opportunity for these beliefs to be expressed in practice. The Qur'an stipulates that Muslims must give: 'As much as you can spare!' which helps to support:

- the poor;
- needy;
- those collecting and distributing zakah;
- converts to Islam;
- the freeing of Muslim captives and debtors;
- travellers experiencing financial hardship.

This was developed into a more precise system where a certain percentage of one's income is given every year for these causes. In Britain (as in many other countries) zakah is voluntary.

Zakah means 'purification'. If a Muslim gives generously and in the right spirit, it is believed that the person's sins are forgiven. Almsgiving, in addition to zakah, is encouraged at other times as well, especially during periods of celebration.

At the public library Rees and Sara are introduced to an increasingly popular way of giving alms through donating money to Muslim aid agencies. Muslim aid agencies initiate and support many of the same types of activity focused on by non-Muslim aid agencies. Islamic Aid and Muslim Aid are two well-known Muslim aid agencies.

Activities

Our environment

Muslims believe that it is their duty to look after the natural world. They are motivated to do this because of their beliefs about Allah (see teachers' notes for this chapter). Walk around the school grounds and look for ways that you could look after this area where you spend so much of your time. What motivates you to be responsible?

Caring for nature

Do the activity on the 'Write a play' worksheet.

Muhammad taught that animals belong to Allah and people should look after animals for Allah. Animals are there for a reason and they are all part of Allah's plan for the world. If people treat animals well, people and animals can live and work well together.

People and animals do a lot of different things together and animals give a lot of things to people. Ask pupils to think of animals which would fit into the following groups, e.g. guide dogs fit 'helping people' (to differentiate this activity, a list of animals could be given to pupils to place in groups):

pets	food	helping people
clothes	sport	enjoyment of nature

Islam teaches that animals should be treated well because of its beliefs about Allah. What reasons would you give for treating animals well?

Caring for others

Using the internet, learn about a Muslim aid agency in more detail (for example, Muslim Aid or Islamic Aid). The following questions will help to focus the activity.

- Does the aid agency have a mission statement which explains what it tries to do?
- Name the projects in which the aid agency is involved.
- In which areas of the world does the aid agency work?
- How can Muslims support the aid agency?

Some pupils could be challenged with a further question.

- Is there anything on the website which points to the aid agency's religious background (Muslim)?

Pupils can relate this to their own lives by doing the 'Make a money box' activity, and, as a class, choose an aid agency to support.

Chapter 5 Learning about halal and haram

Diversity in Muslim practice

Rees and Sara learn that Muslim practice is influenced by:

- how the Qur'an is interpreted;
- the culture in which a Muslim lives.

Different interpretations of the Qur'an and different cultural influences account for much of the diversity found in Muslim practice. However, whatever a Muslim does, it should be halal (permitted by Allah) and not haram (forbidden by Allah).

Food

Muslims eat many different kinds of foods, which reflect the various culinary traditions from diverse cultures around the world. The dishes prepared by a Muslim from Malaysia are very different from those prepared by a Muslim from Morocco, for example. However, Muslims around the world are linked by one common requirement: they are required to eat foods which are halal under Islamic law. Muslim food laws are based on the food rules found in the Qur'an.

Halal foods include:

- all kinds of fish;
- all kinds of vegetables;
- meat and other edible products from halal animals slaughtered in accordance with Islamic law.

Haram foods include:

- pig meat;
- blood;
- meat from carnivorous animals (excluding most fish and sea animals);
- meat and other edible products from halal animals not slaughtered in accordance with Islamic law;
- alcohol.

Some Muslims believe that the meat of fish without scales (for example, shellfish) and the meat of amphibians are also haram.

The slaughter of an animal in accordance with Islamic law involves checking the animal for any signs of ill-health, giving it a drink of water, turning the animal to face Makkah, and reciting the words: 'In the name of Allah, Allah is the Greatest.' The animal's main arteries in the neck and its oesophagus are then severed in a single cut with a non-serrated blade. The words, 'In the name of Allah, Allah is the Greatest', recognise that all created things belong to Allah, and that Muslims are allowed to take the life of animals only by using Allah's name.

Finding foods which are halal or haram can be particularly difficult in non-Muslim countries, in a world increasingly dependent on pre-prepared and processed foods. This is why companies distributing clearly labelled halal foods are important.

Dress

Different interpretations of the Qur'an and different cultural influences are found in Muslim dress. The Qur'an stipulates what is halal (permitted), advocating modesty in dress for both Muslim men and Muslim women. However, how this modesty is interpreted varies considerably among Muslims. It is interesting to compare the dress of male and female Muslims from different countries, for example, Indonesia, Pakistan, Palestine, Saudi Arabia, and Muslims wearing Western-style dress.

Activities

Difference in Islam map

Display a map of the world and mark the countries where there is a large population of Muslims. Illustrate the map with pictures from the internet of famous mosques, locations, and statues. You could also show traditional styles of dress in different Muslim countries.

Dress in Islam

In the Qur'an it says that Muslim women and men should dress modestly. Different Muslims understand what this means in different ways.

Use the internet to find out about women's different dress codes in Islam, and answer the following question.

- How do Muslims understand 'modesty' differently?

These search words may be helpful (the information in brackets is for the teacher):

- abaya (outer garment covering the whole body and head, but leaving face visible);
- jilbab (loose outer garments which are usually worn with a headscarf);
- khimar (headscarf);
- niqab and burqa (covers the whole face);
- chador (outer garment worn over clothes covering the whole body);
- Islamic swimwear or Islamic sportswear.

NOTE: It is important that pupils also know that many practising Western Muslims wear modest Western style dress. There are many differences in the way Muslims dress and how they interpret what the Qur'an says about Muslim dress.

A halal shopping list

Buy a selection of different foods. Include a variety of tins and packets with lists of ingredients on them, food with the halal symbol on it, and fresh fruit and vegetables. Give pupils a piece of paper with 'Rashid and Fatima's shopping list' as a heading. Ask pupils to identify foods which could be put on Rashid and Fatima's shopping list.

Did pupils find the task difficult? What were some of their problems?

Keywords

adhan the call to prayer

Allah the Islamic name for God

Arabic a Semitic language; the Qur'an is written in Arabic and ritual prayer (salah) is conducted in Arabic

Eid-ul-Fitr the festival which celebrates the end of the fast during the month of Ramadan

ghusl a more comprehensive ritual washing than wudu which involves taking a bath or shower before prayer or the recitation of the Qur'an

hadith traditions about what the Prophet Muhammad said and did during his lifetime

halal permitted or allowed

hajj pilgrimage to Makkah: the fifth Pillar of Islam

haram forbidden

Islam the name of the religion followed by Muslims; means submission (to the will of Allah)

Jumah prayer Friday noon prayer

madrassah an Islamic school which is attached to the mosque

Makkah the most sacred city and pilgrimage site in Sunni Islam

minaret a mosque tower from which Muslims are traditionally called to prayer

Muhammad the prophet who received the Qur'an from Allah

Muslim person who submits to the will of Allah

mosque a place of prostration; it is the Muslim place of worship

Ramadan the ninth month of the Muslim year; it is the month of fasting

salah prayer: the second Pillar of Islam

sawn the fast during the month of Ramadan: the fourth Pillar of Islam

Semitic relating to a particular language family including Arabic and Hebrew

shahadah the creedal statement testifying that there is no Allah but Allah and that Muhammad is Allah's prophet: the first Pillar of Islam

shirk the most serious sin of placing anything or anyone on the same level as Allah

Qur'an the most important sacred text in Islam

wudu ritual washing before prayer or the recitation of the Qur'an; not as comprehensive as ghusl

zakah almsgiving: the third Pillar of Islam.

Write a story

Imagine you have visited a mosque with a Muslim friend. Write a story about it, giving details of all the places you visited and the things you saw there. The pictures and descriptions below will help you.

dome

Most mosques have a round roof. This is often decorated with beautiful patterns.

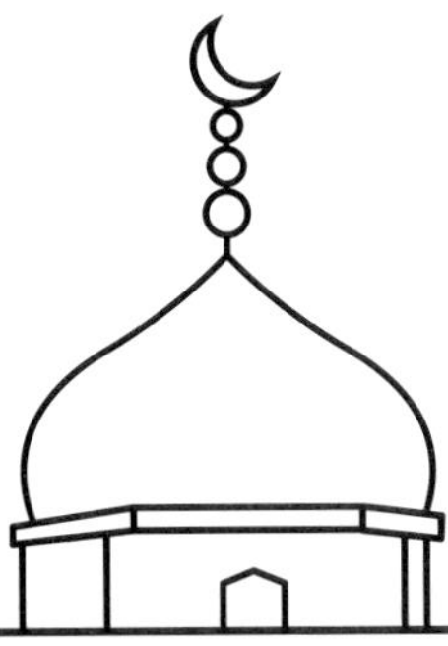

minaret

Next to the dome there may be a tall tower. The times of prayer are called from here.

shoe rack

To keep the place of prayer clean, all shoes are taken off before entering.

wash room

To show respect for Allah, Muslims must be clean to pray. They wash hands, face, arms and feet.

prayer room

The floor is covered in carpet for people to pray or sit on. Women pray at the back or in a different room.

mihrab

Muslims pray facing Makkah. A hollow in the wall shows them the right direction to face.

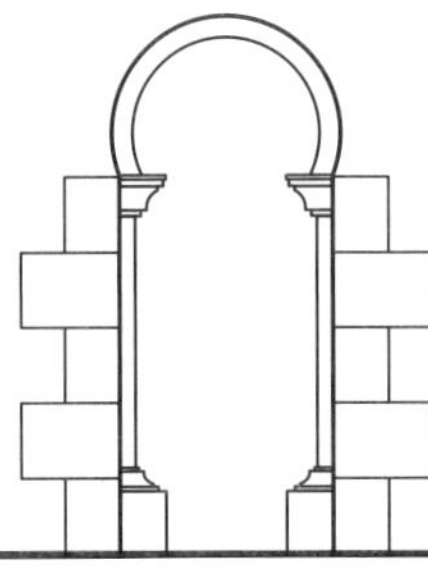

minbar

The imam (leader of the mosque) stands on a raised part of the floor so he can be seen when he teaches.

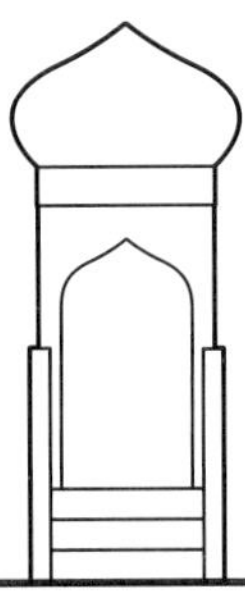

madrassah

Muslims go to school to learn to read Arabic so they can read the Qur'an in its original language.

library

In many mosques you will find study rooms or libraries with books to answer questions about Islam.

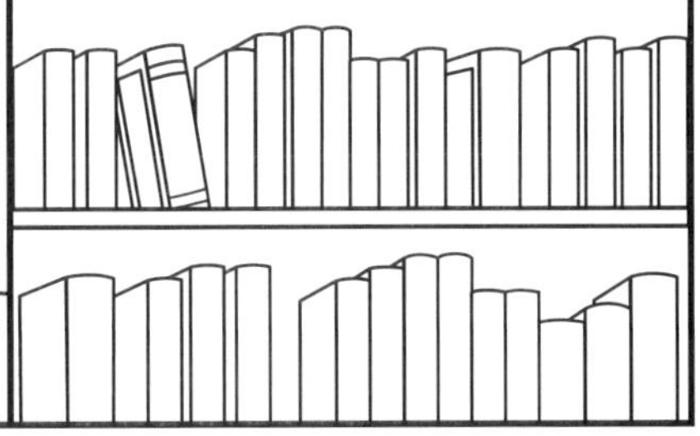

Make a headscarf

Most Muslims keep their heads covered. Men wear caps; women wear headscarfs. Make your own headscarf.

You will need

fabric

dye, fabric crayons or felt tip pens

What to do

1. Cut your fabric in a long strip. (Old white cotton sheets can often be bought cheaply at charity shops. One sheet will make many scarves.)
2. Decorate the fabric by dyeing it or by using fabric crayons or felt tip pens. If you use crayons or pens, choose a pattern that has some meaning for Muslims. You could design a geometrical pattern or a pattern from the moon and stars. Just as the moon and stars show the right path to take at night, so Muslims believe Allah shows them the right way to live. Remember that Muslims do not draw pictures of people or animals.
3. Look at pictures to discover different ways of wearing the headscarf.

Practise Muslim prayer positions

Muslims pray five times a day. Prayer for Muslims is not just in the mind; it involves the whole body. Special words of prayer are said in each prayer position.

1. Be clean

Before praying, Muslims must be clean. They wash their whole body each day. Before prayer they wash hands, mouth and throat, nose and face, arms, head and ears, feet and ankles. Next they must find a clean place in which to pray.

2. Face Makkah

Muslims always face in the direction of Makkah to pray. Mosques show this direction. Many Muslims carry a special compass to help them work out the correct direction for when they pray outside of a mosque.

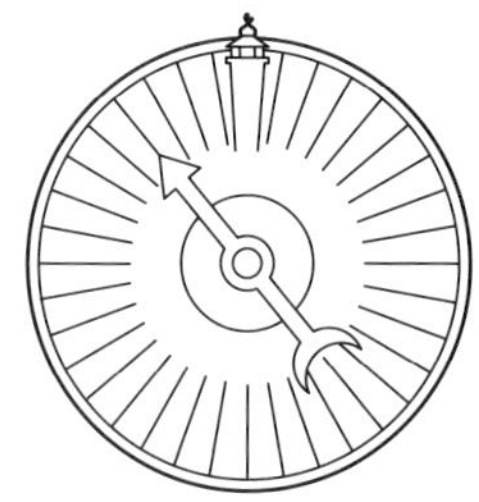

3. Stand

Stand straight. Raise your hands to your ears. Fold your arms over your breast, right arm over left arm.

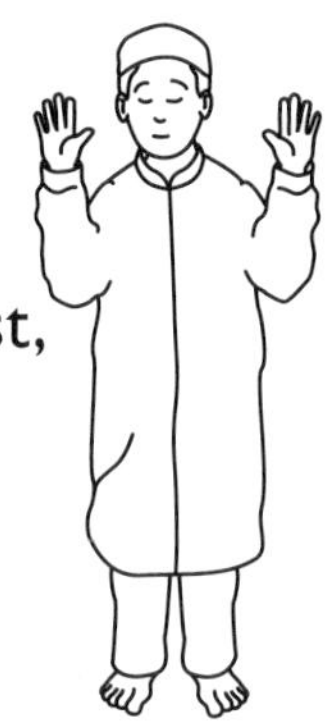

4. Bow down

Bow down, placing your hands on your knees. Return to a standing position.

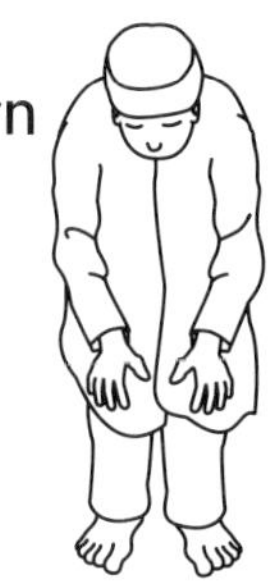

5. Prostrate yourself

Kneel down, then lie forward with your head on the ground. Sit up briefly, then lie forward again.

6. Sit

Sit again and pass the greeting 'Peace on you and the mercy of Allah' to each side of you.

Make an Eid card

1. Fold your card

English and Welsh are read from left to right, and so books and cards open from the right. Arabic is read from right to left, and so books and cards open from the left.

2. Write a caption

This card is to celebrate Eid-ul-Fitr.
You could write:

Happy Eid
Happy Festival
an Arabic greeting

عيد مبارك

3. Decorate your card

Muslim patterns are very beautiful and intricate. Copy a pattern from one of the activity sheets, or design your own.

4. Sign your name

Don't forget to say who the card is for and who is sending it.

عيد مبارك

This says EID MUBARAK in Arabic.
This means Blessed festival.
Trace over it, copy it underneath, then write it on your card.

Plan some fasting activities

For this activity you will need to work with some friends, thinking, discussing and writing.

Fasting in Ramadan

Every year during the month of Ramadan, healthy adult Muslims fast during daylight hours. This means that for twenty-nine days they do not have anything to eat or drink between sunrise and sunset. It is a time when they learn how it feels to be hungry and thirsty and remember how lucky they are to have food and water. It is a time for them to thank Allah.

It is a time to think of other people. During Ramadan Muslims give money to poor people who do not have enough food all year round. During the fast they try to live good lives, not arguing or being angry or telling lies.

It is a time when Muslims need to rest more than usual. Without food and water for the long daylight hours, they cannot work as hard as they do during the other months.

If you were Muslims, fasting during the month of Ramadan, what could you do at meal times instead of eating? How could you use the time in a positive way? **Plan some activities for a week**. You would need a mixture of activities, some to help you learn more about Allah, some to help other people, and some to help you become a kinder person.

Scale drawing of a pattern

Muslim patterns are very beautiful and intricate. This type of artwork is found in Muslim houses and mosques. Use the large grid to copy and enlarge a pattern. Do the copying section by section.

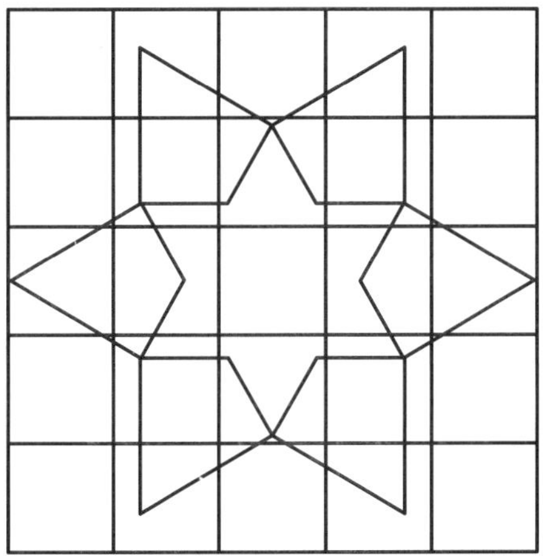

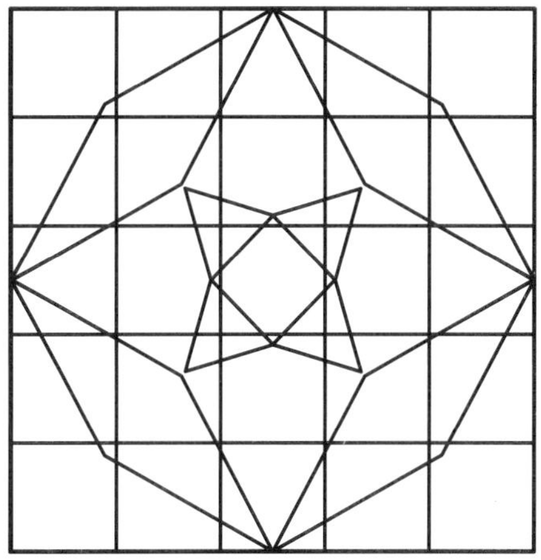

Write 5 rules

Muslims have five important rules to follow. These are called the Five Pillars. Muslims believe that the Five Pillars were given to them by Allah to teach them how to live.

Imagine you have the job of deciding five rules for a group to which you belong. (This could be your family, school, class, club or a friendship group.) Write the rules you would choose, along with your reasons for choosing them.

Rule 1 ______________________________

Reason ______________________________

Rule 2 ______________________________

Reason ______________________________

Rule 3 ______________________________

Reason ______________________________

Rule 4 ______________________________

Reason ______________________________

Rule 5 ______________________________

Reason ______________________________

Find out about Muhammad

Muhammad is very important to Muslims. They believe that Allah taught the Qur'an to him and he then taught it to those around him. He understood what the Qur'an was about and he lived like a perfect Muslim.

Use the story book *Exploring Islam* to answer these questions about Muhammad. Look in other books or on the internet to find out some more information to write, in the bottom two boxes.

When and where was Muhammad born?	*What task was Muhammad given?*	*Why do we not know what Muhammad looked like?*

Muhammad

Write a play

Read the story of Muhammad and the camel, and work with three friends to write it as a play. Begin to write on this sheet, adding as many other pages as you need.

Muhammad and the camel - a story

Muhammad was walking in a garden in Madinah. It was a very hot day. Both humans and animals were feeling the heat. He saw a man trying to keep cool under a tree.

Muhammad heard a camel nearby making a dreadful sound. Muhammad went over to it and gently stroked it. The camel was crying. The camel was far too thin. It worked hard, but it was not given enough food and water.

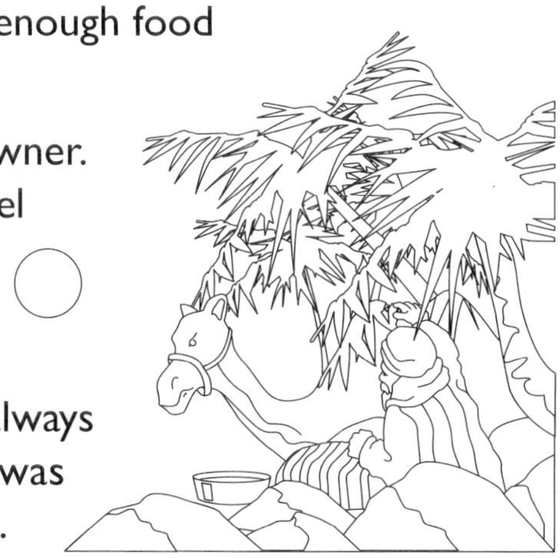

The man sitting under the tree was the camel's owner. Muhammad told him that Allah had made his camel and he was being cruel to it. It was his duty to look after the camel. If the camel had enough food and water, it would work better. The owner felt ashamed and very sorry. After this, the man always looked after his camel properly. And Muhammad was right! He did get a lot more work from the camel.

Muhammad and the camel - a play

Characters: ______________________________

____

Scene: ______________________________

Narrator: ______________________________

____

Camel: ______________________________

____

Muhammad: ______________________________

____

Make a money box

Muslims believe they have a duty to look after one another. As one way to do this, they give money to aid agencies to provide clean water, education and health care for people around the world. You can help people in need too. Make a money box for loose change and start collecting for an aid agency of your choice.

You will need

- construction set such as Polydrons
- card
- scissors
- decorations or coloured pens
- ruler
- pencil
- glue or tape

What to do

1. Select a shape for your money box. You could choose a pyramid, a cube, a cuboid or a prism.
2. Make that shape from a construction set such as Polydrons.
3. Open up the shape to form a flat net of the object. This will show you how to draw it yourself.
4. Draw the net on card. You will need to measure carefully to get each face the correct size.
5. If you intend to glue your box together, add tabs to each face to be joined.
6. Cut a money slot on one face.
7. Cut out the net, decorate it and assemble it with glue (on the inside) or tape (on the outside).

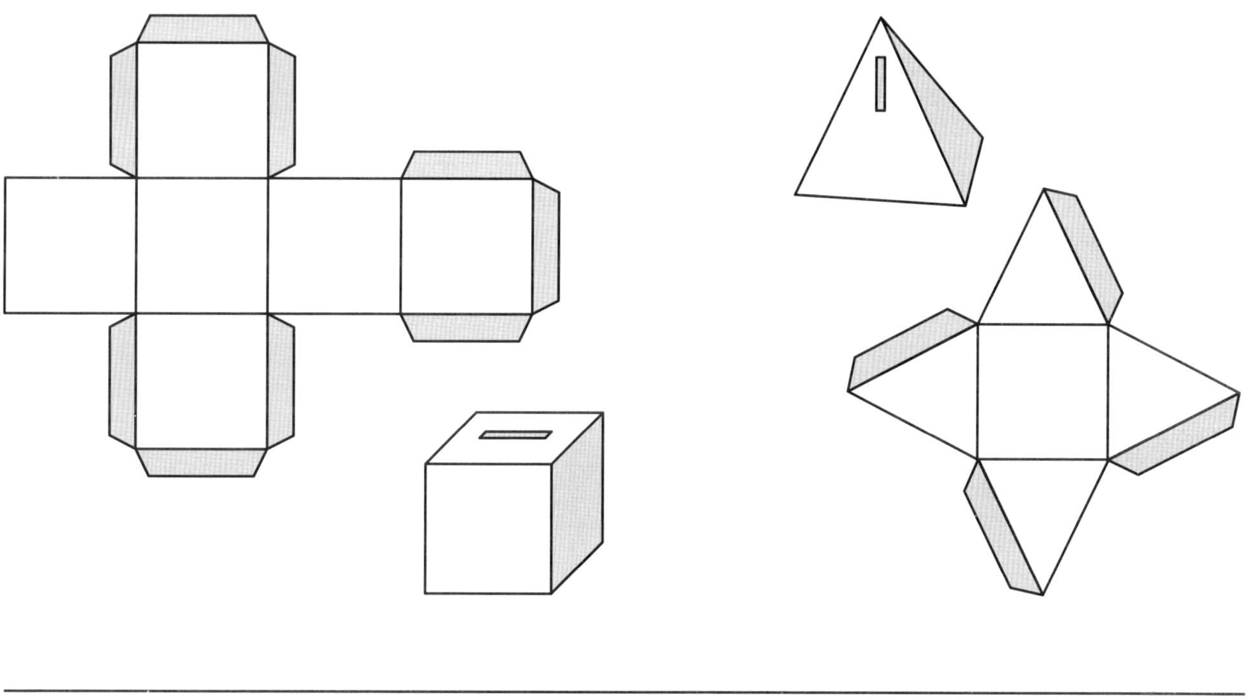

Write a shopping list

Fatima and Rashid were given the task of shopping for the family. What do you think they bought? Write a shopping list for their family. Look in recipe books from the local library to find out the ingredients used in Indian food and put these on the list.

If you were shopping for your family, what would you need to buy? Write a shopping list for yourself. Compare the two lists.

Fatima and Rashid's shopping list	**My shopping list**

Fatima and Rashid went to a special shop which sold halal food. Where would you go to shop?

I shop at ________________________________

Make date sweets

Eid-ul-Fitr is the celebration at the end of Ramadan, the month of fasting. As part of the festival, children have a day off school. They are given new clothes to wear. In the morning they go to the mosque to pray. After this they visit friends and family, perhaps taking gifts and cards. They may go to a party or eat special sweets.

Date palms are common in Arabia, the home of Muhammad. Here is a recipe for date sweets.

You will need

- dates (without stones)
- nuts or seeds
- water

What to do

1. Place the dates in a saucepan and just cover them with as little water as possible.
2. With the help of an adult, cook the dates slowly on a low heat until they are soft and like a cream. You will need to stir them often with a wooden spoon so that they do not stick to the saucepan.
3. Leave the date mixture to cool.
4. Wash your hands! Take spoonfuls of the date mixture and roll it into balls.
5. Roll the date balls in chopped nuts. (If you are allergic to nuts, roll them in sesame seeds.)

My dictionary

You will meet many new words in *Exploring Islam*. Some of these will be English words and some will be Arabic words. Keep a record of them, along with their meanings.

mosque	the place where Muslims worship Allah, learn how to be good Muslims, and get together with Muslim friends
madrassah	mosque school
wudu	washing arms, feet, faces and heads before entering the mosque
____________	____
____________	____
____________	____
____________	____
____________	____
____________	____
____________	____
____________	____
____________	____
____________	____
____________	____
____________	____
____________	____

Search the internet

The internet has a lot of information, but you need to know how to find it. Here are some guidelines.

1. Some companies provide **search engines** to help you with this, such as 'google' (www.google.com) or www.yahoo.co.uk or www.msn.co.uk. Ask your teacher which one he or she prefers.
2. On the internet page you will find a box in which to type **keywords**.If you type in a general word (for example, Islam) you will find thousands of articles. If you type in more specific words you will find fewer articles to work through.
3. Next you will find a description of the articles containing your keywords. You will see that many of them do not seem to be what you want. You could make your search more clear. For example, instead of typing words like **parts of a mosque pictures,** try **"parts of a mosque" pictures** and then you will only be shown articles that contain the words **parts of a mosque** as a phrase instead of as separate words. Even better would be to name a part of the mosque and use it as a key word, like **mihrab pictures.**
4. Click on the section that seems most helpful. If it is not what you want then click the 'back' button (top left of your screen) to go back to the previous page and try another article.
5. If you find a picture you want to copy for further work, move the cursor over it and click the right button. Next click on 'copy' and select which file to copy it to.

Here are some keywords to get you started. Choose some more of your own

- mihrab pictures
- Islamic art pictures
- Muslim clothes pictures
- Muslims "how to pray" pictures
- Muslim aid agencies

Keywords I have tried

Exploring

Judaism

Exploring Judaism

The story

Rees and Sara have two Jewish friends called Dan and Rebecca who introduce them to key beliefs and practices in Judaism. The children explore a synagogue and take part in a Shabbat service. They celebrate the festival of Sukkot and hear the story about Dan and Rebecca's ancestors travelling to the Promised Land. Rees and Sara learn about the main source of authority in Judaism, the Torah, and how Jewish rabbis help Jews to understand what it says. They investigate Jewish beliefs about the environment in Jewish scriptures, and see how belief can relate to practice in the support of charities. The children learn about kashrut (Jewish food laws) and how Jews interpret these rules differently in their daily lives.

Aims

Exploring Judaism provides opportunities for pupils to:

- **engage** with fundamental questions;
- **explore** religious beliefs, teachings, and practices;
- **express** personal responses in relation to the material studied.

Learning outcomes

Pupils should be able to:

- discuss questions raised by life and aspects of Judaism;
- name and describe selected beliefs, teachings, and practices of Judaism;
- explain through examples the relationship between belief and practice in Judaism;
- discuss their own views and the views of others in relation to some of the themes and issues covered, and relate these to their own lives;
- relate symbol to meaning in some Jewish contexts.

The basics

Defining 'Jewish' and 'Judaism' is not an easy task and there are no generally accepted definitions. It is possible to be Jewish without being religious, and traditionally, the line of Jewish descent is continued through the mother, which tends to emphasise the cultural and racial aspects of being Jewish. However, religion plays an important role in the identity and lives of many Jews throughout the world, and it is possible to convert to the religion which we call Judaism.

Historically, parts of what is now called Judaism may stem back as far as 1,500-2,000 BCE. Theologically, in the Torah, Abraham is presented as the father of the Jewish people and the special relationship (covenant) between Abraham and God was marked by the circumcision of Jewish males, which is a practice which continues today. Subsequently, the Torah says that God led the people from slavery in Egypt to the Promised Land (Canaan) where they settled and built a Temple in Jerusalem dedicated to God. The land was invaded and occupied by the Assyrians, the Babylonians, and eventually the Romans, who destroyed the Temple for the final time in 70CE. This is seen as a critical moment in Jewish history because the sense of being a people or a nation was very much tied up with the Temple. However, the rabbis (Pharisees) successfully managed to reconstruct Jewish religious and cultural life by focusing attention on synagogues and shifting religious practice away from the elaborate Temple sacrifices to prayer, scriptural reading, and teaching. This was the emergence of the religion which we call Judaism today.

Today, it is estimated that around 75% of Jews live in the USA or Israel. Other significant Jewish communities exist in Russia, France, Canada, and the UK, and there are smaller communities in many other countries in the world. In terms of ethnicity, the majority of Jews are either Ashkenazim Jews or Sephardim Jews, and in terms of religion, there are three basic religious movements or traditions represented in Britain: Orthodox (the most conservative and traditional); Conservative (between the Orthodox and the Reform), and Reform (the most liberal). In this story, Rees and Sara explore Reform Judaism.

Reform Jews believe that:

- there is one God, who created the universe and who continues to work within the universe;
- there is a special understanding (covenant) between God and religious Jews – in response to God's activity in the world, they adhere to God's laws, and should present a good example to others. Care is often taken not to present this in an exclusive way;
- God and God's laws are revealed in the Torah which are the collected writings of different individuals who were inspired by God;
- the Torah needs to be interpreted in an appropriate way for the time and place;
- every person has an immortal soul which will experience eternal happiness or eternal unhappiness after the death of the body; however, unlike other religions, beliefs about the afterlife are not focused on in Judaism because Jewish scripture does not deal with it in detail.

Reform Jews practise:

- prayer which is a central practice at the synagogue or at home – prayer focuses on praise, thanksgiving, and supplication;
- congregational worship in the synagogue which focuses on prayer, scriptural reading, and teaching.
- following the laws in the Torah in a way that is relevant and meaningful for today.

Chapter 1 Visiting a synagogue

Shabbat

In the Torah it says that Jews are allowed to work for six days a week, but the seventh day should be a day of rest and set apart for God. This day is called Shabbat or the Sabbath. Exactly how 'work' is defined differs among the various Jewish groups. Many Orthodox Jews understand 'work' literally and strictly, and include driving cars, walking more than a certain distance, turning on electricity for lights, gardening, or cooking as 'work', for example. As a result, they may use automatic timers for electrical appliances and plan ahead carefully to ensure that they do not 'work' according to this definition. Dan and Rebecca's family are Reform Jews and their family do not understand 'work' so strictly. They see Shabbat as a joyful time when they can spend time together as a family and remember and thank God for God's gifts. In whatever way 'work' is understood, if life is in danger, that life takes priority over Shabbat laws.

Shabbat begins at home on Friday evening for Dan and Rebecca, with their mother welcoming Shabbat with the lighting of two candles. Their father blesses his children and blesses bread and wine (Kiddush), before the family enjoys a Shabbat meal together. On Saturday morning, Dan and Rebecca's family visit the synagogue to take part in a special Shabbat morning service, and they invite Rees and Sara. After the service two more Shabbat meals are eaten. At dusk a special Havdalah candle is lit to symbolise the light which God created on the first day of creation. A combination of spices in a spice box is also smelt symbolising the hope that the benefits of Shabbat may continue on into the forthcoming week.

Special clothes

When Rees and Sara enter the synagogue they notice that members of the congregation are wearing special clothes. The kippah (cap) is worn as a sign of respect and the tallit or prayer shawl reminds Jews of their obligations to keep God's commandments which are revealed in the Torah. The command to wear the tallit is found in Numbers 15:38-40. Males will normally begin wearing the tallit at their initiation ceremony called Bar Mitvah which takes place around the age of thirteen when they become full members of the Jewish congregation and commit themselves to keeping God's laws in the Torah. Bar Mitvah means 'Son of the Law'. In Reform Judaism females can also begin wearing the tallit after an equivalent initiation ceremony called Bat Mitvah which takes place around the age of twelve. Bat Mitvah means 'Daughter of the Law'. Orthodox females do not wear the tallit.

The Torah

The focus of the service is on the Torah which is written on scrolls in Hebrew and kept in a cupboard called an ark, facing the city of Jerusalem. The ark symbolises the portable Ark of the Covenant which housed the Ten Commandments given to Moses on Mount Sinai, and later the most sacred holy of holies in the Temple in Jerusalem. Different portions of the Torah are read at different services until the Torah reading cycle is completed. The importance of the Torah scrolls is shown by the level of care and respect Jews give to them. For example:

- they are carefully written by hand by scribes without any mistakes;
- any spoiled scrolls or scrolls which are too old to use are ceremonially buried;
- the scrolls are 'dressed' with mantles, breastplates, and finials to protect them as well as to portray important symbols in Judaism;
- a yad or pointer is used to read the scrolls in order to avoid touching and damaging them;
- as the Torah is walked around the synagogue, members of the congregation stand as a sign of respect.

Popular Jewish symbols which appear on the ark curtains, mantles, breastplates, and finials include:

- two stone tablets: represents the Ten commandments given to Moses on Mount Sinai;
- menorah: 7-branched candelabrum which was lit in the Temple to symbolise the presence of God. Today, the ner tamid lamp fulfils the same purpose;
- lions on either side of the stone tablets: represents the cherubim which guarded the Ark;
- pomegranates: these were prized as the best fruit in Israel and they hung from the High Priest's robes in the Temple;
- flowers and leaves: symbolises the flowering of the Torah;
- crown: symbolises the 'crown of the Torah' and the Torah's high royal status. Also, the High Priest in the Temple wore a crown;
- tree of life: symbolises that the Torah provides the foundations of life;
- star of David: this is also known as the shield of David;
- bells: the High Priest in the Temple had bells attached to his robes;
- images depicting stories from the Torah, such as Noah's Ark.

A great variety of decorations exist, both traditional and contemporary, and these can be viewed easily on on-line shopping sites using search words like 'Torah mantles', 'Torah breastplates' and 'Torah rimonim'.

The rabbi

A rabbi is an ordained Jewish teacher. In Reform Judaism both males and females can be rabbis. A rabbi can lead prayer, teach, and help to explain the meaning of the Torah and the law to congregations as well as fulfil pastoral responsibilities.

Synagogue choirs are also popular in many synagogues and they sing prayers.

Activities

Mix and match

Cut out the nine boxes on the 'Write a story' worksheet, and then cut each box into three sections: the heading, the information, and the picture. Mix up all the sections and place them in an envelope. Divide pupils into pairs or groups and give each pair or group an envelope. Pupils need to match heading, information, and picture correctly.

Do the task on the 'Write a story' worksheet (the story can easily be adapted to another genre such as a diary entry or newspaper article, if needed).

Visiting a synagogue

Visit a synagogue and identify the places mentioned in the story. How does it differ from the places in the book and how is it the same?

Faith jewellery

In the story book, Rebecca wears a Star of David necklace. Across the world and throughout history, jewellery has been used for religious purposes. When a person wears such jewellery, they are often making a public statement about who they are and what they believe.

Explore other Jewish symbols found in jewellery by doing an internet search using the search words: Jewish jewellery. Pupils should be able to find the following Jewish symbols incorporated into jewellery in online shops.

- Star of David: it is also known as Magen David. A common claim is that it represents King David's shield which was the same shape. The evidence supporting this claim is not strong, but it remains the most recognisable Jewish symbol.
- Menorah: this candelabrum burned in the Temple in Jerusalem before the Temple's destruction by the Romans in 70CE. It symbolises God's presence and the biblical ideal that Jews should be 'a light to the nations', drawing people to God through setting a good example.
- Mezuzah: a Hebrew scroll containing important verses from the Torah called the Shema. Read the teachers' notes for chapter 4 which contains additional information.
- Chamsa (or hamsa): 'chamsa' means 'five' and it appears in the shape of a hand. This hand is often called the Hand of Miriam. Symbolically, it symbolises the protective hand of God. The chamsa is Middle Eastern in origin and is also found in Islam where it is called the Hand of Fatima.
- Shema: see information about the mezuzah and teachers' notes for chapter 4. Part of these Hebrew words can be found on items of jewellery.
- Chai: it consists of two letters from the Hebrew alphabet, 'het' and 'yod', which together spell 'living'. 'Living' could be a reference to the 'life' focused Judaism or the living God.
- Shofar: this is a ram's horn which was used for rituals in the Temple in Jerusalem. Today, it is particularly associated with celebrations of the Jewish New Year. In Jewish scripture, the shofar was blown at the beginning of battle and the shofar was used when Joshua captured Jericho.

Explore the meanings behind the symbols. Write the name of each symbol on a small card. Working in groups and using the cards, ask pupils to rank the symbols according to how powerful they are.

After feedback, mention that the Star of David is currently the most popular symbol of Judaism, and complete the 'Star of David' worksheet.

Chapter 2 Celebrating Sukkot

The pilgrimage festivals

Judaism celebrates many festivals, and three of these are called the pilgrimage festivals. The pilgrimage festivals are very useful for introducing the period in Jewish history before the Israelites settled in the Promised Land. Pesach or Passover is connected to Moses and the escape of the Israelites from Egypt; Sukkot or the Feast of Tabernacles or Booths is connected to the wandering of the Israelites in the wilderness when they lived in portable huts; and Shavuot or the Feast of Weeks is connected to the giving of the commandments to Moses on Mount Sinai. The interpretation of this history has had a notable effect on Jewish theology. For example, a number of major theological themes are present: the existence of a special relationship between God and Jewish ancestors; the protection given to this people by God; the trust of the people in God; the giving of God's commandments; and the importance of these commandments in Judaism today.

We use the Gregorian calendar which is a solar calendar. Jewish festivals are based on a combined solar and lunar calendar, which means that the dates for the festivals changes from year to year when they are placed in the Gregorian calendar. The Jewish calendar has the following months: Nissan (March-April); Iyar (April-May); Sivan (May-June); Tammuz (June-July); Av (July-August); Elul (August-September); Tishri (September-October); Cheshvan (October-November); Kislev (November-December); Tevet (December-January); Shevat (January-February); and Adar (February-March).

Other important Jewish festivals include: Hanukkah (the Festival of Lights), Rosh Hashanah (New Year), Purim (celebrates the victory over Haman's persecution), and Yom Kippur (the Day of Atonement).

The festival of Sukkot

The festival of Sukkot falls sometime in the months of September and October. According to the Jewish calendar, it begins on 15 Tishri and lasts for seven days. The name Sukkot means 'huts' (sukkah is a single hut), and this relates to the main feature of the festival: a hut, which is built and inhabited over the festival period.

Building a sukkah

A sukkah must have at least 2 walls and half of a third wall, and be large enough to fulfil the command to dwell in it. The walls can be made from any material, but it should be remembered that the hut is supposed to be makeshift. The roof must be made from any plant or tree which has grown in the earth – tree branches are a common material. When the roof is placed on the hut, it is important that the materials are placed so that the rain can enter the hut and the stars can be seen.

It is possible to buy different types of huts on-line which meet these requirements, and then assemble them at home.

The sukkah is usually furnished and decorated. Today many Jewish families do not dwell in the sukkah for the whole seven-day period, but they try to have meals in the sukkah. It is usual to furnish the sukkah with a table and chairs for this purpose. Fruit and vegetables are often hung in the sukkah for decoration, which links the festival with its harvest roots.

The lulav and etrog

Rejoicing with the lulav and etrog is one of the rituals performed in the sukkah. The lulav is made up of the branches of three plants: the palm, myrtle, and willow, which are tied together. An etrog is a yellow citrus fruit. The waving of the Four Species is a ritual which takes place in the sukkah and in the synagogue, and it is waved on each day of the festival. This symbolises God's presence everywhere.

The symbolism behind the number and choice of plants which make up the Four Species is unclear. Some Jews believe that they represent various parts of the body (etrog being the heart; palm, the spine; myrtle, the eyes; and willow, the mouth). Just as the lulav and etrog are waved to rejoice before God, so the whole body worships God. Other Jews believe that the Four Species represent four different types of Jews in their community, based on the metaphors of taste and smell: an etrog has taste and smell like Jews who have learning and do good actions; palm has taste but no smell like Jews who have learning but do no good actions; myrtle has no taste but has smell like Jews who have no learning but do good actions; and willow has neither taste nor smell like Jews who have no learning and do no good actions.

The meaning of Sukkah

Sukkah:

- celebrates God's care for the ancestors of the Jews in the harsh conditions of the wilderness, where God provided for their needs;
- reminds Jews of the precariousness of life and the need to rely on God to sustain them through reconnecting modern lives with the natural world;
- celebrates and thanks God for the abundance of

the harvest;

- reminds Jews of those who are less fortunate than themselves, prompting them to give charity, which is an important commandment;
- helps Jews to keep God's commandments in the Torah, where God asks them to build a sukkot in Leviticus 23:42 and to rejoice with the lulav and etrog in Leviticus 23: 39-40 (the commandments are central to Judaism).

Activities

Then and now

Complete the 'Story of Sukkot' worksheet to familiarise pupils with the story behind the festival of Sukkot.

Identify the differences between the life of Dan and Rebecca's family and that of their ancestors in the wilderness many years ago (for example, permanent home/makeshift tents and homeless, enough food and drink/lack of provisions). How did God look after Dan and Rebecca's ancestors? (for example, provided food and drink, guided them to a permanent home, gave them strength/ protection on their journey)

Rebecca tells Rees and Sara that God also looks after them today, which can be easy to forget when you are living in a comfortable home. In what ways might God look after Dan and Rebecca today?

Festivals across religious traditions

Work on a calendar or book of festivals from all religions. This would need to be a loose-leaf folder, or pages joined together with treasury tags so that pages can be added as needed in chronological order.

Talk about the importance of organising material well so that people can find quickly the information they need. With the pupils, decide on a useful structure for the book, for example, section headings could include stories, how the festival is celebrated today, recipes, and so on.

Chapter 3 Understanding the Torah

Information about the presentation and ritual use of the Torah in the synagogue as well as the role of the rabbi is provided in the teachers' notes for chapter 1.

The Torah within Jewish scripture

The Torah refers to the first five books in the Bible (the Pentateuch). These books are:

- Genesis
- Exodus
- Leviticus
- Numbers
- Deuteronomy

It is these writings which are written in Hebrew on the Torah scrolls used in synagogues.

The Torah forms a part of a larger body of biblical texts which include the Nevi'im (the prophets) and the Ketuvim (the writings). The Nevi'im includes:

- Joshua
- Judges
- Samuel
- Kings
- Isaiah
- Jeremiah
- Ezekiel
- and other prophets

The Ketuvim includes:

- Psalms
- Proverbs
- Job
- Song of Songs
- Ruth
- Lamentations
- Ecclesiastes
- Esther
- Daniel
- Ezra
- Nehemiah
- Chronicles

Taken together, Torah, Nevi'im, and Ketuvim are called the TeNaKh. Readings from the three sections of the Tenakh are a central important part of synagogue services, and are organised in planned cycles. The main reading is always from the Torah, and the readings from the Nevi'im and Ketuvim are selected to complement the Torah reading, drawing on similar themes.

Another important Jewish text is the Talmud. The Talmud is not scripture; it contains authoritative interpretations of the Tenakh by rabbis. As with all religious texts, the Tenakh needs interpretation and this vast work of interpretation was codified around the third century CE. A religion also needs to ensure that its texts and their teachings remain relevant to society. In Judaism, another set of texts contained in the Halakhah provides the resources to do this.

In the story, rabbis are described as 'Jewish teachers and experts in the law' who help Jews to understand how to apply God's commandments in scripture to their everyday lives. On a practical level, rabbis have an important role to play in the community.

Repentance

In the story, Rees asks an important question: what happens if you break a commandment? In response, Rebecca answers that you need to repent and then be forgiven by whoever you have wronged.

Repentance and forgiveness are understood in specific ways in Judaism. It is possible to sin against God and to sin against other human beings when one breaks commandments. When a person sins against God, there are ways provided for God to formally forgive the person who repents, for example, during Yom Kippur, the Day of Atonement. However, if the wrong has been done to another human being, the forgiveness of that person is also required, and it is hoped that the reparation given for the damage caused will elicit the necessary forgiveness.

Activities

What's so important about language?

The Torah is written in a very old language called Hebrew. Hebrew is one of the official languages of the State of Israel, and it is also used in Jewish worship. Outside Israel, Jews live in many different countries around the world – if they are practising Jews, many learn how to read Hebrew because the Torah and parts of Jewish worship are in Hebrew.

Complete the 'Hebrew writing' worksheet so pupils can appreciate the vast difference between the Hebrew language and a European language like English or Welsh, for example.

Ask pupils to imagine that they are young Jews living in this country and they are expected to learn Hebrew so that they can read and listen to the Torah in the synagogue. Imagine the challenges and the motivations. Divide the class into groups, focusing on creating arguments to support the following statement:

• It is very important to use Hebrew in the synagogue for reading the Torah.

Each group can record its ideas on a large piece of paper as a spider diagram, which can then be presented to the whole class. In the process of doing this activity, the groups will find that they are asking questions which need to be answered before they can create some of their arguments. It is essential that sources of information are available, either in the form of books or the internet.

How hard is it to forgive?

Complete the worksheet 'Righting wrongs'. In Judaism, it is important to be forgiven by the person that you have wronged as well as feeling sorry for what you have done and repairing the damage. Complete forgiveness can be one of the hardest parts in righting wrongs. This is because when a person wrongs another person, it causes negative feelings. Even when someone says sorry and the apology is accepted, it can take a bit more time for the negative feelings to be repaired. Ask pupils to identify the possible negative feelings which could be experienced by the person wronged in the following scenario:

One morning before the start of the school day, Ed was playing with a group of friends in the playground. Everyone was having a good time. As a joke, Billy grabbed Ed's bag and threw it over a wall into someone's garden. Everyone laughed, so Billy threw Ed's coat over the wall too. Ed was not very pleased. Luckily, another friend helped Ed get his bag and coat back. Unluckily, they both got shouted at by the owner of the garden and reported to the headteacher. At first, Billy refused to admit that it was his fault, but the truth was discovered eventually and Billy said sorry for his unkind behaviour. He promised never to do something like that again.

Pupils should list the possible feelings Ed may have had towards Billy and what Billy did to him. They should be able to explain why they have chosen those feelings. Even when Billy said sorry and Ed accepts the apology, these feelings will probably take a little longer to heal.

Chapter 4 Caring for others and the world

Mezuzah

Mezuzah means 'a doorpost', and it refers to a scroll that is placed in a box and nailed to the doorposts of Jewish homes or buildings, apart from bathroom doorposts. The mezuzah is touched by Jews when they pass through the doorpost, reminding them of God's presence and the need to keep God's commandments. It also identifies a home or building as Jewish.

The practice obeys the commandment in the Torah that two sections from Deuteronomy should be nailed to Jewish doorpost (Deuteronomy 6:9). The two passages are:

- Deuteronomy 6:4-9;
- Deuteronomy 11: 13-21.

The passages must be handwritten in Hebrew by a qualified scribe (sofer). In order for a mezuzah to be legitimate, it must also be copied perfectly and looked after appropriately. These two passages are called the Shema and they contain central Jewish beliefs. The opening verses are particularly important:

> Hear, Israel, the Lord is our God, the Lord is one. And you shall love the Lord your God with all your heart, with all your soul, and with all your might.

The verses focus on the belief that there is only one God, and that God should be worshipped. The main practical expression of worship in Judaism is following God's commandments which are found in the Torah. Tzedakah (charity) is an important commandment, and this is the subject of the chapter.

Charity

The Hebrew word tzedakah is often translated as charity, which can misrepresent how Jews themselves understand tzedakah. 'Charity' suggests that the attitudes of generosity, kindness, and altruism lie behind acts of giving to others. However, in Hebrew, tzedakah means 'righteousness', which suggests that the attitudes of justice and fairness lie behind acts of giving to others. This identifies two important points about Jewish tzedakah or charity:

- tzedakah is a religious duty, not a choice to be generous;
- justice and fairness requires that people have their basic needs met.

The commandment in the Torah for tzedakah is viewed by many Jews as one of the most important commandments, and it plays a central part in the lives of many Jewish families. The charity box depicted in the story is a familiar sight in Jewish homes. Tzedakah is given for the benefit of Jews and also for the benefit of non-Jews.

Jewish law says that 10% of a person's income should be given to those in need, in addition to the taxes paid. Those in need usually includes:

- the poor;
- healthcare institutions;
- educational institutions;
- a synagogue.

The Talmud (an important commentary on the Torah) provides an interesting list of the different ways of giving tzedakah, which are organised according to quality. The lowest type of tzedakah is when a person gives unwillingly. The highest type of tzedakah is when a person gives in a way which enables the recipient to become self-reliant.

The environment

There are a number of laws in the Torah which relate to the correct treatment of animals and land. Many of these rules make sense from the perspective of agricultural production, economics, and health, for example, leaving land to rest, not cutting down trees, and keeping water sources clean. God provides what human beings need in terms of natural resources, but human beings are expected to cultivate and use these resources properly. Human beings are required to work with God by maintaining and not destroying God's creations.

In addition, by remembering that natural resources belong to God and not to people, there is a requirement to share these resources, which takes us back to the practice of tzedakah.

Activities

Why do I care?

Complete the 'Caring for the world' worksheet where pupils are asked to identify what they care about and how, in practice, they show that they care.

What we care about is connected to our beliefs about the world and other people. In the story, the Jewish children care about the environment and other people. Their beliefs about God and God's creation help to explain why these things are important to them. People following other religions or no religion at all will have different beliefs which explain why they care about the environment and other people.

Ask pupils to look carefully at what they care about on the worksheet and to consider the reasons why they care. As an example, it might be helpful if the teacher shares with pupils one thing which s/he cares about with a short reason why.

Supporting a charity

In the story, the Jewish children discuss as a family which charities to support. Gather together leaflets and information about charities which work in a number of different areas. As a class, discuss the various charities and decide which charity to support by a democratic vote.

Plan a fund-raising event to take place during a lunch break or break time. Prepare posters advertising the event and the work of the charity to display around the school.

Chapter 5 Learning about kashrut

Kosher and non-kosher food

In the story, Dan introduces Jewish food laws called kashrut to Rees and Sara. Very detailed food laws are found in the Torah. Dan explains that the food laws can be divided into two main groups. The first group of food laws identifies permitted (kosher) food and prohibited (non-kosher) food for Jews. Kosher foods are:

- meat from mammals which have cloven hooves and chew their cud (cows, goats, deer, and sheep);
- birds (all birds, apart from those which are prohibited in Leviticus);
- dairy products from kosher animals;
- fish with fins and scales;
- eggs from kosher birds;
- all fruit and vegetables;
- grains and cereals (unprocessed or with a kashrut label).

Non-kosher foods are:

- meat from pigs and mammals which do not have cloven hooves and do not chew their cud;
- cheese making use of animal rennet;
- scavenging birds;
- all sea animals which do not have fins and scales, for example, shellfish (lobster, crabs, prawns), sea mammals (whales, seals, and dolphins), squid, and octopus.

The second group of food laws concerns how food is prepared; a food is kosher only if it is prepared in a particular kind of way. Food preparation which makes a food kosher includes:

- highly prescribed slaughtering procedures for all kosher animals;
- the separation of meat and dairy products in the same meal;
- care that no contaminating product enters kosher food.

The slaughterer must be qualified and use a non-serrated blade to slice through the throat to sever the arteries, veins, nerves, trachea, and oesophagus. Death is said to be almost instantaneous when a qualified slaughterer is used. After slaughter the animal must be checked for signs of disease and all its blood removed.

The separation of meat and dairy products in the same meal involves more than simply not eating the products together. Strict Jews will use different cooking utensils, cutlery, and dishes for milk and dairy products to avoid any mixing of products.

Many processed foods are prepared in conditions where it is difficult to guarantee that the mixing of kosher and non-kosher products, or the mixing of meat and dairy products, does not take place.

Following a very strict kosher diet can be difficult. For this reason, Jews can buy food products marked with a special label, certifying that it is kosher.

Difference in Judaism

It is important that difference within a religion is recognised, to avoid the creation of stereotypes. On a simple level, recognising difference should begin at primary school. In the story book, Dan and Rebecca are introduced as Reform Jews (not just Jews) and a particular form of Judaism is then presented to the reader in the following chapters. In the last chapter, 'Learning about kashrut', Dan and Rebecca's diet as Reform Jews is explicitly compared with Uncle Reuben's diet as an Orthodox Jew. In fact, some Reform Jews would be less strict than Dan and Rebecca.

This makes the point that although practising members of a particular religion share essential similarities, there are also significant differences. In this case, both Reform and Orthodox Jews maintain the centrality of the Torah and commandments but both approach and interpret scripture in very different ways.

Activities

Mapping Judaism

Pin up a large map of Wales. Mark on the map the locations of synagogues in Wales, noting the Jewish traditions to which they belong. This information is easy to find on the internet using a search phrase like 'synagogues in Wales'. Where in Wales are most practising Jewish communities located today?

Create a bar chart displaying the number of synagogues belonging to each Jewish tradition. Which Jewish tradition has the most synagogues in Wales?

Difference in Judaism

The worksheets 'Kashrut food', 'Food rules', and 'Make a menu' explore Jewish food laws. Different Jewish traditions understand these laws in different ways. In the story book, examples of these differences are provided from the Reform tradition and the Orthodox tradition.

Research with pupils other differences between a more liberal Reform tradition and a more conservative Orthodox tradition. (Remember that not all Orthodox Jews or Reform Jews are the same either!) Useful areas to explore include:

- dress (for example, distinctive dress of some Orthodox Jewish men, and only men wear the tallit and kippah in the Orthodox tradition);
- role of women in the synagogue (for example, women and men sit separately in Orthodox synagogues, and the position of female rabbis);
- views about the Torah and laws (for example, many Orthodox Jews believe that the Torah is the exact word of God. This means that they often keep as closely as possible to the text when they interpret it. Reform Jews believe that God inspired human beings who wrote the Torah. This means that they are often more liberal in their interpretation of the Torah, which can be seen in their approach to Jewish laws such as kashrut and Shabbat laws).

Keywords

ark	cabinet containing the Torah scrolls
covenant	an agreement between two parties where each party agrees to do certain things
etrog	a citrus fruit
kashrut	Jewish food laws which are found in the Torah.
kippah	a small circular cap worn by Jewish men
kosher	meets the requirements demanded by Jewish food laws
lulav	the branches of three plants: the palm, myrtle, and willow, which are tied together
mantle	material cover for the Torah scroll
mezuzah	a scroll with verses from the Shema written on it, which is nailed to the doorposts of Jewish houses and buildings
ner tamid	the lamp burning in front of the ark
rabbi	an ordained Jewish teacher
Shabbat	the Jewish Sabbath which begins on Friday evening and ends on Saturday evening
Shema	part of the Torah which contains central Jewish beliefs and the command to nail these words to Jewish doorposts
star of David	one of the symbols for Judaism
sukkah	a makeshift hut symbolising the huts used by the Jewish people in the wilderness
Sukkot	a Jewish festival celebrating God's care for the Jewish people in the wilderness
synagogue	a place of worship in Judaism
tallit	a prayer shawl worn by Jewish men (and women in Reform Judaism)
Torah	most important scripture in Judaism
tzedakah	the Jewish religious duty to provide charity

Write a story

Imagine you have visited a Jewish synagogue with a friend who attends there. Write a story about it, giving details of all the places you visited and the things you saw there. The pictures and descriptions below will help you.

star of David

This sign shows people that the synagogue is Jewish. It might be seen in stained glass windows or on candlesticks or in patterns on the walls.

ark

On the wall that faces towards Jerusalem, is a cupboard where the scrolls of law are kept. It is covered with a beautiful curtain.

ner tamid

A special lamp hangs over the ark. This is alight at all times as a symbol of God being present.

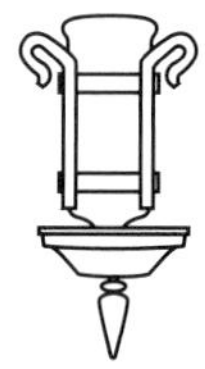

Torah scrolls

The books of the law (the first five books of the Hebrew Bible) are written on long scrolls in the Hebrew language. The handles of the scrolls are often decorated with silver crowns or bells.

bimah

In the middle of the prayer hall is a small stage with a reading desk. During services the Torah is read from here.

yad

When the Torah is read, a special pointer is used to follow the words, so that the scrolls are not touched by anyone's hand.

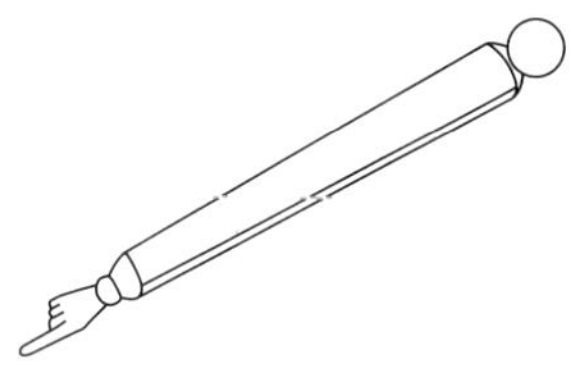

Hebrew writing

The Jewish commandments were written in Hebrew. Often synagogues have Hebrew words above the entrance door or the ark as a reminder of these.

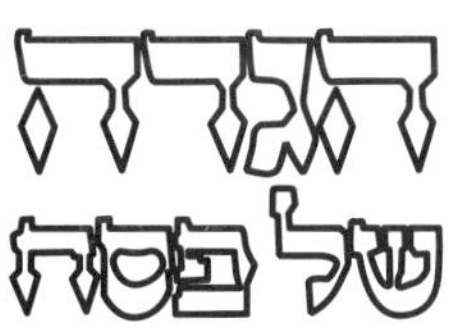

kippah

Inside the synagogue men cover their heads with a small circular cap.

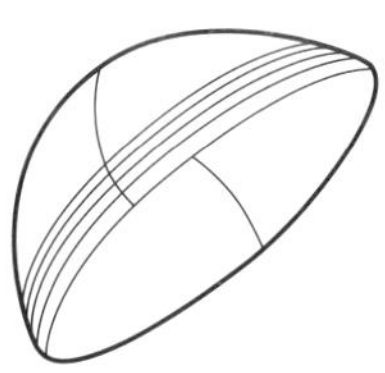

tallit

All men, older boys and some women wear a prayer shawl to cover their heads. This shows their respect and humility before God.

Star of David

The star of David is an important symbol for Jewish people. Draw and decorate your own six-pointed star, or series of stars, beginning with a hexagon.

What to do

1. Trace the hexagon from this page onto a new sheet of paper.

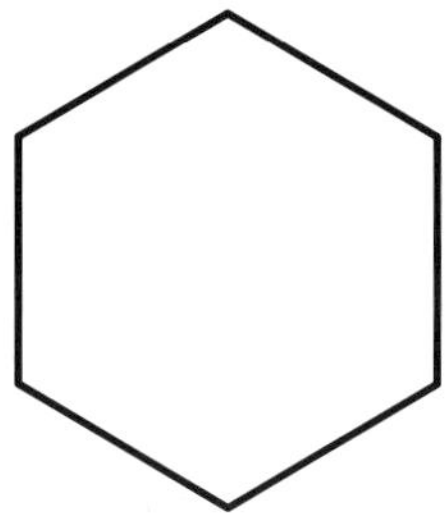

2. Rule lines to connect one vertex with the two next closest vertices. (You will need to miss the first vertex, which is the outside line, and go to the next one.) Make sure you use a ruler.

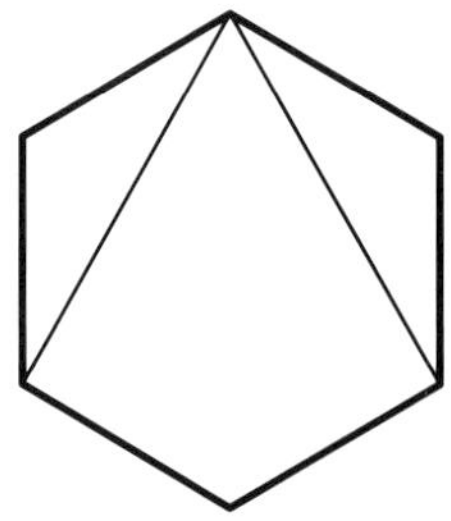

3. Repeat this process with all the other vertices. Make sure that each vertex has two lines coming from it. By the end you will see the Star of David.

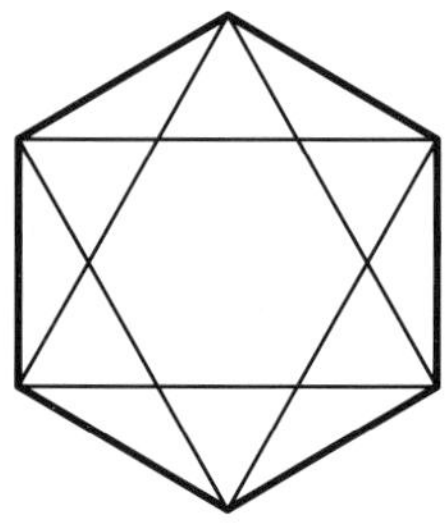

4. In the centre of the star is a new hexagon. Repeat the process to give you a new star in the centre.

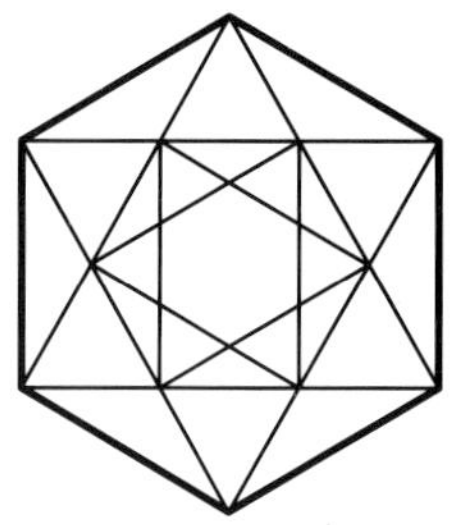

5. You can stop here and colour in the stars you already have, or you can continue to draw new stars. To do this, extend the lines of the central star out to the edge.

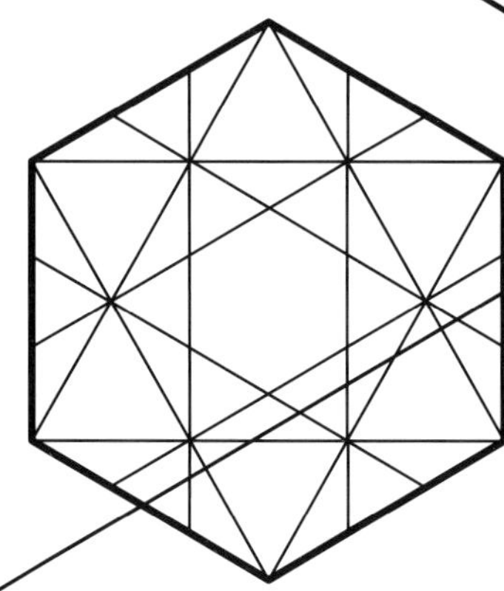

6. You will find a new hexagon at each vertex, and can make a new star in that, and a star at the centre.

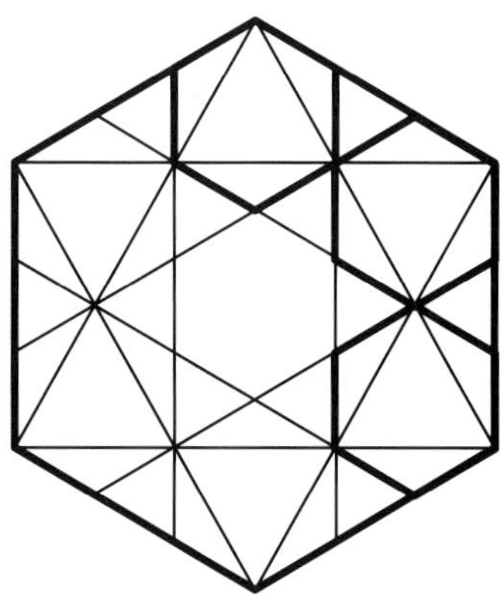

Write a poem

Write a poem about Sukkot. Here are three ideas to choose from.

1. ***Acrostic:*** Write the word SUKKOT vertically down the page. Choose words or lines about the festival that begin with those letters.
2. ***Shape poem:*** Very faintly draw the outline of a hut or a palm branch. Choose words and phrases about Sukkot that fit into this shape.
3. ***Feeling poem:*** Pretend you are sitting in your hut, remembering the Jewish people thousands of years ago wandering through the wilderness for 40 years. Write your feelings as a poem.

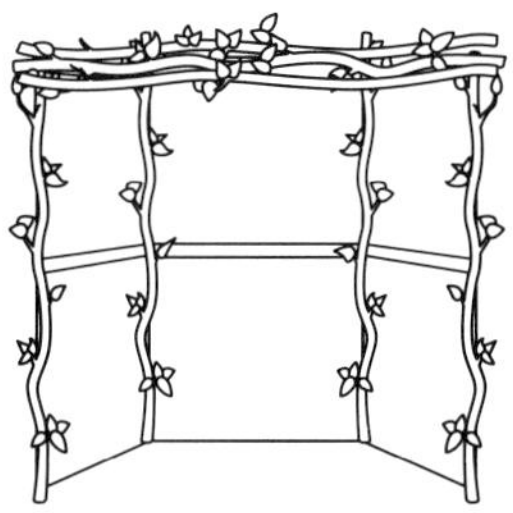

Make a Sukkot card

During Sukkot, Jewish people spend part of their time in a sukkah (a simple hut). This helps them to remember the time when their ancestors lived in huts for 40 years while travelling in the wilderness. They remember that God looked after them then and that God also looks after them today.

Make a Sukkot card in the shape of a sukkah.

You will need

- card
- scissors
- coloured pencils or felt tip pens
- sticky tape or glue
- leaves and sticks

What to do

1. Fold the card in half.

2. Glue or tape the sides together.

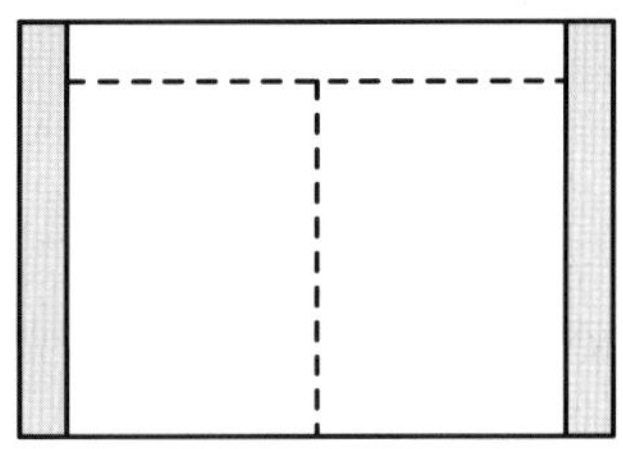

3. Cut doors in the front.

4. Write a Sukkot greeting inside.

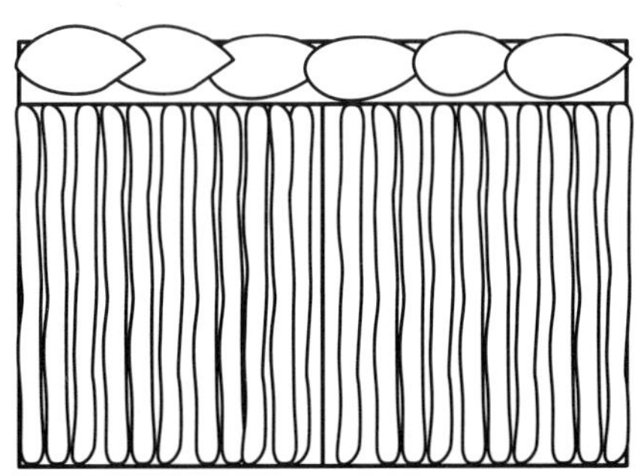

5. Decorate the outside to look like a sukkah, either by drawing or by gluing on leaves and sticks.

The story of Sukkot

> The Hebrew language was originally written without any vowels. Imagine trying to read words and sentences written with only consonants! In later years Hebrew was often written with dots under the consonants to show the sound of the vowels. This made it easier. Here is a story for you to read where some words are written with only consonants. Work out what the words are and write them in the blank spaces.

Over thr (____________) thousand yrs (____________) ago the Jewish people were slaves n (_____) Egypt. Their lives were difficult. They were treated harshly. They hd (_______) no hope. They prayed to God for hlp (__________).

Moses was snt (__________) to thm (__________) wth (__________) a message for the Pharaoh to st (_______) the Jewish people fr (__________). They were told to st (_______) ff (_______) for a special lnd (__________) that would be their own. After many prblms (____________________) they lft (__________) Egypt for freedom.

For forty yrs (____________) they wandered n (_____) the wilderness, waiting to rch (____________) their new lnd (__________). They hd (_______) n (_____) houses. They carried wth (__________) them frames tht (__________) could be used to build hts (__________) whn (__________) they stppd (__________________). Alng (____________) the way God provided fd (__________) nd (_______) water.

Jewish people stll (____________) remember ths (__________) time and celebrate by building hts (__________) and lvng (________________) in thm (__________) for part of each day during Sukkot. A sukkah mst (__________) have at least thr (______________) walls. It must have a rf (__________) made of branches. The roof mst (__________) give shade but must also allow the sky to be sn (__________).

Righting wrongs

When Jewish people break the commandments, they are expected to put things right. If you were Jewish, you might follow these steps.

1. Realise you have broken one of God's commandments.
2. Repent: feel sorry and decide not to do that again.
3. Try to put things right by saying sorry and by repairing any damage you have caused.

At times we all do things we know to be wrong. With your friends, discuss some of the wrong things that happen at school. Write the steps you could take to put things right again.

Some wrong things

Some steps we could take

Hebrew writing

The Jewish laws were originally written in the Hebrew language. This is very different from English. It is a much older language than English.

letter	*name*	*sound*
א	Aleph	Silent
ב	Bet	B/V
ג	Gimel	G
ד	Dalet	D
ה	He	H
ו	Vav	V
ז	Zayin	Z
ח	Chet	Ch
ט	Tet	T
י	Yod	Y
כּ	Kaf	K
ך	Khaf	K
ל	Lamed	L
מ	Mem	M
ם	Mem	M
נ	Nun	N
ן	Nun	N
ס	Samech	S
ע	Ayin	Silent
פּ	Peh	P
ף	Feh	F
צ	Tsadeh	Ts
ץ	Tsadeh	Ts
ק	Qof	Q
ר	Resh	R
שׁ	Shin	Sh
ת	Tav	T

The Hebrew language

- Hebrew letters are written differently from English.
- There are only consonants, no vowels.
- Hebrew is written from right to left.
- A book written in Hebrew begins at what we think of as the back. Pages are turned from left to right.
- Some of the Hebrew letters can be used for two sounds in English, and some are for sounds that English does not have.
- There are two ways of writing five of the letters. Look at Kaf, Mem, Nun, Pe and Tzade. The top version is used in the middle of a word. The bottom version is used at the end of a word.
- The first two letters of the Hebrew alphabet are Aleph and Bet, so it is often called the alefbet. (Does this word sound familiar to you?)

Write some Hebrew words

Use the Hebrew alefbet to write the following words. Remember to start at the right of the page.

ner tamid ____________________

bimah ____________________

yad ____________________

kippah ____________________

tallit ____________________

your name ____________________

Different laws

We have many different laws or rules in our world. Think of some of these.

Jewish laws

Where can you read them? ______________________

Name two laws. ______________________

____

Who helps Jewish people understand them? ______________________

Family rules

How do you know what they are? ______________________

Name two rules. ______________________

____

Who helps you understand them? ______________________

School rules

Where can you read them? ______________________

Name two rules. ______________________

____

Who helps you understand them? ______________________

Road rules

Where can you read them? ______________________

Name two rules. ______________________

____

Who helps you understand them? ______________________

Make a mezuzah

Outside Jewish homes you may see a small box on the right hand side of the doorpost. This is a mezuzah. Inside Jewish homes you may see a mezuzah on other doors. Jewish people touch the mezuzah as they pass through the door, as a reminder that God is always there.

Inside the Mezuzah is a tiny scroll with a special prayer written on it. This prayer, from the Bible, is called the Shema. It begins like this.

> Hear, Israel, the Lord is our God, the Lord is one.
> And you shall love the Lord your God
> with all your heart, with all your soul, and with all your might.

You will need

cardboard	ruler	scissors
sticky tape	pencils	paper

What to do

1. Cut out a small rectangle of cardboard. Fold it in thirds, longways. Fold a similar amount at top and bottom.
2. Cut out the four corners along the folds.
3. Fold each of the four cross sections in half. These folds need to be upwards, in the opposite direction of the other folds.
4. Tape the corners together, so you have an open box with tabs to attach it to a surface.
5. Plan what to write for your mezuzah. Jewish people write their special prayer. You could write what is most important to you. It could be about people who are important to you or about the type of person you want to be. Write this on a small piece of paper.
6. Roll up the paper and put it inside the mezuzah. Tape the mezuzah to a place you can see it and touch it most days. It could be inside your school tray or at home on your doorpost.

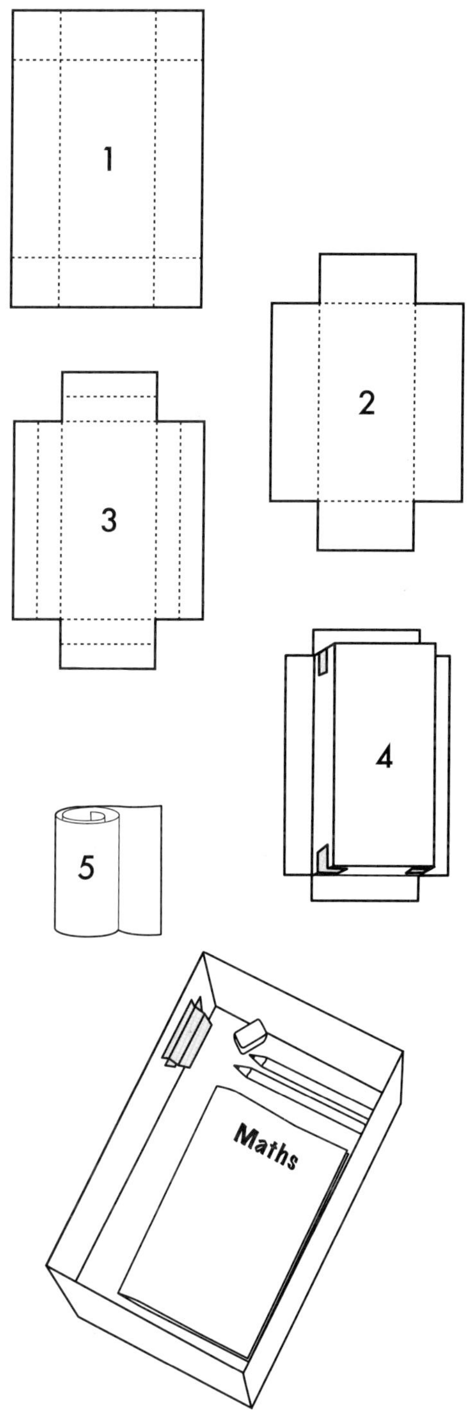

Caring for the world

Jewish people believe that their love for God is shown in the way they act. One way they can show their love is by looking after the things that God has made. This means looking after people, animals, and the environment.

We make choices like that too. Read what the children below say. Which do you agree with? Which are most important to you? Cut out the boxes and arrange them in order of importance to you. Discuss your choices with a friend.

Nia cares about dolphins.

I heard that sometimes dolphins are caught and killed when people fish for tuna. Since then my family has only bought dolphin-friendly tuna.

David cares about lonely children.

Sometimes in the playground at school I see children who are all alone. I ask them if they want to play with our group.

Nick cares about poor children.

Every Christmas my family buys extra presents and sends them to an orphanage overseas where the children do not have many toys.

Catrin cares about animals.

I saw a fur coat once and thought it was lovely until my mother told me about the animals that were killed for the fur. I will never wear a fur coat.

Shannon cares about recycling.

At home we recycle everything we can. In our kitchen we have different boxes for paper, cardboard, plastic bottles, and vegetable scraps.

John cares about pollution.

I always ride my bike to school. Mum rides her bike to work but Dad has too far to go so he takes his car. He drives other people to work to save petrol.

Emrys cares about cancer research.

My grandfather has just recovered from cancer. Now my whole family raises money for research into cancer. We want doctors to find a cure for it.

I care about

____

____

____

Kashrut food

Jewish people have strict food laws. Write down all the food you have eaten in the last 24 hours and work out if it is kashrut (allowable). Put a tick next to the food if it is kashrut and a cross if it is not.

Food Laws

- All fruit and vegetables are allowed, but check them carefully to make sure there are no insects on them.
- Fish with fins and scales are allowed, but shellfish are not.
- Many birds are not allowed, but chickens, turkeys and ducks can be eaten.
- Dairy foods (butter, milk, cheese, yoghurt) are allowed.
- Meat from cows, sheep, goats and deer are allowed, but not meat from pigs, rabbits or camels. (Allowed animals chew their cud and have hooves divided in two.)
- Some Jewish people will not eat dairy foods and meat at the same time

My food

Food rules

Some Jewish people keep the food laws more strictly than others. Orthodox Jews like Uncle Reuben in the story will not eat meat or milk products in the same meal. (This means no butter in meat sandwiches.) If they have eaten meat, then they will not eat milk products for a few hours. They even have two complete sets of cooking pots, plates and cutlery. Reform Jews like Dan and Rebecca believe that it is important to be able to mix with people who are not Jewish and to eat with them. They are careful to eat the correct foods but they are prepared to mix meat and dairy.

Plan the food for a day for Dan and Rebecca and for their Uncle Reuben, allowing for the difference in the way they live.

Menu for Dan and Rebecca

Menu for Uncle Reuben

My dictionary

You will meet many new words in *Exploring Judaism*. Keep a record of them, along with their meanings.

Shabbat	one special day each week to worship God and rest; it goes from sunset on Friday to sunset on Saturday
kippah	a skull cap worn by Jewish men to cover their heads as a sign of respect and humility to God
Torah	the first five books of the Hebrew Bible

Make a menu

Imagine you are opening a café that serves only kashrut foods. Your first job is to plan and type a menu.

1. Plan the food

Look at the Jewish food laws. (See the worksheet on 'Kashrut food'.) What food can you serve in the café?

2. Group the food

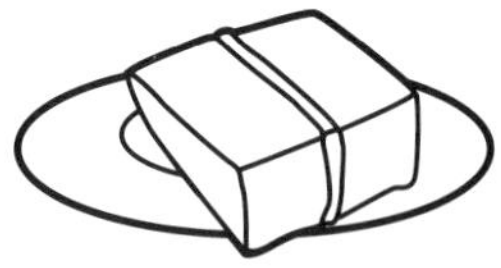

Menus often organise the food in sections such as 'drinks', 'snacks', 'vegetarian food', 'cakes'. Choose headings that suit the food you plan to sell.

3. Type the menu

Here are some reminders to make your menu look more attractive.

- Decide if your paper orientation will be portrait or landscape. If it is landscape, you might type it in two columns and fold it in half.
- Vary your headings. Try different fonts, different sizes, different colours, bold, centre.
- Choose the font and size carefully for the menu items. Make sure it is clear and easy to read.
- If you include prices, experiment with a 'right tab' or a 'left tab' to find the best place to set them.
- If you want pictures of a few of your menu items, look in Clip Art.

Exploring
the Orthodox Church

Exploring the Orthodox Church

The story

Rees and Sara have two Christian school friends called Anna and Michael who introduce them to key beliefs and practices of the Eastern Orthodox Church. Anna and Michael's grandparents had grown up in Russia. When the children visit the Orthodox church, they hear the singing, savour the incense, and gaze at the beauty. They celebrate the festival of Easter, and learn about the significance of the midnight service. They study the icon screen and examine the detail of the icons, and listen to the stories behind the icons. They investigate Christian commitment to care for the disadvantaged by studying the activity of an Eastern Orthodox charity organisation in St Petersburg. They learn Christian commitment to development education by examining why Anna and Michael's family is so keen on 'Fairtrade' and 'Tradecraft'.

Aims

Exploring the Orthodox Church provides opportunities for pupils to:

- **engage** with fundamental questions;
- **explore** religious beliefs, teachings, and practices;
- **express** personal responses in relation to the material studied.

Learning outcomes

Pupils should be able to:

- discuss questions raised by life and aspects of Christianity;
- name and describe selected beliefs, teachings, and practices of Christianity;
- explain through examples the relationship between belief and practice in Christianity;
- discuss their own views and the views of others in relation to some of the themes and issues covered, and relate these to their own lives;
- relate symbol to meaning in some Christian contexts.

The basics

There are a number of different strands within the Eastern Orthodox tradition of Christianity, just as there are a number of different denominations within the Western tradition (like Catholics, Anglicans, Methodists, and so on). The two strands of the Orthodox tradition best known are the Russian Orthodox Church and the Greek Orthodox Church. Other strands include the American Orthodox Church and the Ethiopian Orthodox Church. As these names show, the strands are named after countries. To the Western eye these different strands may look very much alike, but they are in fact separated by some very important differences.

Eastern Orthodox Christians believe in:

- one God, who is understood through the persons of God the Father, God the Son, and God the Holy Spirit;
- the opportunity of redemption for human beings, made possible by the death and resurrection of Jesus Christ, through which the relationship between human beings and God is re-established;
- the authority of scripture and tradition;
- the importance of the saints who are still active in heaven, and with whom it is possible to connect;
- the aim of mystical union with God.

In their religious practices, Eastern Orthodox Christians place emphasis on the sacraments (Holy Mysteries) through which human beings are drawn into a closer relationship with God. The sacraments are:

- baptism: usually infant baptism;
- chrismation: an anointing with oil which follows baptism, and admits a person fully into the Eastern Orthodox community;
- communion: viewed as the most important sacrament, which can be shared by those who have undergone baptism and chrismation;
- unction: the anointing of the sick;
- confession: involves confession of one's wrongdoings to a priest, who pronounces God's absolution, and usually takes place before the sacrament of communion;
- marriage;
- ordination: for those called to be priests.

Chapter 1 Visiting the Orthodox Church

Eastern Orthodox Church in Wales

When families have moved to Wales and England from countries where the Orthodox Tradition has been strong, it is natural that they have wanted to bring their distinctive Christian tradition with them. This has meant establishing churches and ensuring that such churches can be properly serviced by Orthodox priests. In the story, Anna and Michael's grandparents had grown up in Russia, and their parents had remained loyal to the Russian Orthodox Church. Now living in Wales, this meant that they had to travel a considerable distance to attend their Sunday service.

Some argue that the Orthodox Tradition was established in Wales in the very early days of Christianity before the Western Tradition became dominant there. This view is consistent with the argument that St David, the Patron Saint of Wales, was consecrated Bishop by the Patriarchs of Jerusalem. When the Great Schism between east and west occurred in 1054, the Christian Church in Britain, being under Rome, became clearly separated from the Orthodox Church.

Some trace an important step in the re-establishment of the Orthodox Tradition in Wales to 1973 when Barnabas was ordained priest in Paris and returned to Wales to live the monastic life and to engage in mission to the Welsh nation. Archimandrite Barnabas died in 1996 at the age of 80.

The Orthodox Church re-emerged in modern Wales at the close of the nineteenth century with the establishment of St Nicholas' Church near the docks in Cardiff by the Greek shipping families. This remains the home of the oldest and largest Orthodox community in Wales, serving possibly 2,000 parishioners, mainly of Cypriot origin, in south-east Wales.

Other significant orthodox churches in Wales include the Church of All Saints of Wales in Blaenau Ffestiniog, the Chapel of St David and St Nicholas in Llanelli, and the Orthodox community of St Zechariah and St Elizabeth who worship in the Church of St Mary in Swansea.

Orthodox leaders in Wales

In 1979 another Welshman (and Welsh-speaker), Iqoumen Deiniol, was ordained as an Orthodox priest to undertake mission in Wales. Father Deiniol established the congregation of Orthodox Christians who worship at Blaenau Ffestiniog. Archimandrite Deiniol is priest of the Church of All Saints of Wales and abbot of the Monastery of the Church of the Holy Protection, both in Blaenau Ffestiniog. Services are largely in Welsh, but also in Greek, English, and Slavonic. Rees and Sara visit the Church of All Saints of Wales and are made very welcome by Father Deiniol.

Designing an Orthodox Church

Design and atmosphere are very important aspects of an Orthodox Church. The church building and the worship conducted in the church are intended to offer people a glimpse of heaven. The sweet smell of the incense and the highly distinctive sound of the music are all intended to transport the worshippers to the gateway of heaven.

The east end of the church (the end where the sun rises each morning) is separated from the rest of the church by a great screen. To the east of the screen is heaven where the walls and ceiling are richly decorated, often with golden stars. The screen (known as the iconostasis) is where the icons are displayed. Doors in the screen allow the priest to pass to and fro between heaven and earth, and allow the people to glimpse the mystery of heaven behind the icons. The priest is moving constantly between heaven and earth, drawing people closer to God through administering the sacraments.

Traditionally, the main body of the Orthodox church is kept uncluttered by furniture. The congregation stands for the service. There are seats placed around the edges of the church for the elderly and for the infirm.

Ritual within the Orthodox church

Rees and Sara were introduced to three important aspects of the ritual of the Orthodox community when they entered the church.

First, they made the sign of the cross in the traditional way across their bodies. They held the thumb and first two fingers of their right hand bunched together, and held their other two fingers close to their palm. They brought their thumb and first two fingers to their forehead, then to their chest, then to the right shoulder, and last of all to the left shoulder. Symbolically, the sign of the cross is very significant in the Eastern Orthodox Church. It reflects the central Christian belief in God as Trinity: there is one God whose nature and activity is best understood through the persons of God the Father; God the Son; and God the Holy Spirit. The shape of the cross is a reminder of God's pivotal redemptive work in the death and resurrection of Jesus Christ, which allowed channels between God and human beings to be opened once again. Christians show their commitment to this relationship with their whole selves by touching their forehead (mind), heart (soul), and shoulders (strength).

Secondly, they lit a candle which they found at the back of the church and carried the lighted candle slowly to the front of the church. They placed their candle before the screen alongside candles already placed there by other members of the congregation. Light is an important Christian symbol, reflecting the light Jesus Christ brought and still brings into the world.

Thirdly, they kissed one of the special icons placed by the great screen, before walking back to take their place in the body of the church. Devotion is given to the saints in heaven who are depicted in the icons ; devotion is not given to the physical images. The physical images provide a connection between heaven and earth.

Orthodox Christians believe that God makes use of material resources as a means of drawing humans closer to God (for example, icons, water, oil, bread, and wine). It is unnecessary to explain exactly how this happens; it is a Holy Mystery. Orthodox Christianity places emphasis on truth found in experience rather than complex theological arguments designed to rationalise and explain how the Mysteries work.

Activities

Mix and match

Cut out the nine boxes on the 'Write a story' worksheet, and then cut each box into three sections: the heading, the information, and the picture. Mix up all the sections and place them in an envelope. Divide pupils into pairs or groups and give each pair or group an envelope. Pupils need to match heading, information, and picture correctly.

Do the task on the 'Write a story' worksheet (the story can easily be adapted to another genre such as a diary entry or newspaper article, if needed).

Visiting an Orthodox church

Visit an Orthodox church and identify the places mentioned in the story. How does it differ from the places in the book and how is it the same?

Using senses in worship

Complete the 'Investigate the senses' worksheet. Some Christian denominations make more use of the senses than other Christian denominations in their worship. The Orthodox Church believes that using the senses is an important part of worship because they can help to draw people closer to God.

Explore with pupils the worship of another Christian denomination which makes less use of the senses, for example, a plainer non-Conformist (Free Church) tradition (where candles, incense, images etc. do not feature). Arrange a visit to a chapel so that pupils can compare these very different approaches to worship.

Chapter 2 Celebrating Easter

Easter is the main festival of the Christian year – Jesus' death and resurrection lie at the heart of Christianity. Like the Eastern Orthodox Christmas, the Eastern Orthodox Easter falls at a different time from the Western Church because it follows a different calendar: the Eastern Orthodox Church uses the Julian calendar while Western churches use the Gregorian calendar.

Preparing for Easter

As with many other Christian churches, the celebrations of Easter Sunday take place after an important period of preparation. Many Orthodox Christians fast from certain foods during the 40-day period of Lent (for example, meat, eggs, and dairy products). Fasting is important in the Orthodox Church because it helps to develop self-discipline.

In addition, there are services taking place in the week leading up to Easter Sunday, which mark important events in the biblical story leading up to the empty tomb. For example:

- Palm Sunday is the Sunday before Easter Sunday. Crosses made from palm leaves are distributed among the congregation to remember Jesus' Entry into Jerusalem when palm branches were laid in Jesus' path.
- Great Thursday recalls the story of Jesus washing the disciples' feet at the Last Supper as an act of humility and service. In the Orthodox Church, bishops will re-enact this by washing the feet of their priests.
- Great Friday marks the day when Jesus was crucified and died. In Orthodox churches, a cloth bearing an icon of Jesus is processed and placed in the middle of the church. Some of the rituals are the same as funeral rituals, for example, gathering around the deceased with candles, kissing the icon of Jesus, and bringing flowers.
- Great Saturday marks the day after Jesus was crucified. Just before midnight, the cloth bearing the icon of Jesus is taken out of the church, at which point the church symbolises the empty tomb.

Easter Sunday

Before midnight, there is a procession led by the priest outside the church. At midnight, the priest chants the Easter hymn three times announcing the resurrection of Jesus and his victory over death. The doors are flung open and the priest and people enter the building. This symbolises the opening of the sealed tomb and the discovery that it is empty. The darkened church becomes flooded with light. This symbolises the light of the resurrection and the life it brings. Throughout the Easter period, people greet one another with the words, 'Christ is risen!' followed by the response, 'He is risen indeed!'

Activities

The feelings of Easter

Easter celebrations in the Orthodox Church stimulate a number of different emotions, and those participating symbolically walk with and feel with the very first Christians during this period. Explore with pupils the possible feelings of the very first Christians at the crucifixion and burial of Jesus. Make a list of emotions. Then, explore with pupils the possible feelings of the very first Christians when they discover the resurrection of Jesus. Make a list of emotions.

Create a poem, using these emotions. The following structure may be useful:

From (crucifixion and burial emotion) to (resurrection emotion),
From (crucifixion and burial emotion) to (resurrection emotion),
From (crucifixion and burial emotion) to (resurrection emotion),
From (crucifixion and burial emotion) to (resurrection emotion).
Christ is risen!
He is risen indeed!

Complete the 'Make a twist-out card' worksheet and include the poem on the card.

The meaning of Easter

Today, Easter means different things to different people. Conduct a simple survey of key stage 2 pupils to discover what it means to pupils in your school. Ask pupils to finish ONE of the following.

For me, the most important thing about Easter is ...

OR

Easter is not important to me because ...

After completing the survey, devise categories into which the responses to the first question can be placed. These categories can be detailed (such as eating chocolate eggs, Easter egg hunts, the death/resurrection of Jesus, new life, holidays etc.) or more general (such as religious/non-religious). Do the same with the second question.

Count the number of responses in each category and display the results in a number of different formats; for example, a numerical table, a bar chart, or a pie chart.

The results from this survey could be used as part of a school assembly about the meaning of Easter for young people today. You could also ask key stage 2 pupils in neighbouring schools to complete the survey and feed back the results to you, if you want a larger number of responses. The survey can be made more complex by adding additional fields such as male/female and Christian/non-Christian.

In the story book, Rees and Sara take part in a very powerful celebration of Easter, rich in symbolism. Complete the 'Celebrating Easter' worksheet about Orthodox Easter celebrations, and explore the symbolism with pupils.

Linking practice with story

Make links between the celebration of the Orthodox Easter today and the biblical accounts of the death and resurrection of Jesus. This can be approached in different ways, for example, write individual aspects of the celebrations on small cards and do the same with relevant parts of the celebrations today. Ask pupils to match up the celebration cards with the story cards. Suggested content for the cards:

story	**celebration**
the loss and sadness felt by Jesus' friends after his death	the darkened church
the sealed tomb in which Jesus was buried	the closed doors of the church
Jesus' friends going to visit the tomb on Easter morning	the procession around the church
Jesus' friends discover the stone rolled away and enter the tomb	the opening of the church doors and the procession into the building
the joy of the resurrection of Jesus	the church flooded with light and the greetings, 'Christ is risen!' 'He is risen indeed!'

Chapter 3 Studying the icons

What is an icon?

In the Orthodox Church, icons are religious pictures used as an aid to prayer. Icons are made of the saints, Jesus, the apostles, angels, and scenes from the Bible, and these can be found in the Orthodox home as well in the Orthodox church. The Orthodox Church believes that God the Father and God the Holy Spirit should never be directly portrayed in icons. However, God the Son is portrayed in the incarnated form of Jesus Christ – common representations in icons show a small Christ with Saint Mary (page 17 of the story book) and Christ as Pancrator (page 9). These two important icons are usually placed on either side of the middle doors in the icon screen (page 3).

Icons can be made of different materials, but they must always be flat or flattened. This prevents them from becoming three-dimensional statues to which the offering of reverence and devotion would be inappropriate. It is important to note that Orthodox Christians do not worship the icons; they show reverence and devotion to the figures portrayed in the icons. God alone is worshipped. The figures represented in the icons are in heaven and the physical icons offer a doorway to heaven, so when the Orthodox children in the story say that the saints in their icons are 'really here with us', it is understood in this sense. The figures and scenes depicted in the icons look unusual; they are never depicted in a realistic way. That is because they are highly symbolic and they show the characters in their heavenly forms. The haloes around their heads indicate God's presence with them.

The icon screen

The paintings on the doors of the icon screen are shown on page 12. These paintings depict the Annunciation (when the Angel Gabriel appeared to Saint Mary to announce that she would give birth to the Son of God) and the four Gospel writers, which show the centrality of the teaching in the four Gospels. Together with the two icons of Jesus Christ on either side of the middle doors, Orthodox Christians are reminded that the way to God is through Jesus Christ, who has opened up the doors between heaven and earth.

Saint Anna

Saint Anna was the mother of Saint Mary, the Mother of God. This tradition is found in the apocryphal Gospel of James. Anna was married to Joachim, and the couple were childless. After a visit from an angel, Anna gave birth to Mary, whom she dedicated to the service of God in the Temple. Various aspects of this story are often depicted in icons. One popular depiction of Saint Anna is shown on page 13 of the story, where she is holding a small Mary. In other icons, the small Mary holds a small Jesus.

Saint Cadwaladr

Saint Cadwaladr lived in the seventh century CE, and was the last Celtic King of Britain. We have few details relating to his life and death, but the general points presented in the story provide a useful summary of the main traditions. Saint Cadwaladr is venerated in the Orthodox Church because he represents the ideal of Christian kingship which serves God and God's people. In the Mediaeval source, The Triads, Cadwaladr is identified as one of the three 'blessed'.

The red dragon on Cadwaladr's standard was used by Henry Tudor, who claimed to be a descendant of Cadwaladr, and it is still an important symbol in Wales today.

Saint Cadwaladr is associated with Llangadwaladr Church (originally called Eglwys Ael), where tradition records that he was buried.

Saint Melangell

A fuller version of the story about the seventh-century Saint Melangell and the Prince of Powys is provided in one of the worksheets.

Saint Mary as Theotokos

The icon of St Mary on page 17 depicts her as Theotokos (the mother of God), because she carries a small Jesus. Mary is called the 'mother of God' in the sense that she gave birth to the incarnate Son of God. The incarnation lies at the heart of Orthodox Christianity, and everything else should be understood in relation to it. The symbolism of the careful positioning of icons in Orthodox churches reflects this alongside the symbolism of the rituals.

Due to her status as 'mother of God', Mary is particularly important in the Orthodox tradition, and she has a number of major feast days dedicated to her in the Orthodox year.

The iconographer

Icons are said to be 'written' rather than 'painted'. The writing of an icon is an act of worship and devotion on the part of the iconographer, which is demonstrated by the preparation and approach taken. For example, the iconographer fasts and prays before starting and will not sign the icon. The iconographer must follow strict rules which have been passed down through the centuries. These rules determine every aspect of the icon, for example, facial shapes, features, and expressions, gestures, colours, and accompanying objects. For this reason, the characters depicted in icons should be easily recognisable to those brought up in the Orthodox tradition.

Activities

Seeing the bigger picture

Ask pupils to share some of their favourite photographs of people with the class (the photographs may show family, friends, themselves, or people they admire). Pupils need to be able to explain:

- who is in the photograph;
- why they like the photograph;
- how they feel when they look at the photograph;
- where the people in the photograph are now.

Why do people take photographs? Photographs of people are more than just pictures – they mean something to those who own them.

Link this to the icons in the story book, using the information provided in the teachers' notes. In this case, the people shown on the icons are special people from Christian history. Today, Orthodox Christians believe that the people in the icons are in heaven. Praying before the icons is like looking through a window and getting a glimpse of heaven. Icons are used in Orthodox worship, to draw people closer to God.

Complete the 'Make an Icon' worksheet.

Signs of something special

Complete 'The story of Saint Melangell' worksheet. Look carefully at the reassembled story of Saint Melgangell and the image of Saint Melangell in the story book (other images of Saint Melangell can be found on the internet). What signs or clues can you spot which show that Saint Melangell is very special?

Chapter 4 Helping others

Orthodox charity

Like other Christian traditions, the Eastern Orthodox Church lives out its faith in the world by providing help and support to those in need. This is rooted in biblical example and teaching. In the story, charity is seen as a response to the most important biblical commandments to love God and to love your neighbour.

This chapter is based closely on the work of the Pokrov Community in St Petersburg, Russia, which cites these commandments in relation to its mission. There are many other Eastern Orthodox charities involved in Christian service in various parts of the world, which can be researched on the internet.

The Pokrov Community

The Pokrov Community became a registered charity in 2000, and focuses its work on helping the elderly, homeless, and sick of St Petersburg. Michael and Anna's Aunt Natasha is a member of that community which comprises mostly women. The charity has a non-church status which has helped it to work collaboratively with both religious and non-religious organisations.

Members come from a variety of backgrounds, bringing with them various skills which they can contribute to the Community. Some are doctors and nurses; others are architects, builders, lawyers, designers, directors, and photographers who can work as volunteers, offering their time as well as their skills.

Activities

Write to Aunt Natasha

In the story book, the children receive a letter from Aunt Natasha who belongs to a special community in St Petersburg, Russia. Write a letter to Aunt Natasha, thanking her for the letter. You may wish to mention some of the following things:

- what you found interesting in her letter;
- any questions you have which you would like answered;
- examples of things you have done recently (or intend to do) to help other people (Rees and Sara decided to visit their grandmother who had been ill).

What are our needs?

Identify a person's physical needs (for example, food, water, sleep, clothes, medical care, warmth, and money). Identify a person's other needs which are not physical (for example, friendship, love, guidance, feeling valued, feeling of belonging/ purpose and meaning in life).

In the story, the community looks after the physical needs of sick, elderly and homeless people in St Petersburg and also the community looks after their non-physical needs. What does the community do to look after the physical needs of the people they help? What does the community do to look after the non-physical needs of the people they help?

After reading Aunt Natasha's letter, Rees and Sara decide to visit their grandmother who has been ill. How can Rees and Sara help with their grandmother's physical needs? How can Rees and Sara help with their grandmother's non-physical needs?

Research an Eastern Orthodox charity

The Eastern Orthodox charity organisation in the story is based on the work of the Pokrov community in St Petersburg, Russia. Search for the 'Pokrov community' using the internet, and find out more about its work and how projects are developing.

Chapter 5 Fairtrade and Traidcraft

Christmas is often associated with the giving and receiving of presents and cards, Christmas trees, decorations, and carols. This chapter reminds readers that, from a Christian perspective, Christmas celebrates the lowly birth of Jesus whose mission was to the poor and socially disadvantaged. Readers also learn how Anna and Michael's family follows the example and teaching of Jesus in their celebration of Christmas through the theme of fairtrade.

Fairtrade

The Fairtrade logo is now a familiar label which appears on many different types of food products such as fruit, vegetables, coffee, and wine as well as non-food products such as cotton and cut flowers. Buying a product carrying the Fairtrade logo is an assurance that the consumer is purchasing a product which conforms to specific basic trading standards which are regularly monitored. Fairtrade labelling first appeared in the Netherlands in 1988.

Traidcraft

Traidcraft is both a fairtrading company and a development charity which was founded in 1979.

Traidcraft's Foundation Principles underpin its work and these are based on Christian principles; in particular, the Christian principles of 'love', 'justice', and 'service' as exemplified by the life and teachings of Jesus. Like the Pokrov Community in the previous chapter, Traidcraft's work is motivated by the biblical commandment to love your neighbour. Like the Pokrov Community, this is translated as practical service to others and concerns spiritual and moral issues as well as material issues. Christians believe that all human beings are made in the image of God (creation story in Genesis) and it is fair that everyone is provided with opportunities to live to their full potential.

Traidcraft's work in fairtrade focuses on establishing long-term partnerships with smaller producers and helping those producers create stable and sustainable businesses. Traidcraft understands sustainability in environmental terms as well as in human terms, and helps its partners to pursue 'responsible stewardship' in relation to the environment.

Christian service

One of the main aims of this chapter is to portray Christian service through learning about fairtrade. The principle and practice of fairtrade is supported by members of many different faith groups and also those who belong to no faith group. Although the general reasons given for supporting initiatives like fairtrade may be broadly similar for those involved, more specific beliefs and values often underpin these. In this case, the focus is on an Eastern Orthodox family and Traidcraft, both of whom are influenced by distinctively Christian beliefs which provide meaning for their actions in the world. Relevant specific Christian beliefs cited include:

- the biblical commandment to love your neighbour;
- following the example set by Jesus' life and teachings and his work with the poor and socially disadvantaged members of society;
- all human beings are made in the image of God.

Activities

Caring for others

Using the internet, learn about the work of Traidcraft in more detail. The following questions will help to focus the activity:

- Does Traidcraft have a mission statement which explains what it tries to do?
- Name the projects in which Traidcraft is involved.
- In which areas of the world does Traidcraft work?
- How can people support Traidcraft?

Some pupils could be challenged further :

- Is there anything on the website which points to Traidcraft's Christian background?

Giving at Christmas

Explore what presents pupils want at Christmas, why they want them, and how they feel when they receive them. Do they know anything about where they are made and who makes them?

Giving presents is a popular tradition at Christmas. The three wise men offered gifts to Jesus in the Christmas story. These presents were not ordinary presents but rather gifts to show that the three wise men had understood who Jesus was. Also, there is the gift-giving St Nicholas who used his wealth to help the poor.

In the story book, Anna and Michael's family believes that Christmas is a time to help the poor and the disadvantaged, following the example of Jesus. This is why they try to encourage people to buy fairtrade products at Christmas from their corner shop.

Keywords

abbess a female in charge of an abbey of nuns

Archimandrite in this case, an honorary title of a monastic priest

fairtrade trading which meets specific basic trading standards

fast abstinence from all or some types of food/drink for religious purposes for a specific period

Gregorian calendar the most popular calendar used in the world today, named after Pope Gregory XIII and a reform of the Julian Calendar

halo a circle of light around the head of Jesus and saints, depicting holiness (God's presence)

hermitage a monastery

iconographer an artist who specialises in making icons of Jesus and the saints in the Orthodox Church

iconostasis screen separating the main part of the church (earth) from the altar (heaven)

Julian calendar introduced by Julius Caesar and still used in some parts of the world today as well as in the Orthodox Church

priest an ordained minister, responsible for administering the sacraments

icon in the Orthodox Church, a picture of religious significance (showing Jesus, the saints, and biblical scenes) used in devotional prayer

sacrament a Christian ritual believed to have been instituted by Jesus which uses outward physical elements such as water, bread, and wine as a sign of inner spiritual grace

saint a person of exceptional holiness, living with God in heaven, and a focus for religious devotion

Saint Anna the mother of Saint Mary

Saint Cadwaladr the last Celtic King of Britain and Patron Saint of the Wales Orthodox mission

Saint Mary the mother of God (i.e. God in the incarnated form of Jesus)

Saint Melangell a seventh-century abbess who was given land by the Prince of Powys to build a hermitage in the well-known story about Saint Melangell and the hare

Write a story

Imagine you have visited an Orthodox Church with a friend who attends there. Write a story about it, giving details of all the places you visited and the things you saw there. The pictures and descriptions below will help you.

icon screen

The screen separates the area in which the altar is placed from the congregation. The doors and curtains are opened and closed at different times.

icons

Pictures of saints are on display to help people to pray. Haloes of light around the heads of the saints remind people of God's presence with the saints.

choir

Music is an important part of worship. The choir sings the words of the liturgy with the priest.

candle stands

As people enter they light a candle and place it in a special rack or a basin of sand. This candle is a symbol of their prayers.

icon stand

Some icons are at a low level for people to kiss as they enter the church.

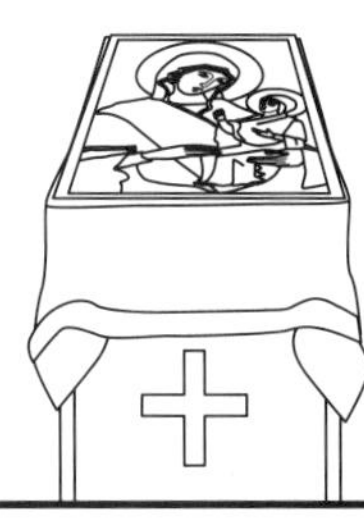

seats

There are a few seats in the building but most of the people stand. It is thought important to stand when worshipping God.

Bible

To show how important the Bible is, it is carried around the people in a procession before it is read as part of the service.

incense

During the service the priest swings the thurible so that the smoke and smell of the incense is carried to every part of the building.

robes

The priest is dressed in rich robes as a symbol of the importance of the time of worship. These robes are only used during worship times.

Investigate the senses

When Rees and Sara visited the Orthodox Church they needed to use all of their senses to fully appreciate what was happening. Read chapters 1 and 2 of the story again to find all the ways in which their senses were used.

sight

hearing

smell

touch

taste

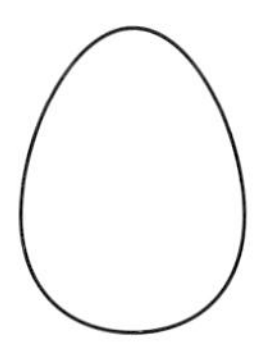

Make a twist-out card

Easter is the time of year when Christians remember that Jesus was put to death on the cross and rose to new life on Easter Sunday. Some Christians give cards at Easter with pictures of eggs as a symbol of new life.

You will need

sheet of A4 card
cutting knife and mat
ruler
pencils

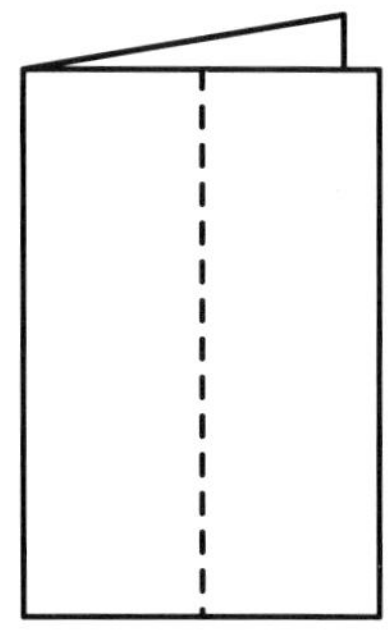

What to do

1. Fold the card in half. On the front, draw a faint pencil line down the centre.

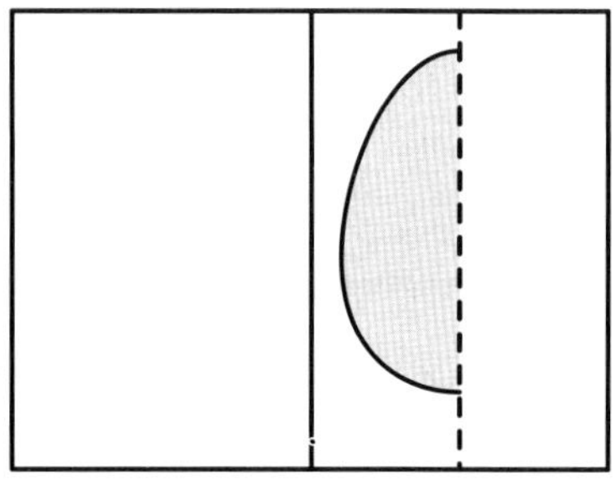

2. Open out the card. On the front, draw half of an egg shape on one side of this line, beginning 1cm from the top and ending 2cm from the bottom. Cut the curved line with the blade.

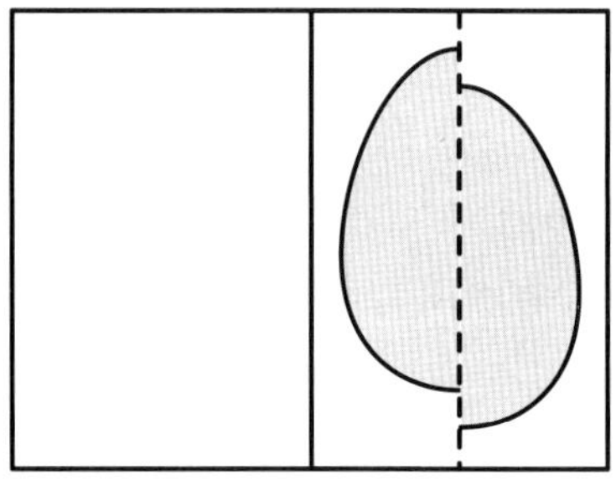

3. Draw the other half of the egg shape on the other side of the line, beginning 2cm from the top and ending 1cm from the bottom. Cut this curved line.

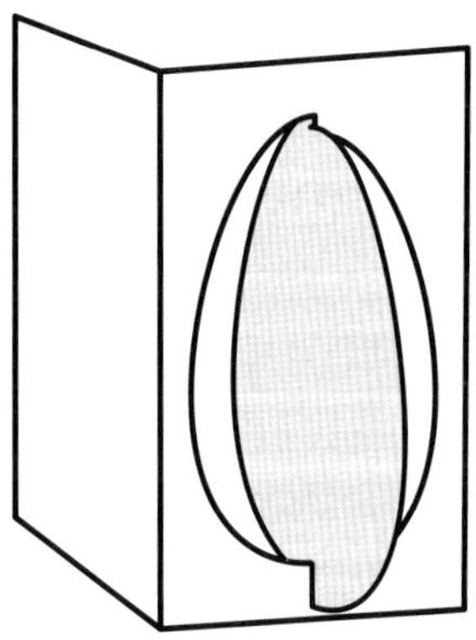

4. Pull one side of the egg towards you and push the other side away, making creases where marked.

5. Decorate the egg shape by colouring it red or by drawing patterns.

Easter eggs

In the Orthodox church, real hard-boiled eggs coloured red are served on Easter Day. The red colour is said to remind us of the blood of Christ. The eggs are usually prepared on the Thursday before Easter.

You will need

- uncooked eggs
- ¾ cup vinegar
- vegetable oil
- water
- red food dye or colouring
- cotton balls and cloth

What to do

1. Half fill a large pot with water. Add the red dye and vinegar to the water.
2. Put on plastic or rubber gloves before touching the uncooked eggs (for health and safety reasons). Carefully put the eggs into the water.
3. Bring the water to the boil and then lower the heat. Simmer for 15 minutes.
4. Ask an adult to remove the eggs from the boiling water.
5. Polish the cooked eggs with a cotton ball soaked in oil, then wipe each egg with a clean dry cloth.
6. Serve the eggs cold.

A game to play

Lightly tap your egg against a friend's until one egg cracks. The person with the uncracked egg is the winner. Keep playing against other people to see how many eggs you can crack.

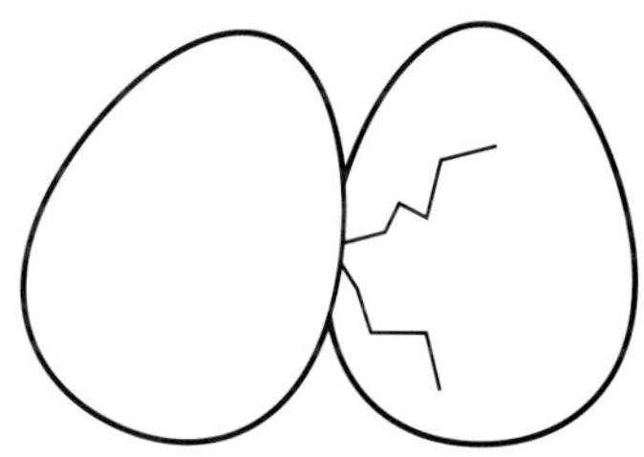

You can dye eggs in other colours too. Instead of using red dye, try some other natural ingredients for the colour of your choice.

pale red: fresh beets or cranberries, frozen raspberries
light yellow: orange or lemon peel, carrot tops, celery seed
yellow: ground turmeric
orange: yellow onion skins
pale green: spinach leaves
green-gold: Yellow Delicious apple peels
beige to brown: strong brewed coffee
blue: canned blueberries or red cabbage leaves

Celebrating Easter

Read chapter 2 of *Exploring the Orthodox Church* to find out how Easter is celebrated. For each time given below, write or draw where the people are and what they do.

Saturday night, just before midnight

midnight

Sunday morning, just after midnight

3:00 Sunday morning

Make an icon

An icon represents one of the saints of the church. It is a picture of a person who lived close to God. Icons are not decorations; they are used to bring people closer to God. The haloes of light painted around their heads are symbols of God's presence with the saints.

When an icon is made for the Orthodox Church, the iconographer (icon maker) first prays. The icon may be painted with a mixture of natural mineral colours, egg yolk and olive oil, so that it is made from animal, vegetable and mineral products (representing all parts of the world).

You will need

- wood or thick card
- brushes
- poster paints
- white paint
- scrap paper and pencil
- PVA glue

What to do

1. Prepare the wood or card by painting it with white emulsion or poster paint. (By doing this first, the colours in your painting will be clear.) Leave until dry.
2. Choose a person or saint to draw for your icon. Select someone who teaches people about God. Make sketches of how you want your icon to look.
3. Paint the picture. If appropriate, paint a gold halo around the head.
4. When the paint is completely dry, varnish it with a coat of PVA glue to add shine and to protect it.

The story of Saint Melangell

This story has been printed in the wrong order. Cut out the boxes, read the story parts and arrange them in the correct order.

The hare disappeared into the undergrowth and as the riders started to follow, strange things happened. The dogs turned back in fear. The chief huntsman could not remove the horn from his lips, yet could not make any sound on it.

Prince Brochwell was impressed. He returned to his home without killing any animals that day. He gave to Melangell the valley as a place of prayer and refuge forever.

The huntsmen set off towards the small, wooded valley filled with wild game. They pushed their way through the thick, green undergrowth. Within minutes the dogs started barking as they caught the scent of a hare. The chief huntsman sounded the horn. The riders laughed at the thought of the sport to come.

To his surprise he found a clearing, with a young woman standing in the centre praying. The hare was crouched down at her feet for safety. Prince Brochwell felt a sense of great peace.

It was a fine day for hunting in the Pennant Valley in central Wales. Prince Brochwell, prince of Powys, called together his friends and huntsmen. 'Come hunt!' he called. 'Bring the dogs. Let us see what we can find.'

Prince Brochwell was a brave and proud man. He refused to show fear in front of his friends. He leaped from his horse, drew his sword and cut his way through the brambles and shrubs. What would he find?

Who was this woman? The prince questioned her and discovered she was the daughter of an Irish chieftain. When her father had arranged a marriage for her with an old warrior chieftain she had fled to Wales and instead had chosen a life of prayer, living in a cave in the Pennant Valley. As she prayed and grew closer to God, the animals had grown to trust her.

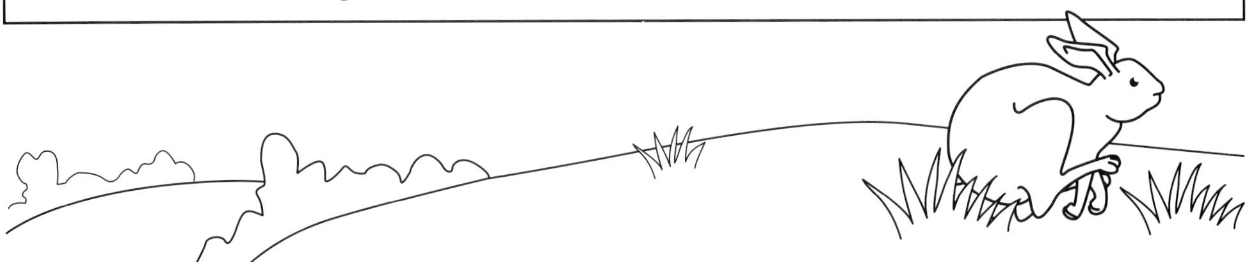

Find out about the community

Read and think about chapter 4 of *Exploring the Orthodox Church* to answer these questions about the community to which Anna and Michael's aunt belongs.

1. In which Russian city is the community based?

2. What commandment in the Bible is important to this charity organisation?

3. Name two problems the hospital faces.

4. How do the sisters care for the patients' physical health?

5. How do the sisters care for the patients' spiritual health?

6. How do they use some of the money that is donated to them?

7. Name three ways the community helps elderly homeless people.

8. How would you describe the people who work in the community?

Helping others

Think of different ways that our government or different charity organisations help the following people in need.

old people

sick people

homeless people

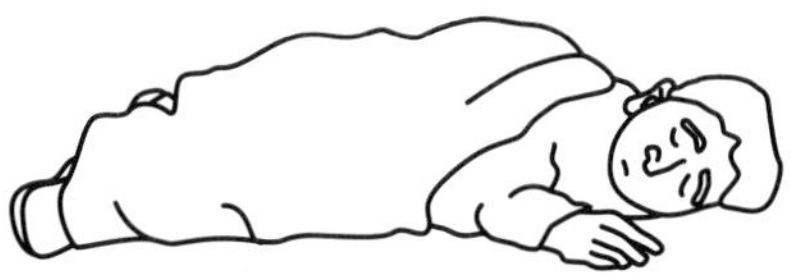

Fairtrade food

Find out about the fairtrade food available at your local supermarket or shops. List all the products you can buy.

Fairtrade products

Look at the food available. Look through recipe books. What could you prepare with just fairtrade products?

Fairtrade recipe ideas

fruit salad
chocolate dipped fruit

Compose an acrostic

Compose an acrostic based on the words below. You could select the names of fairtrade products or you could use the names of countries that sell fairtrade products or words that have anything to do with fairtrade. The given letters may appear anywhere within the word.

______________ F ______________

______________ A ______________

______________ I ______________

______________ R ______________

______________ T ______________

______________ R ______________

______________ A ______________

______________ D ______________

______________ E ______________

Write a letter

Imagine you are a person who grows bananas and sells them through the fairtrade system. Write a letter to the people of Wales, telling them about your life and saying why you would like them to buy fairtrade bananas.

My dictionary

You will meet many new words in *Exploring the Orthodox Church*. Keep a record of them, along with their meanings.

icon	a picture of a saint, used to draw people closer to God
congregation	a group of people meeting together in church for worship
incense	a sweet-smelling smoke produced by burning a gum or spice
____________	____
____________	____
____________	____
____________	____
____________	____
____________	____
____________	____
____________	____
____________	____
____________	____
____________	____
____________	____
____________	____

Make a class book of icons

1. Find out about icons

Research in the library or on the internet to find out about Orthodox icons.

2. Select your saints

Find out about people who are considered saints in the Orthodox Church. Search on the internet using keywords such as "orthodox church saints". Decide which saints you want in the book. Decide who will write about each saint.

saints

3. Write a page

Include pictures of icons and information about the life of the saint. You could write the life of the saint as a story or as a series of bullet points. Make your page look attractive by using WordArt, borders, different fonts and different colours. When you are happy with the appearance, print the page.

A handy hint

There are many ways to copy pictures from the internet to your document. One way is to have a text window open on the computer as well as the internet browser. Highlight the picture and then click and drag it straight to the text window.

4. Make a book

Bind everyone's pages together as a class book.

Exploring *the* Parish Church

Exploring the Parish Church

The story

Rees and Sara have two Christian school friends called Bethan and Tomos who introduce them to key beliefs and practices of the Anglican Church. Bethan and Tomos' mother, Mrs Davies, serves as an Anglican priest. The children explore the parish church and learn about what happens when Bethan and Tomos receive communion for the first time. They celebrate the festival of Christmas and learn about the significance of the midnight mass. Rees and Sara meet a key source of authority in Christianity in the form of the Bible, and they learn about the Old Testament and the New Testament. They investigate Christian approaches to development education by studying the activity of Christian Aid, and by exploring fairtrade products. They learn about the close sacramental connection between the material world and the spiritual world in Christian teaching by celebrating harvest festival, where they connect the fruits of the earth, the work of human hands, and the sharing in communion.

Aims

Exploring the Parish Church provides opportunities for pupils to:

- **engage** with fundamental questions;
- **explore** religious beliefs, teachings, and practices;
- **express** personal responses in relation to the material studied.

Learning outcomes

Pupils should be able to:

- discuss questions raised by life and aspects of Christianity;
- name and describe selected beliefs, teachings, and practices of Christianity;
- explain through examples the relationship between belief and practice in Christianity;
- discuss their own views and the views of others in relation to some of the themes and issues covered, and relate these to their own lives;
- relate symbol to meaning in some Christian contexts.

The basics

In the middle ages Wales and England were part of the Catholic Church owing allegiance to the Pope in Rome. As part of the Catholic system, the whole country was divided into parishes served by a parish church. Everyone was assumed to belong to their parish church and to have rights and responsibilities in respect of the ministry provided there. At the Reformation the Church of England replaced the Catholic Church as the official and 'established' religion in England and Wales and took over responsibility for the parish churches. The Church of England remains the established religion in England, but was disestablished in Wales in 1920 and renamed the Church in Wales. The Church in Wales is now part of the worldwide Anglican Communion, the family of Churches derived from the Church of England.

The Anglican Church sees itself as a broad and inclusive Church which is both Catholic and Reformed. It is Catholic in the sense of holding to some beliefs and practices shaped by the Catholic tradition before the Protestant Reformation of the fifteenth and sixteenth centuries. It is Reformed in the sense of holding to some beliefs and practices introduced by the Protestant Reformation. During the early nineteenth century these two strands in Anglicanism were re-emphasised and sharpened by the Tractarian Movement (Catholic) and by the Evangelical Movement (Reformed). Individual parish churches are still shaped by those divergent traditions. Bethan and Tomos attend a parish church shaped by the Catholic tradition.

Anglicans believe in:

- the three-fold revelation of God as Holy Trinity: Father, Son and Holy Spirit;
- the three-fold authority of scripture, tradition, and reason;
- the three-fold ministry of deacons, priests, and bishops.

In their religious practices Anglicans place importance on two main sacraments (outward signs of God's presence):

- the sacrament of baptism marks the beginning of the Christian life. Anglicans practise infant baptism. The outward sign is water.
- the sacrament of communion sustains the Christian life. The outward signs are bread and wine.

Chapter 1 Visiting the parish church

Parish church

Everywhere in Wales and England has a local parish church. The land is divided up in this way. Some of these parish churches date back to medieval times. Many were built in new areas in the nineteenth century to reflect movements in the population. In the same period some of the old medieval churches were replaced and re-modelled. New parish churches continued to be built during the twentieth century to serve new residential developments. When a parish church is closed (or declared redundant) the area once served by that church is taken over by a neighbouring parish church. The parish church attended by Bethan and Tomos was built in the second half of the nineteenth century in the neo-Gothic style to imitate medieval church architecture.

Ministry

The Anglican Church believes in the three-fold ministry of deacons, priests, and bishops. Clergy generally serve as a deacon for one year before they are ordained as priests. As deacons they cannot preside at communion, they cannot pronounce forgiveness (absolution) of sins, and they cannot proclaim God's blessing. Some dioceses promote the permanent diaconate for people who wish to serve the whole of their ministry as deacons.

Priests can take responsibility for local parishes as vicars, as rectors, or as priests-in-charge. They are appointed and licensed for their work by the Bishop of the Diocese in which they serve. Within the Church in Wales there are six Diocesan Bishops (the Dioceses of Bangor, Llandaff, Monmouth, St Asaph, St Davids, and Swansea and Brecon). Bishops will have served as priests first (often for many years). Consecration to episcopacy (being made bishop) enables them to administer two additional sacraments: confirmation (when those who have been baptised as infants reaffirm their promises) and ordination (the making of deacons and the ordination of priests).

Women in ministry

For many years in the Anglican Church only men could be recognised in ordained ministry. The decision to ordain women is now taken independently by the different Provinces of the Anglican Church. The Church in Wales first agreed to ordain women as deacons in 1980 and the Church of England first ordained women as deacons in 1987. Women were first ordained as priests by the Church of England in 1994 and by the Church in Wales in 1997. The issue of consecrating women as bishops continues to be debated in Wales and England. Women have been consecrated as bishops in other Provinces of the Anglican Communion, including New Zealand and the United States of America, although these women bishops are not allowed to exercise their episcopal ministry in Provinces which have not agreed to consecrate women as bishops.

Clerical dress

Anglican clergy (deacons, priests and bishops) like Catholic priests and many Free Church ministers choose to wear the white clerical collar as the distinctive badge of their ministry. Traditionally this clerical collar has been worn with a black shirt, but now a wide range of coloured shirts are also acceptable. Bishops can choose purple shirts to signify their special office. The long black cassock is worn on more formal occasions, although it has become less and less common to see Anglican clergy walking about their parish dressed in a cassock.

When presiding at the communion service, Mrs Davies chooses to wear a chasuble. This very distinctive vestment, only worn by priests for the communion service, is shared by Catholic priests and demonstrates that Mrs Davies' church has been influenced (to some extent) by the Tractarian Movement. Under the chasuble she wears a long white vestment known as an alb and a narrow scarf known as a stole. The stole and chasuble come in four main colours, signifying different seasons in the Church's year. Green is the basic colour worn most often. White is used at major festivals like Christmas and Easter as a sign of celebration. Purple is worn during Advent and Lent as a sign of penitence. Red is worn on festivals of the Holy Spirit (Pentecost) or to celebrate martyrs.

Communion service

The communion service stands at the heart of Anglican worship. The communion service re-presents the 'Last Supper' that Jesus held with his disciples before his crucifixion and death. At that Last Supper, Jesus took bread, gave thanks, broke the bread and shared it among his disciples. He said, 'This is my body'. Then Jesus took the cup of wine, gave thanks, and shared it among his disciples. He said, 'This is my blood'.

Receiving communion

Traditionally in the Anglican Church, people were baptised as babies and then confirmed when they were old enough to reaffirm their baptismal promises for themselves. Traditionally only those who had this to give people the opportunity to learn more about the text of the Bible and to explore how this text interacts with and influences their lives. They may also allow the text to stimulate a period of silent meditation, open prayer, and praise.

Children's clubs

On most Thursdays after school the children from the church come round to Bethan and Tomos' house for a club. Many Christian churches run groups like this to give children the opportunity to help prepare for the next Sunday service. They can hear one of the readings used in the service and make posters or models to display in the church. They can prepare songs, drama or dance on the theme of the reading to share in the service.

Activities

Showing that something is special

When something is special to us, we show that it is special by how we treat it. Explore with pupils some of their special things. How do they show that these things are special by how they treat them?

The Bible is a special book for Christians and it has a special place in many Christian services, although this is shown in different ways by different denominations. In Tomos and Bethan's church, they do a number of things which show that the Bible is special to them. Read pages 14-17 of the story book carefully and look at the pictures. How do these Christians show that the Bible is special by how they treat it?

Different types of books

There are many different types of books which have been written for different purposes. Place pupils in groups and give each group a wide selection of books taken from the school or class library (include a variety of genres and subjects). Ask each group to sort the books physically into different piles which make sense to them. They need to be able to explain how the books have been sorted.

Link this to the Christian Bible. The Bible is a religious book for Christians which teaches them about God and God's relationship with the world. The Bible is made up of different types of books by different authors (for example, law books, 'history' books, poems, letters, and myths). An example of poetry is the Psalms in the Old Testament. Complete the 'Create a Psalm of praise' worksheet. What do you think Psalm 104 teaches Christians about God?

Chapter 1 Visiting the parish church

Parish church

Everywhere in Wales and England has a local parish church. The land is divided up in this way. Some of these parish churches date back to medieval times. Many were built in new areas in the nineteenth century to reflect movements in the population. In the same period some of the old medieval churches were replaced and re-modelled. New parish churches continued to be built during the twentieth century to serve new residential developments. When a parish church is closed (or declared redundant) the area once served by that church is taken over by a neighbouring parish church. The parish church attended by Bethan and Tomos was built in the second half of the nineteenth century in the neo-Gothic style to imitate medieval church architecture.

Ministry

The Anglican Church believes in the three-fold ministry of deacons, priests, and bishops. Clergy generally serve as a deacon for one year before they are ordained as priests. As deacons they cannot preside at communion, they cannot pronounce forgiveness (absolution) of sins, and they cannot proclaim God's blessing. Some dioceses promote the permanent diaconate for people who wish to serve the whole of their ministry as deacons.

Priests can take responsibility for local parishes as vicars, as rectors, or as priests-in-charge. They are appointed and licensed for their work by the Bishop of the Diocese in which they serve. Within the Church in Wales there are six Diocesan Bishops (the Dioceses of Bangor, Llandaff, Monmouth, St Asaph, St Davids, and Swansea and Brecon). Bishops will have served as priests first (often for many years). Consecration to episcopacy (being made bishop) enables them to administer two additional sacraments: confirmation (when those who have been baptised as infants reaffirm their promises) and ordination (the making of deacons and the ordination of priests).

Women in ministry

For many years in the Anglican Church only men could be recognised in ordained ministry. The decision to ordain women is now taken independently by the different Provinces of the Anglican Church. The Church in Wales first agreed to ordain women as deacons in 1980 and the Church of England first ordained women as deacons in 1987. Women were first ordained as priests by the Church of England in 1994 and by the Church in Wales in 1997. The issue of consecrating women as bishops continues to be debated in Wales and England. Women have been consecrated as bishops in other Provinces of the Anglican Communion, including New Zealand and the United States of America, although these women bishops are not allowed to exercise their episcopal ministry in Provinces which have not agreed to consecrate women as bishops.

Clerical dress

Anglican clergy (deacons, priests and bishops) like Catholic priests and many Free Church ministers choose to wear the white clerical collar as the distinctive badge of their ministry. Traditionally this clerical collar has been worn with a black shirt, but now a wide range of coloured shirts are also acceptable. Bishops can choose purple shirts to signify their special office. The long black cassock is worn on more formal occasions, although it has become less and less common to see Anglican clergy walking about their parish dressed in a cassock.

When presiding at the communion service, Mrs Davies chooses to wear a chasuble. This very distinctive vestment, only worn by priests for the communion service, is shared by Catholic priests and demonstrates that Mrs Davies' church has been influenced (to some extent) by the Tractarian Movement. Under the chasuble she wears a long white vestment known as an alb and a narrow scarf known as a stole. The stole and chasuble come in four main colours, signifying different seasons in the Church's year. Green is the basic colour worn most often. White is used at major festivals like Christmas and Easter as a sign of celebration. Purple is worn during Advent and Lent as a sign of penitence. Red is worn on festivals of the Holy Spirit (Pentecost) or to celebrate martyrs.

Communion service

The communion service stands at the heart of Anglican worship. The communion service re-presents the 'Last Supper' that Jesus held with his disciples before his crucifixion and death. At that Last Supper, Jesus took bread, gave thanks, broke the bread and shared it among his disciples. He said, 'This is my body'. Then Jesus took the cup of wine, gave thanks, and shared it among his disciples. He said, 'This is my blood'.

Receiving communion

Traditionally in the Anglican Church, people were baptised as babies and then confirmed when they were old enough to reaffirm their baptismal promises for themselves. Traditionally only those who had been confirmed were invited to receive communion. Increasingly young people are now invited to receive communion before confirmation but after a period of special preparation. The precise age for admission to communion before confirmation varies from one parish to another.

In the present study Bethan and Tomos are receiving communion for the first time. Rees and Sara come to share in their special day. Like other people (adults as well as children) who have not been confirmed nor undertaken the special preparation, Rees and Sara do not receive communion; but they do receive a special blessing when the priest places her hand on their heads.

Assistants

In this service Mrs Davies is assisted by four robed people. The Crucifer leads the procession by carrying the cross. Two Acolytes follow carrying candles. The Acolytes support Mrs Davies at various points of the service. The Reader preaches the sermon and assists in administration of communion. Readers are lay people who have been trained and licensed to preach. Their badge of office in the service is the blue scarf.

Activities

Mix and match

Cut out the nine boxes on the 'Write a story' worksheet, and then cut each box into three sections: the heading, the information, and the picture. Mix up all the sections and place them in an envelope. Divide pupils into pairs or groups and give each pair or group an envelope. Pupils need to match heading, information, and picture correctly.

Do the task on the 'Write a story' worksheet (the story can easily be adapted to another genre such as a diary entry or newspaper article, if needed).

Visiting a parish church

Visit a parish church and identify the places mentioned in the story. How does it differ from the places in the book and how is it the same?

Communion service

Look carefully at the words said to Tomos and Bethan in the story, when they receive the bread and the wine – 'the body of Christ' and 'the blood of Christ'. This ritual is more than 2,000 years old, going back to the time of Jesus, and it has been re-enacted by generations of Christians ever since. Read the story of the Last Supper from a children's Bible to pupils. Note carefully the words and actions of Jesus. Jesus shared this special meal with his twelve disciples (the first Christians), and today Christians share a similar special meal with one another. They are giving thanks to God for the gift of Jesus, and when they share this meal they believe that Jesus is present there with them.

Complete the 'Make a communion set' worksheet. Ask them to think carefully about an appropriate slogan to write on a narrow band of gold paper which can be glued around the circumference of the cup and on to the plate. The slogan should help remind people about the meaning of communion for Christians.

Dressed for a purpose

Explore the purpose of uniforms with pupils (for example, school uniform, cubs, football/rugby teams, karate/judo, firefighters, police, army). Usually uniforms show that you belong to a particular group or have a particular job. Often, they also have a practical purpose, for example, a judo suit is hard-wearing to cope with the contact nature of the sport and it is also baggy to allow freedom of movement.

Complete the 'Dress Mrs Davies' worksheet. As a priest she wears different clothes for different occasions. Explore the colours worn for various times in the Church year (see teachers' notes).

Relate Mrs Davies' clothes to the previous exploration of uniforms. Identify the purposes of Mrs Davies' clothes.

Chapter 2 Midnight mass at Christmas

Celebrating Christmas

Christmas has become a major holiday and time of celebration for most people living in Wales and England, not just a festival for Christians. As a consequence many parish churches have adapted the ways in which they keep Christmas to accommodate the celebrations going on all around them.

Traditionally parish churches may have kept the four-week period of Advent as a sombre preparation for Christmas. Throughout Advent there would have been no flowers in church, the dominant colour would have been purple, and no carols would have been sung before midnight mass. Such a period of preparation would have made the splendour of the midnight service even more spectacular.

Even without the sombre preparations of Advent, the first communion service of Christmas (the midnight mass) remains very special in many parish churches. Now that they were old enough to stay up so late, Sara and Rees were really looking forward to taking part in their first midnight service, going to church with their friends Bethan and Tomos.

Bell ringing

Many parish churches were built with towers that could accommodate bells. Some churches have just one or two bells which are rung to let people know that a service is about to happen. Others have a larger set (or ring) of bells. Six bells comprise a good and useful set. Each bell is tuned to a different note and each bell needs its own bell-ringer.

A simple way to use a set of six bells is to ring rounds with a simple progression of notes being rung from high to low in sequence and then repeated. The much more complex tradition popular in Wales and England is known as change ringing when the order keeps changing according to complex patterns. Change ringing requires a lot of skill, practice and concentration.

The broadcast of change ringing across the winter night sky is one of those very special Christmas sounds.

Christmas carols

Christmas carols embrace a wide range of different themes, traditions and moods. The three carols recognised by Rees and Sara are all well known not only in churches, but also in schools and on the radio and television: 'Away in a manger', 'Silent night', and 'Angels from the realms of glory'. The full set of words for these carols can be found in many different books.

Midnight mass

The midnight mass usually begins a little before midnight so that the service is well underway when the midnight hour chimes. The priest presiding at the eucharist will wear a white (or gold) chasuble to signify that this is a major festival within the Church's year. At the service there will be special readings from the Bible to mark the birth of Jesus. Often the Gospel reading is the famous passage from John's Gospel 1:1-14 which begins, 'In the beginning was the Word, and the Word was with God'.

The collect is the special prayer which sums up the theme for the service. Mrs Davies is using that collect immediately after blessing the Christmas crib.

Christmas story

Inside the parish church Rees and Sara looked at the Christmas story as related by pupils from local schools in huge murals around the walls. This is an excellent way in which to build good links between local schools and the parish church at Christmas time.

The Christian story has its roots in two of the four Gospels included in the New Testament. The Gospel of Mark (which is generally accepted as the oldest of the four Gospels) includes nothing about the birth of Jesus. The two Gospels of Matthew and Luke appear to have added other material to what they learnt from Mark and to have done so from different sources. Both Matthew and Luke include narratives about the birth of Jesus, but these two narratives relate the story from very different perspectives.

Luke sets his story in an atmosphere shaped by the imagery and poetry of the Old Testament. Luke begins by introducing the birth of John the Baptist, who was the forerunner to Jesus. Then Luke introduces the birth of Jesus. According to Luke the Angel Gabriel appeared to the young Mary and told her that the power of the Holy Spirit would overshadow her, that she would conceive and give birth to a boy to be named Jesus. According to Luke, Mary was betrothed to Joseph. Joseph was a descendant of the Great King David and traced his roots to Bethlehem. At that time the land was occupied by the Roman forces and Joseph was forced to travel to Bethlehem, taking Mary with him, to be registered and to be taxed by the Roman officials. In Bethlehem the inns were full, leaving Mary and Joseph to lodge in the stable. It is there in the stable that Jesus was born, and placed in the animals' feeding trough for a bed.

According to Luke the heavenly choir of angels

announced Jesus' birth to the shepherds guarding sheep in the neighbouring fields. The shepherds came to pay homage to the newborn babe.

Matthew sets his story in a different context. It is Matthew who tells of the wise men (magi) who followed the star to find Jesus' place of birth. Matthew does not count the number of wise men who made the journey, but he does associate them with bringing three gifts: gold, frankincense, and myrrh.

Activities

Making sense of Christmas cards

Collect together a variety of different Christmas cards (for example, explicitly religious, Father Christmas, snow scenes, animals/birds, carol singers, Christmas trees, historical, etc.). Place pupils into groups and ask them to study the cards carefully. Task:

- What are the different kinds/types of Christmas cards? Place the cards into different piles according to their type.

Christmas cards can be categorised in a number of ways; there is no single right answer. A sign of a good set of categories is when most of the cards have some place within it, because coherent major themes have been identified. Remember that sometimes you have to use a miscellaneous category, but make sure it is not too big.

Christians often send Christmas cards which have a religious theme. Complete the 'Make a pop-up card' worksheet, choosing appropriate illustrations for a Christian market.

The meaning of Christmas

Today, Christmas means different things to different people. Conduct a simple survey to discover what it means to key stage 2 pupils in your school, by finishing ONE of the following sentences.

For me, the most important thing about Christmas is ...

OR

Christmas is not important to me because ...

After completing the survey, devise categories into which the responses to the first question can be placed. These categories can be detailed (such as receiving presents, eating, the birth of Jesus, Christmas parties, etc.) or more general (such as religious/non-religious). Do the same with the second question.

Count the number of responses in each category and display the results in a number of different formats; for example, a numerical table, a bar chart, or a pie chart.

The results from this survey could be used as part of a school assembly/collective worship about the meaning of Christmas for young people today. You could also ask key stage 2 pupils in neighbouring schools to complete the survey and feed back the results to you, if you want a larger number of responses. The survey can be made more complex by adding additional fields such as male/female and Christian/non-Christian.

In the story book, Rees and Sara learnt that for Christians 'the real meaning of Christmas is not to be found in the cards showing holly, robins, and snow-covered inns, but in the birth of Jesus'.

Complete the 'Tell the Christmas story' worksheet about the birth of Jesus and explore its Christian significance.

Festivals across religious traditions

Work on a calendar or book of festivals from all religions. This would need to be a loose-leaf folder, or pages joined together with treasury tags so that pages can be added as needed in chronological order.

Talk about the importance of organising material well so that people can find quickly the information they need. With the pupils, decide on a useful structure for the book, for example, section headings could include stories, how the festival is celebrated today, recipes, and so on.

The sounds of Christmas

What are the musical sounds of Christmas in the story? (church bells and singing carols)

What other sounds do the pupils associate with Christmas? (for example, sleigh bells, wrapping paper opening, silence of snow falling, crackling fire, laughter, etc.)

Find musical instruments or everyday objects that make sounds like these.

Using your chosen sounds, compose, perform and record a piece of music called 'The sounds of Christmas'.

Chapter 3 Using the Bible

What is the Bible?

The Bible is a collection of books which are of particular significance to Christians. Most Bibles have at least two sections. The first section, a collection of 39 books, comprises the Old Testament. All of these books were written before the birth of Jesus, and Christians believe that they point to God's purposes revealed through the birth of Jesus. The second section, a collection of 27 books, comprises the New Testament. All of these books were written during the early years of the Christian Church, and Christians believe that they reveal God's purposes for the world today. Some Bibles also include a third section, published between the Old Testament and the New Testament, known as the Apocrypha.

How is the Bible used?

The Bible is generally seen as a source of authority by Christians, but what is meant by this varies greatly from one person to another. A conservative view maintains that the Bible is the Word of God in quite a literal sense. Some conservative Christians will accept the account of creation related in the opening chapters of Genesis as describing how the world was literally created in six days. As a consequence they reject the scientific theory of evolution. A liberal view maintains that the Bible is inspired by God in special ways, but rejects the notion that the text has to be taken literally. Some liberal Christians will accept the Genesis account of creation as pointing not to how the world was made, but to why God created the world.

Mrs Davies, the priest of St David's Church, appears to be a relatively liberal Anglican. As an Anglican she is committed to three sources of authority: the Bible; the tradition of the church; and human reason. As a liberal she is placing emphasis on how the Bible is used in the liturgy of the church. Her message to Bethan and Tomos written inside their Bibles is very important. She wrote, 'You are a child of God supported by word and sacrament', reminding them that the Bible is to be used alongside the traditions and sacraments of the church.

Using the Bible in Church

When Rees and Sara visit the parish church, they see the gleaming brass eagle on which the Bible is placed. This is known as the lectern. The eagle symbolises how the Word of God is carried through the world.

When Rees and Sara attend a service in the parish church, they see and hear how the Bible is used in Anglican worship. In the Sunday morning communion service, traditionally three readings are used. The first reading is taken from the Old Testament. The second reading is taken from the New Testament, but not from one of the four Gospels with which the New Testament begins. Both of these passages from the Bible are read by members of the congregation walking up to the lectern from their pews. At the end of each reading, the reader proclaims, 'This is the Word of the Lord', and the people respond, 'Thanks be to God'.

The third reading is treated differently and seems to be more important. This reading always comes from one of the four Gospels (Matthew, Mark, Luke, or John), the books concerned with the life, the teaching, and the works of Jesus. The Gospel is generally read by the priest. In this parish church, influenced by the Anglican Catholic tradition, the crucifer took the Bible from the lectern and carried it to the centre of the church. Mrs Davies kissed the Bible before reading the Gospel. The two acolytes held their candles high while the Gospel was being read. At the end of the Gospel reading Mrs Davies said, 'This is the Gospel of Christ' and the people responded, 'Praise to Christ our Lord'.

Deciding what to read

The Anglican Church follows a fixed pattern of readings from the Bible set for every service in the year. The pattern of readings is set out in the Lectionary. Although there are several different lectionaries in current use, the dominant one is known as the Revised Common Lectionary which proposes a three year cycle, so the same readings come up every three years. The church Bethan and Tomos attend uses this lectionary which is shared not only with Anglican churches across the world but with other churches as well, including the Catholic Church.

Translating the Bible

The books of the Old Testament were written in Hebrew and the books of the New Testament were written in Greek. These books have now been translated into many languages. Moreover, there are a number of different English translations. Some are in an old fashioned form of English like the famous King James Version (also known as the Authorised Version). Many are in very up-to-date forms of English.

Bible Study Groups

On most Tuesday evenings eight or nine people come to Bethan and Tomos' house for a Bible Study Group. Many Christian churches run groups like this to give people the opportunity to learn more about the text of the Bible and to explore how this text interacts with and influences their lives. They may also allow the text to stimulate a period of silent meditation, open prayer, and praise.

Children's clubs

On most Thursdays after school the children from the church come round to Bethan and Tomos' house for a club. Many Christian churches run groups like this to give children the opportunity to help prepare for the next Sunday service. They can hear one of the readings used in the service and make posters or models to display in the church. They can prepare songs, drama or dance on the theme of the reading to share in the service.

Activities

Showing that something is special

When something is special to us, we show that it is special by how we treat it. Explore with pupils some of their special things. How do they show that these things are special by how they treat them?

The Bible is a special book for Christians and it has a special place in many Christian services, although this is shown in different ways by different denominations. In Tomos and Bethan's church, they do a number of things which show that the Bible is special to them. Read pages 14-17 of the story book carefully and look at the pictures. How do these Christians show that the Bible is special by how they treat it?

Different types of books

There are many different types of books which have been written for different purposes. Place pupils in groups and give each group a wide selection of books taken from the school or class library (include a variety of genres and subjects). Ask each group to sort the books physically into different piles which make sense to them. They need to be able to explain how the books have been sorted.

Link this to the Christian Bible. The Bible is a religious book for Christians which teaches them about God and God's relationship with the world. The Bible is made up of different types of books by different authors (for example, law books, 'history' books, poems, letters, and myths). An example of poetry is the Psalms in the Old Testament. Complete the 'Create a Psalm of praise' worksheet. What do you think Psalm 104 teaches Christians about God?

Chapter 4 Christian Aid

A number of organisations and charities have been set up to help improve the lives of others and support the environment. In this chapter Rees and Sara are introduced to Development Education Centres, Christian Aid, Oxfam, and Fairtrade, and they learn how the work of Christian Aid is a practical application of Christian teaching.

Development Education Centres

Development Education Centres are generally independent organisations established to promote understanding about issues like global citizenship and sustainable development. Such Centres are supported by major Development Agencies (non-governmental organisations) like Christian Aid and Oxfam, as well as the Department for International Development (government agency).

Christian Aid

Christian Aid was established in 1945 by churches in the UK and Ireland to respond in a practical way to the needs of those in Europe whose lives had been seriously affected by the Second World War. Today, Christian Aid is involved in a large number of projects which seek to respond to the needs of very poor communities around the world through raising global awareness of the problems and working to help people help themselves.

Oxfam

Like Christian Aid, Oxfam was also established to provide a practical response to the needs created as a result of the Second World War. Today, Oxfam works on the premise that every person, wherever that person lives, has certain basic rights. Every person has a right to healthcare, education, a secure livelihood, a safe environment (for example, clean water and accommodation), freedom from discrimination (for example, on the basis of gender, race, and religion), and a voice which is heard.

Fairtrade

The Fairtrade logo is now a familiar label which appears on many different types of food products such as fruit, vegetables, coffee, and wine as well as non-food products such as cotton and cut flowers. Buying a product carrying the Fairtrade logo is an assurance that the consumer is purchasing a product which conforms to specific basic trading standards which are regularly monitored. Fairtrade labelling first appeared in the Netherlands in 1988.

Christian teaching

A great deal of Christian teaching is concerned with the fundamental issues that inspire development education programmes. The following themes are relevant.

Doctrine of creation Christians generally believe that the world was created by God and that God continues to care for and continues to care about the world. The doctrine of creation is about why the world exists, not about how it exists. Many Christians reject the literal account of creation in six days related by the first book in the Old Testament (Genesis), but accept the view that the world was created by God.

Doctrine of humankind Christians generally believe that men and women were created in the image of God and share in God's concern for the world.

Doctrine of stewardship Christians generally believe that it is their responsibility to be good stewards of God's world and to work with God realising the full potential of the world. According to this doctrine, men and women have a God-given responsibility of conserving and protecting the birds of the air, the fish of the seas, the animals of the land, and all the rich resources of the earth.

Practical application Christian teachings of this nature are clearly seen in the wide range of development initiatives undertaken by Christians throughout the world, including Christian Aid, Catholic Agency for Overseas Development (CAFOD), and World Vision, among others

Activities

Treat others as you would like them to treat you

How do you like to be treated by other people? What do you think is fair treatment and unfair treatment? How do you feel when you are being treated unfairly?

Link this to the passage from the Bible in the story:

> Treat others as you would like them to treat you. If you love only those who love you, What credit is that to you?

Here Jesus was asking people to do a very difficult thing – to treat other people as you would like to be treated even if you might not like them or even know them.

Explore world trade with the pupils. In the story, what is unfair about world trade in many poor countries? What does fairtrade do to improve the situation? What can you do to help people who are not treated fairly in trade?

Complete the 'Make posters' worksheet about fairtrade products. Display the posters prominently to draw attention to unfairness in the lives of people who are not known personally and to advertise what can be done to help.

Caring for others

Using the internet, learn more about the work of a Christian aid agency (for example, Christian Aid or CAFOD). The following questions will help to focus the activity.

- Does the aid agency have a mission statement which explains what it tries to do?
- Name the projects in which the aid agency is involved.
- In which areas of the world does the aid agency work?
- How can people support the aid agency?

Some pupils could be challenged with a further question.

- Is there anything on the website which points to the aid agency's religious background (Christian)?

Chapter 5 Celebrating harvest

Harvest Thanksgiving

Harvest Thanksgiving Services continue to play an important part in the life of Christian churches in Wales and England, across the denominations, and in towns as well as in villages. Harvest Thanksgiving is not part of the Church's year in the same sense as Christmas and Easter, but these services do proclaim some important things about Christian belief and practice.

Christians generally believe that God created the world and established the pattern of seedtime and harvest. Christians generally believe that the harvest symbolises close collaboration between the processes of nature, the work of men and women, and the continuing activity of God. Christians generally believe that they have responsibility to share the gifts of harvest with all God's people throughout the world. Christians generally want to give thanks to God for the gifts of the harvest and to pray for God's blessing on the continuing fruitfulness of the soil.

Linking harvest with communion

In Saint David's parish church, Mrs Davies is making some clear connections between keeping Harvest Thanksgiving and the regular pattern of Communion Services. These connections reveal important insights into Mrs Davies' Catholic and sacramental theology. In chapter one, we met the opening lines of the prayers Mrs Davies offered when she took the bread and when she poured the wine. These prayers go on to make the clear link between the gifts of God, the fruit of the earth and the work of human hands. Taking the bread, Mrs Davies prays:

> Blessed are you Lord God, King of the universe.
> By your goodness we have this bread to offer,
> fruit of the earth and work of human hands.

Taking the wine, Mrs Davies prays:

> Blessed are you Lord God, King of the universe.
> By your goodness we have this wine to offer,
> fruit of the vine and work of human hands.

Harvest Project Day

St David's parish church arranged a whole Saturday for children and young people to be able to explore the connection between Harvest Thanksgiving and the communion service by focusing on bread and wine. The project day was designed to illustrate some of the principles of Catholic sacramental theology.

The visit to the local supermarket highlighted the variety of breads available across the world: the long baguette of France, ciabatta bread from Italy, and naan bread from India. When Christians take bread in the communion service, they are joining with all God's people across the world.

The visit to the farm highlighted the complex processes concealed within a bag of flour. Here is the story of nature, including the seed, the soil, the nutrients, the sun and the rain. Here is the story of human toil, including the people who made the tractor, refined the diesel, harvested the grain, and ground the grain into flour. When Christians take bread in the communion service, they are giving thanks to God for all these processes of nature and for all these human activities.

The experience of baking bread caught Rees and Sara up in the remarkable processes of change that take place. Once the flour was mixed with yeast and with water, the dough began to form and to expand. Once the dough was baked in the oven the bread became firm and the crust crisp.

In the communion service on Sunday Rees and Sara saw the bread which they had made taken by Mrs Davies, the priest. They joined with her in giving thanks to God for fruits of the earth and for the work of human hands. Then in the great prayer of thanksgiving which Mrs Davies offered over the bread and the wine, Rees and Sara heard about another great process of change and transformation. Christians believe that in the communion service the bread and the wine become for them the body and blood of Christ.

Decorating the church for harvest

For Harvest Thanksgiving many churches take a great deal of trouble to decorate the building with signs of the harvest from across the world. In Saint David's church special displays were made around the altar and around the font. The altar is special because that is where the sacrament of communion is celebrated. The font is special because that is where the sacrament of baptism is celebrated. Alongside the apples and pears grown in their back gardens, the congregation at Saint David's had collected and displayed around the altar tins of peaches, grapefruit and pineapples grown in far away places. Alongside the potatoes, carrots, parsnips and leeks grown on their allotments, the congregation of Saint David's had collected and displayed around the font vegetables grown across the world.

For the people in Saint David's church, Harvest Thanksgiving was a time not only to link with people across the world, but also to link with people across the ages. That is why they displayed in the Lady

Chapel (the side chapel dedicated to the Blessed Virgin Mary) spades, hoes and scythes from bygone days, as well as ploughs and spraying equipment used on farms today.

Sharing God's gifts

Harvest Thanksgiving is also a time when Christians express their concern and care for the hungry and for the poor across the world. Often the gifts displayed in the church are distributed to a local charity or to deserving individuals in the local community. Often a special collection is taken to support Christian development agencies across the world.

Activities

Our local parish church

Visit your local parish church at Harvest Thanksgiving time and discover how its congregation celebrates Harvest Thanksgiving. Arrange for the parish priest to be present, and beforehand prepare an agreed list of important questions to ask. In what ways are the celebrations similar to and different from the ones described in the story book?

Investigating food

It is easy to take for granted the food we eat, without thinking of its origins. Ask the children to name a favourite or common food product. Discuss how that product is prepared, listing the ingredients under the heading of 'fruit of the earth' and preparation actions under the heading of 'work of human hands'. After doing this for one product as a class, separate into small groups to do the same for other items. You could provide recipes to help, for children who have little cooking experience. Allow each group to present their findings to the whole class.

Individually or in pairs, complete the 'Investigate your lunch' worksheet. The investigations could form the basis of a display. Use the technique explained in the 'Make a pop-up card' worksheet. A picture of one product could be drawn on the cut-out part. The vertical sheet could have pictures showing the 'fruit of the earth' while the horizontal sheet could have pictures showing the 'work of human hands'.

Types of bread

One basic food is bread. In the story, Rees and Tomos visited the local supermarket to find out about bread. This is a good example of the ingenuity and creativity involved in 'the work of human hands'. Although the basic ingredients are the same, the style of bread is different from country to country and nowadays varies depending on the preference of people.

Give the children five minutes in small groups to list all the different types of bread they can think of. Come back together and share the results to make a class list. The children could discuss which of these are personal favourites and why, but remember that this is a discussion where answers display preference rather than right or wrong.

A quick internet search will reveal types of bread that the children may not have identified. If help is needed, suggest search words such as "bread", "types of bread" or "pictures of bread". (Make sure that the children understand the use of double quotation marks in search engines, and the need to scan text for different types of bread, rather than reading every word.) Add these to the class list.

Bake your own bread using the 'Make your own bread' worksheet or a recipe discovered during your search.

Growing food

Invite a keen gardener to talk to the class about his or her work growing food in a garden or allotment. After the talk, put the children into groups to work out questions to ask the gardener. If the children are unsure of questions, one suggestion is to think of questions beginning with 'what', 'when', where', 'why' and 'how'. You may like to keep in touch with the gardener and develop a display board in one part of the room with month-by-month descriptions of the work being done and the plants growing.

Keywords

acolytes persons who carry the candles in procession

alb long white robe worn under chasuble

altar table at front of church where priest presides at communion

baptism sacrament of Christian initiation using water

Bible collection of books of special significance for Christians

blessing prayer pronouncing God's goodwill

cassock distinctive long black robe worn by priests

chalice special cup (usually silver) used to hold the communion wine

chasuble toga-like vestment worn by the priest presiding at communion

Christmas festival celebrating birth of Jesus

communion service bread and wine are offered to God and consumed as the body and blood of Christ

clerical collar distinctive white collar worn by priests

crucifer person who carries the cross at the front of processions

font large basin to hold water for baptism

Gospel the four books (Matthew, Mark, Luke, and John) telling the life, words, and works of Jesus

Harvest Thanksgiving celebration to thank God for the fruits of the earth

hymn songs used in worship

Lady chapel side room in church with altar dedicated to St Mary, mother of Jesus

lectern special stand from which Bible is read

mass another name for communion service

organ pipe organs make the distinctive church music

parish geographical area served by the Anglican church

pews long wooden benches

priest person authorised to preside at communion

sacrament an outward sign symbolising God's activitiy

surplice long white robe worn over cassock

Write a story

Imagine you have visited a parish church with a friend who attends there. Write a story about it, giving details of all the places you visited and the things you saw there. The pictures and descriptions below will help you.

porch

The porch is a place to wipe dirty feet and quieten down, ready to enter the church for worship.

bell-tower

The bells are rung to call the people to worship. Long bell-ropes are pulled so that the bells, high in the tower, sound out to people all around.

organ

Music is an important part of worship. It may be played on a large pipe organ.

pews

Inside most churches there are long wooden pews for the people to sit on during the service. The pews will have racks in which people can put service books and hymn books.

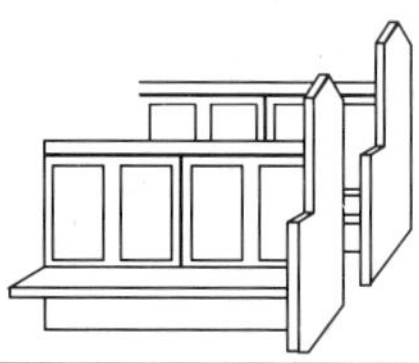

processional cross

At the start of the service the priest and choir enter in a procession. This is led by the crucifer carrying a tall cross. The cross is displayed during the service.

lectern

The Bible is kept on a special stand. The top of the lectern may be in the shape of an eagle with wings outstretched to carry the word of God to the world.

pulpit

During the service the priest or the reader will teach the congregation about the Christian faith. This is done from high in the pulpit where all can see and hear.

altar

At the front of the church is the altar where the people go to receive communion. On the altar there are candles and a cross.

aumbry

Near the altar is a special place where the blessed sacrament of bread and wine is kept. A light burns above it to symbolise Jesus, the Light of the world.

Make a communion set

As a sign of respect, and to show the special place that communion holds in the parish church, the chalice and plate used for communion are often made of silver.

You will need

cardboard plate
foil
plastic drinking or wine cup
scissors

What to do

1. Cut a piece of foil just over twice the size of the plate. Crinkle it slightly by creasing it into a loose ball. Open it up. Fold the foil over the plate so that it is completely covered. (The crinkles will give an antique effect and will match the accidental crinkles on the chalice.)

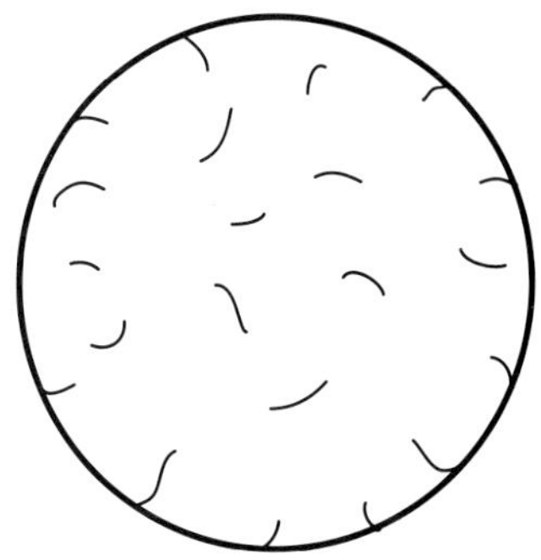

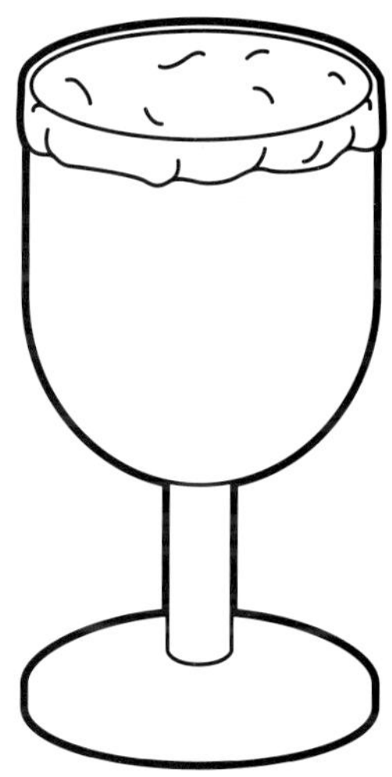

2. Cut a piece of foil just slightly longer than the cup. Arrange this around the inside of the cup, folding and creasing about 1cm over the top.

3. Cut another piece of foil and arrange it around the outside, folding about 1cm over the top, into the inside. If you are covering a plastic wine cup, heavily crease the foil around the stem. Use a separate piece of foil for the foot of the cup.

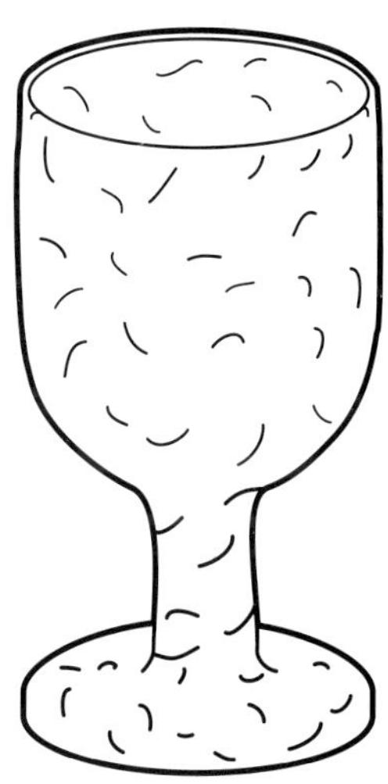

Dress Mrs Davies

Mrs Davies is a priest in the local parish church. She has special clothes to wear for different parts of her work.

What to do

1. Photocopy this page on thin card.
2. Colour Mrs Davies and her clothes.
3. Cut them out.

4. Think of different things that Mrs Davies might need to do and put the correct clothes on her.
   Bend the support on the dotted lines to make her stand up.

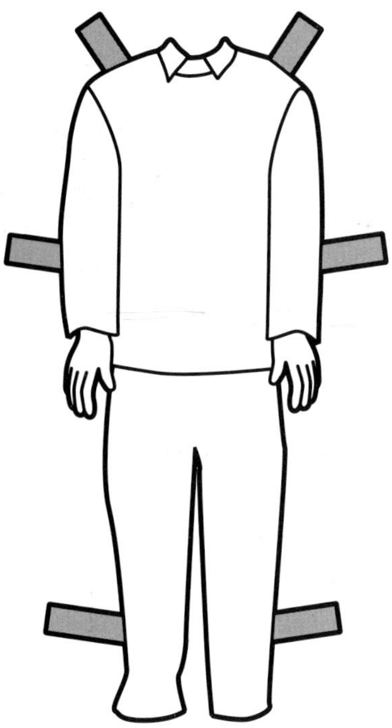

The special clerical collar shows that Mrs Davies is a priest. She can wear it with a black shirt or a colourful shirt. She wears this for meetings, visiting people, or working around the church.

Mrs Davies wears this black cassock when she needs to conduct a funeral. Sometimes she wears it for walking around town.

When Mrs Davies leads the communion service she wears a golden chasuble over her white alb.

Make a pop-up card

Christmas is the time of year to celebrate the birth of Jesus. At this time people give cards and gifts to family and friends, remembering the gifts given to Jesus by the wise men, and remembering that Jesus is the gift of God to us. Many Christians choose cards with pictures of the first Christmas, to show Jesus' birth and the visits of the shepherds and wise men.

You will need

scrap paper
scissors
½ sheet of A4 card
pencils

1.

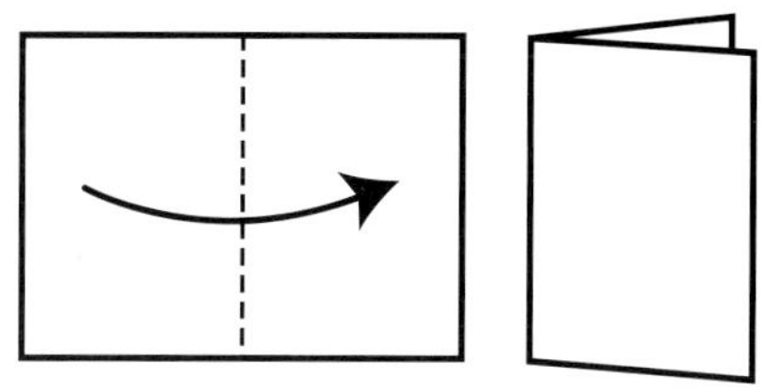

What to do

Practise steps 1-4 on scrap paper before you try it out on card.

1. Fold the card in half.

2. Make two cuts from the fold almost halfway across the sheet. (Make sure you cut from the fold, not from the open ends.)

3. Fold the cut section over to the edge and crease it firmly, then unfold it.

4. Open the card. Keep a valley crease (pointing in) on the outer edges but lift the centre cut part to make a mountain crease (pointing out).

5. Decorate the card. You could draw scenery on the uncut part and Mary, Joseph and Jesus on the pop-up.

2.

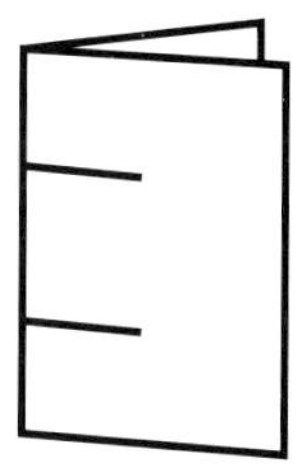

3.

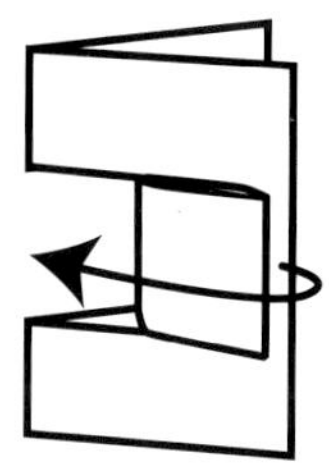

4.

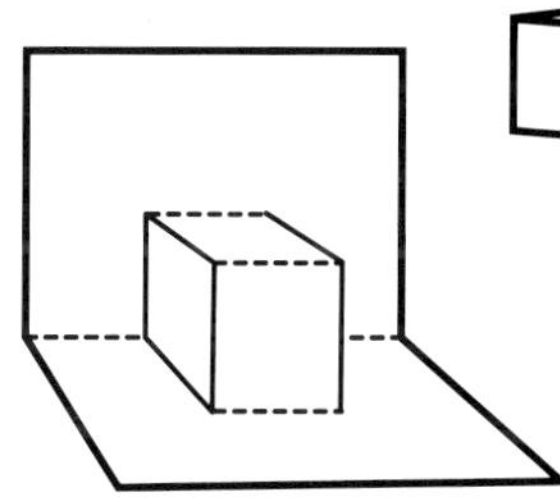

5.

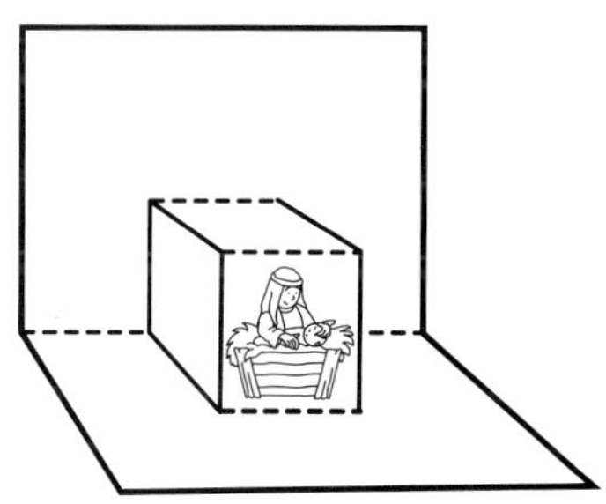

Experiment with different shapes of pop-ups. Make angled curves, or cuts of different shapes, or add a second pop-up by cutting into the front crease.

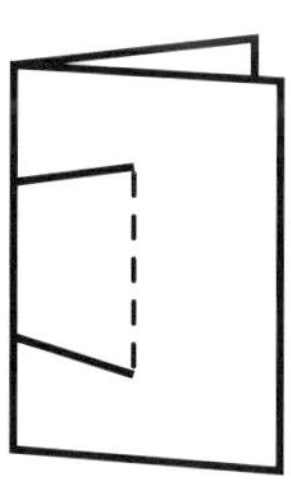

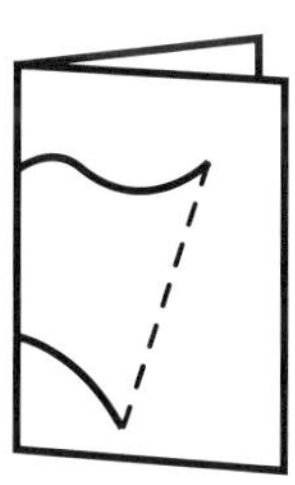

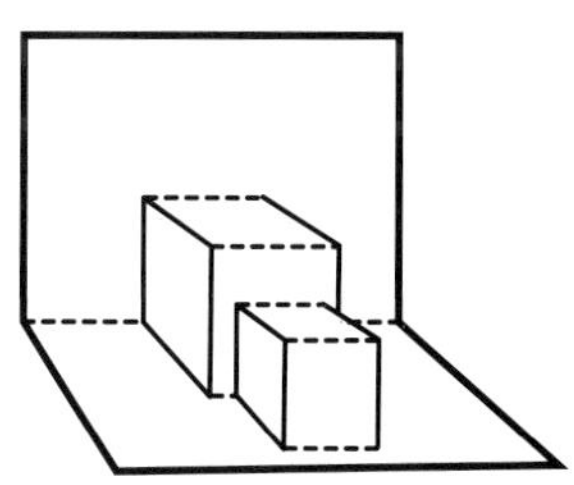

Tell the Christmas story

Christmas is the time when Christians celebrate the birth of Jesus. The Christmas story is told in words, pictures and song. Below are six parts of the Christmas story. Retell the events in your own words.

When you have finished, you could cut out the boxes and mix up their order. Give them to a friend to put back in the correct sequence.

Think about the Bible

How is the Bible part of daily life for Bethan and Tomos and their family?

In order to give a good answer to this question, you will need to be a detective and look at all the clues in chapter 3 of *Exploring the Parish Church*. Answer the questions below to help you find the clues.

1. Name three places in the Davies home where you would find a Bible.

____

____

____

2. Name three events during the week when the Bible is used.

____

____

____

3. Write what Tomos said about how reading the Bible helps Christians.

____

4. Write what Mrs Davies said about Christians reading the Bible at home.

____

5. How does St David's Church show that the Bible is important?

____

____

6. After the Bible is read in church, what is said each time?

____

____

7. What did Mrs Davies do before reading from the Gospel of Mark?

____

Now answer the main question on a new sheet of paper. How is the Bible part of daily life for Bethan and Tomos and their family?

Create a psalm of praise

The book of Psalms in the Bible reminds its readers of the greatness of God. Some of the psalms use images from the world around them. Read the beginning of Psalm 104 below. You can find the rest of it in the Bible.

Psalm 104

Bless the Lord, my soul
Lord my God, you are very great,
    clothed in majesty and splendour,
    and enfolded in a robe of light.
You have spread out the heavens like a tent,
    and laid the beams of your dwelling on the waters;
you take the clouds for your chariot,
    riding on the wings of the wind;
you make the winds your messengers,
    flames of fire your servants.

(The Revised English Bible)

Draw the scene that comes to mind when you read this psalm of praise to the greatness of God.

Think of a part of the world that you consider to be beautiful. Choose something natural, rather than made by people. Draw a picture of it and then use your picture to help you write a psalm of praise to God.

Write prayers

There are many people involved in the production of our food. Some of them live in poverty. Although they produce food for us to eat (and sometimes for us to throw away) they may not have enough food to eat themselves.

On the pictures below write prayers that Bethan and Tomos could say. You might write a prayer for Bethan and Tomos thanking God for food, or thanking God for the work of the people involved in preparing our food, or a prayer about the lives of the people who bring this food to you.

Make posters

Work as a group to make posters encouraging people to buy fairtrade products.

1. Research

Find out about the fairtrade products available in your area.

- Look at online supermarket stores and search for fairtrade. (If you work with friends, each of you could check a different local store.)
- Contact local charity shops to see what they sell.
- Compare the prices of fairtrade products with those of normally traded products.
- Compare your findings with those of your friends to see which store has the best selection.

places to research	person to do the work

2. Design

Here are some things to consider as you design.

- Audience: are you designing it for people your age or for the adults in your life?
- Size: do you want a large poster or a small leaflet for your fridge or car to remind your family each time you go shopping?
- Clear design: make sure you have only a few words and make them large enough to be read from a distance.
- Eye-catching colours: choose colours that will make the poster noticed.

Audience: ______________________ **Size:** ______________________

Design ideas

3. Distribute

Display your posters for maximum effect.

Make your own bread

In *Exploring the Parish Church*, Rees and Tomos made bread for the communion service to symbolise the fruits of the earth and the work of human hands.

You will need

- 650g strong white bread flour
- I teaspoon sugar
- I sachet dry yeast
- 2 teaspoons salt
- I tablespoon vegetable oil
- 400ml warm water

What to do

1. Wash your hands.
2. Mix together the flour, salt, sugar, yeast and oil.
3. Prepare warm water by mixing together one third boiling water and two-thirds cold water. Add this to the flour mixture and mix to a soft dough.
4. Knead the dough for 10 minutes on a clean, floured surface.
5. Divide the dough into 50-75g balls and shape into rolls. Place these on greased baking trays. (Alternatively, use the dough to make two loaves, placing it in 450g bread tins.)
6. Cover the rolls and leave them in a warm place for about 30 minutes until they have doubled in size.
7. Place the trays in the middle of a pre-heated oven at 230°C (450°F or gas mark 8). Bake for 15 minutes for rolls or 30-35 minutes for loaves.
8. Remove the bread from the oven and cool it on a wire rack.

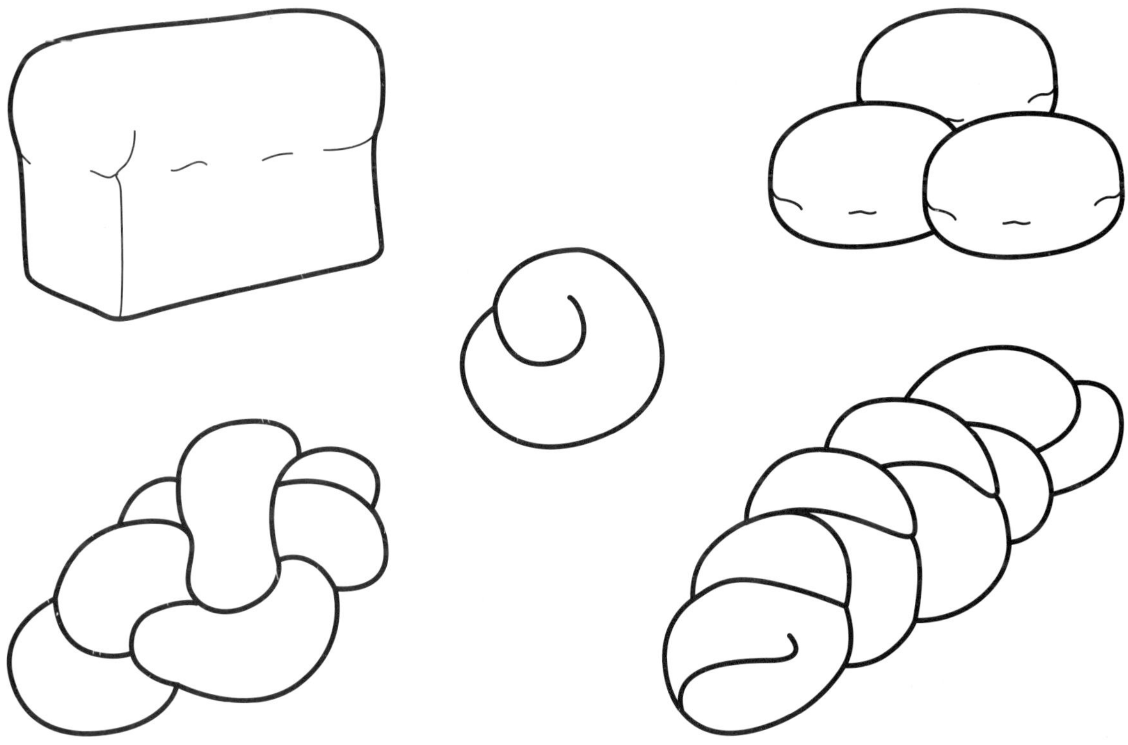

Investigate your lunch

The food we eat is a mixture of 'fruits of the earth' (the gift of God) and 'work of human hands'. With some friends, investigate a typical lunch to see this mixture. (Continue on another page if you need to.)

1. Write down all the food in your chosen packed lunch or school dinner.
2. Write every ingredient in it that you can identify.
3. Write the original 'fruit of the earth' from which it came (for example, butter comes from milk).
4. Identify the 'work of human hands' involved in preparing it.

My lunch

Ingredients	**fruit of the earth**	**work of human hands**

Create a dance

Create a dance about one special food you enjoy. The dance should show the steps involved in growing the basic ingredients and combining them to produce the food.

1. Choose the food

Think of something basic like bread or something special like chocolate. Choose food that has several steps involved so that your dance will be interesting.

The food we choose: ______________________________

2. Identify the steps involved in producing it

Think of all the people and steps involved in producing this food. This might include planting crops, feeding and milking cows, mixing ingredients and so on.

The steps involved:

____

____

____

____

____

____

3. Select music

Listen to different music to find a piece that best fits your idea of the work involved.

4. Experiment with ways to show these steps

Try out different movements, with individuals or groups, to show these steps in food production. Choose who will portray each part.

My dictionary

You will meet many new words in *Exploring the Parish Church*. Keep a record of them, along with their meanings.

cassock	long black garment worn by the priest and choristers
crucifer	robed chorister who carries the cross at the head of the procession during a service
surplice	three-quarter length full white garment worn over the cassock by priests and choristers
__________	____________________________________
__________	____________________________________
__________	____________________________________
__________	____________________________________
__________	____________________________________
__________	____________________________________
__________	____________________________________
__________	____________________________________
__________	____________________________________
__________	____________________________________
__________	____________________________________
__________	____________________________________
__________	____________________________________

Find out about your class and fairtrade

1. Design a questionnaire

Rees and Tomos' class used a pencil and paper questionnaire at the supermarket. You can use a computer questionnaire to find out about the use of fairtrade products in your class or in several classes.

First you need to design simple questions. Here are some suggestions. Change these to suit your needs and add your own questions. (Your choice of questions will need to fit in with what you want to find out in step 3.)

- Name (or give each child a number if you want it to be confidential)
- Sex (male or female)
- Class
- Do you use fairtrade products?
- Which fairtrade products have you tried?
- Have you tasted fairtrade chocolate?
- Will you look for fairtrade products in future?

2. Construct a data base

Choose a computer programme that allows you to construct a data base. Set up the fields with your chosen questions. Invite children to come one at a time to each fill in a record.

3. Use the data base

When the data base is complete you can use it to find out information. Think of things you would like to know, and construct searches. Here are some examples.

- How many pupils use fairtrade products? What fraction is this of the total in the data base?
- Have more boys or more girls tasted fairtrade chocolate?
- Are there more people in Red Class or Blue Class who will look for fairtrade products in future?

I would like to find out this information

____

____

____

____

____

Exploring Sikhism

Exploring Sikhism

The story

Rees and Sara spend their holiday with two Sikh friends called Sanjit and Yasmin who introduce them to key beliefs and practices in Sikhism. The children explore a gurdwara and learn about God (Waheguru) in Sikhism and how their friends worship God. They celebrate the festival of Baisakhi and attend a Khalsa initiation ceremony which teaches them about belonging in a Sikh community. Rees and Sara are introduced to special teachers and guides, and they learn about how God guides Sikhs through these gurus. They investigate Sikh attitudes to the environment through a visit to a planetarium and a visit to a park. The children learn about how Sikhs practise serving others in a Sikh kitchen.

Exploring Sikhism provides opportunities for pupils to:

- **engage** with fundamental questions;
- **explore** religious beliefs, teachings, and practices;
- **express** personal responses in relation to the material studied.

Learning outcomes

Pupils should be able to:

- discuss questions raised by life and aspects of Sikhism;
- name and describe selected beliefs, teachings, and practices of Sikhism;
- explain through examples the relationship between belief and practice in Sikhism;
- discuss their own views and the views of others in relation to some of the themes and issues covered, and relate these to their own lives;
- relate symbol to meaning in some Sikh contexts.

The basics

Sikhism is the youngest of the six major world faiths portrayed in this series. Sikhism emerged in the sixteenth century in the Punjab in response to the life and teachings of its founder, Guru Nanak. In the Punjab at this time tensions existed between the Hindu communities and the Muslim communities, and Guru Nanak was a Hindu. After a three-day mystical experience where Guru Nanak was in the presence of God, he uttered the famous words of his first teaching:

There is no Hindu and no Mussulman [Muslim], so whose path shall I follow? God is neither Hindu nor Mussulman and the path I shall follow is God's.

Guru Nanak rose above the sectarian divisions around him, and spent the rest of his life teaching the Sikh 'path' as it was revealed to him through his mystical experiences with God.

Today, around 90% of Sikhs reside in the Punjab (their traditional homeland), although Sikh communities are found increasingly in different countries around the world, with a large, established community in Britain.

Sikhs believe that:

- there is only one God who is creator of the Universe;
- God is present in creation and in every living thing;
- all living beings have a soul which is trapped in a continuous cycle of rebirth, which is determined by people's good and bad actions (karma); the ideal is liberation (mukti) of the soul from the cycle of rebirth to experience eternal union with God;
- liberation is possible if a person stops being self-centred (manmukh) and becomes God-centred (gurmukh) which means letting go of pride (haumai) and replacing it with humility (nimrata), but this can happen only through God bestowing grace (darshan);
- everyone is equal before God, and unfair divisions in society are wrong (for example, inequality on the basis of social group, race, or gender) because everyone has the same origins and possesses the divine spark (jot);
- God as supreme guru has always made God known to the world through teachers, including the ten Sikh gurus;
- the Sikh sacred scripture, the Guru Granth Sahib, is an important medium through which God guides the Sikh community.

Sikhs practise:

- focusing on God in their lives through meditation on God's Name and congregational worship in the gurdwara;
- seva (service) to others;
- equality;
- membership of the Khalsa (to become full members of the Sikh community) where Sikhs wear the Five Ks and vow to adhere to a code of conduct.

Chapter 1 Visiting a gurdwara

Flag

The Sikh flag is called the Nishan Sahib. The symbol on the flag is called the Khanda, and it is the symbol most frequently associated with Sikhism. At its centre is a double-edged sword called a khanda and a circle called a chakar. On each side is a sword called a kirpan.

- The khanda represents God's power separating truth and falsehood.
- The chakar represents the eternal God, who (like a circle) has no beginning or end.
- The two kirpans represent earthly power and spiritual power.

God

God is called by a number of different names in Sikhism. In the story book Waheguru is used, which means 'Wonderful Lord'. Waheguru is a popular title for God, and Waheguru contains the word 'guru' which can be linked to the belief that God is the supreme teacher, guide, and source of the teachings provided by the Ten Gurus (and the Guru Granth Sahib) in Sikhism.

The main beliefs about God in Sikhism include:

- God is without form and cannot be portrayed in any image (from the inception of Sikhism, the Hindu portrayal of God through image or murti was rejected);
- God is creator and sustainer of the universe;
- the universe came from God because God willed it, and one day it will return to God;
- God is present in God's creation;
- God reveals God through the gurus and in personal devotion.

In a gurdwara, pictures of the gurus and places of pilgrimage are normally kept away from the central platform on which the Guru Granth Sahib is placed to avoid the temptation to commit idolatry.

Guru Granth Sahib

In the story, Rees and Sara learn that Sikhs come together to worship God in a building called a gurdwara, and that 'gurdwara' means 'guru's house'. A guru provides access to the teachings of God. Guru Granth Sahib means 'Guide/Teacher' (Guru), 'Book' (Granth), and 'Master' (Sahib). It is also referred to as the Adi Granth (Adi means 'First' in a chronological sense, and Granth means 'Book'). The Guru Granth Sahib is written in the Gurmukhi script which is a written form of Punjabi.

The Guru Granth Sahib is treated with great care and reverence, for example:

- heads must be covered in the book's presence;
- shoes must be removed;
- Sikhs bow before the book;
- during a service, the book sits on a special throne with a canopy covering it;
- during a reading, a chauri is waved over the book;
- when not in use, in the evening, the book is placed carefully in a bed in a separate room;
- when the book is moved, strict rules have to be met.

Few Sikhs have a copy of the Guru Granth Sahib in their homes because it requires so much care, though occasionally, to mark a special time, a Guru Granth Sahib may be installed in a Sikh's home for a short period. This makes the gurdwara and congregational worship particularly important in Sikhism because they provide access to the Guru Granth Sahib.

Officials working in the gurdwara are selected by the local congregation to serve the local community. However, these individuals should not be given any special privileges because of the Sikh belief in equality. In the story book, a male Sikh has been given the role of Granthi (keeper and reader of the Guru Granth Sahib), but a woman could also be selected to serve the community in this role.

Further information about how the Guru Granth Sahib is used and how it acts as a guru is found in chapter 3 of the story book and teachers' notes.

Congregational worship

Singing hymns (kirtan) is a popular way to worship and meditate on God in Sikhism. Many of these hymns come from the Guru Granth Sahib. The importance of singing can be traced back to the first guru, Guru Nanak, who was accompanied by a musician as he received revelations from God.

Activities

Visiting a gurdwara

Visit a gurdwara and identify the places mentioned in the story. How does it differ from the places in the book and how is it the same?

Flags

Look at flags for the different countries of Britain and explore their symbolism (or focus on your national flag).

Where do they see flags flying? (for example, official buildings, outside hotels, or at international sporting events)

Why do you think countries have flags? (for example, to unite people under a common banner, to show ownership, or to say something about your identity)

Other flags, such as the European flag, are broader in reference, and represent the drawing together of different nations committed to a set of agreed ideals and practices.

Sikhs have prominent flags outside their gurdwaras.

- What does the Sikh flag tell people about the building?
- What does the khanda on the Sikh flag tell people about Sikhism?

Complete the 'Make a Khanda' worksheet. (If pupils have a good knowledge of Sikh beliefs and practices, challenge them to consider how useful the khanda is as a symbol for Sikhism.)

Pupils could also design a flag for their school. They will need to consider carefully what represents the school and be able to explain the thinking behind the design to the class.

Mix and match

Cut out the nine boxes on the 'Write a story' worksheet, and then cut each box into three sections: the heading; the information; and the picture. Mix up all the sections and place them in an envelope. Divide pupils into pairs or groups and give each pair or group an envelope. Pupils need to match heading, information, and picture correctly.

Do the task on the 'Write a story' worksheet (the story can easily be adapted to another genre such as a diary entry or newspaper article, if needed).

Alternatively, cut out the nine boxes on the 'Write a story worksheet' and organise them into three groups:

- cleanliness (being clean);
- service (seva) to others;
- the Guru Granth Sahib.

Working in pairs, ask pupils to place the three groups in order of importance, explaining the reasons behind their choices. There is no right answer to this question; the emphasis is on the ideas and quality of argument.

Chapter 2 Celebrating Baisakhi

The Khalsa

The story book outlines the historical origins of the Khalsa which date back to Guru Gobind Singh in 1699. The Khalsa means the 'Pure' signifying Sikhs who have undergone the special amrit initiation ceremony (sometimes this is called 'baptism').

Amrit/initiation ceremony

For the initiation ceremony to be valid, 5 Khalsa Sikhs have to be present as well as the Guru Granth Sahib. At the initiation ceremony, Sikhs promise to wear the Five Ks as symbols of their faith. They also promise to adhere to a more demanding set of rules than non-Khalsa Sikhs.

Becoming a Khalsa Sikh is a real commitment to taking one's faith to the next level.

Baisakhi celebrations

The festival of Baisakhi falls on the first day of the month of Vaisakhi in the Sikh calendar (April-May). It marks the beginning of a new year. Traditions include:

- 'bathing' the Guru Granth Sahib with milk and water with special readings in the gurdwara;
- sharing karah prashad and eating a vegetarian meal as a community in the gurdwara;
- community processions.

In northern India, Baisakhi is also a harvest festival when God is thanked for the bountiful harvest.

The Five Ks

The Five Ks are a reminder of the commitment and faith displayed by the first 5 Sikhs initiated into the Khalsa in 1699. They also remind Khalsa Sikhs of key facets of their faith.

Kesh (uncut hair)

Both the physical world and the non-physical world are special because both come from God, and they should be respected. Leaving all human hair uncut symbolises a Sikh's commitment to living according to God's will.

Kangha (comb)

Keeping hair clean and neat is also very important in Sikhism. The comb keeps the hair tidy under a turban.

Kirpan (sword)

The sword reminds Sikhs of their duty to defend truth and justice. As the story shows, in Sikh history, there were times when Sikhs needed to defend themselves against oppressors in physical terms. However, today, as Sunita Kaur emphasises, defending truth and justice takes other forms, and the sword is viewed as a powerful symbol rather than a weapon. Today, Khalsa Sikhs wear miniature swords which can take the form of jewellery or an emblem on the Kangha (comb).

Kachera (shorts)

The white shorts are often worn as undergarments today and they are a symbol of modesty.

Kara (bracelet)

The steel bracelet has no break or joint and it is worn on the right wrist. This reminds Sikhs to do only good with their hands (actions).

Although not one of the 5 Ks, for many, the turban is a distinctive part of Sikhism. Turbans come in a variety of colours. Traditionally, turbans were worn by those who were held in high regard in society, and turbans keep long hair tidy. Wearing a turban is a clear statement of a person's commitment to God.

Activities

Festivals across religious traditions

Work on a calendar or book of festivals from all religions. This would need to be a loose-leaf folder, or pages joined together with treasury tags so that pages can be added as needed in chronological order.

Talk about the importance of organising material well so that people can quickly find the information they need. With the pupils, decide on a useful structure for the book, for example, section headings could include stories, how the festival is celebrated today, recipes, and so on.

Symbols of belonging

Choose a uniform with which you are familiar (either one you wear yourself or have seen someone else wearing). Examples could include: school uniform, brownie/cub uniform, football kit, martial arts suit (for example, karate/judo).

Think carefully about the different parts of the uniform and their purpose (most will have both practical and symbolic purposes).

Make a list of the 'good' and 'bad' experiences of wearing a uniform.

Complete the worksheet 'Dress Amrit Singh', exploring the symbolism of the 5 Ks (these also have both practical and symbolic purposes – in Sikh history, the uniform was practical in times of battle, defending the rights of the oppressed; today, the 5 Ks simply retain their symbolic significance). What might be the 'good' and 'bad' experiences of Sikhs wearing the 5 Ks?

This activity can be extended to explore symbols of belonging in dress codes of different religious traditions (for example, Christian monastic orders/priests, Buddhist monks/nuns, Muslims on Hajj, and Jews in a synagogue).

Defending fairness and justice for all

Sikhs believe in the importance of defending the basic human rights of all people, whether or not they are Sikhs. They believe in fairness and justice for all.

Injustice and unfairness exist everywhere in the world, but individuals and organisations exist who also believe in defending basic human rights. Research the work of Amnesty International which focuses specifically on these concerns (www.amnesty.org.uk).

There are many reasons why people are concerned with the fight against unfairness in the world – some are explicitly influenced by religious beliefs and philosophies while others are not. In the story book, the Sikh belief in freedom and justice is explored.

Chapter 3 Leaders

Gurus in Sikhism

God is the supreme Guru (teacher/guide). God is self-revealing and leads humans towards enlightenment and liberation. However, God works through chosen individuals who reveal God's Word (Shabad) in the world. Sikhs believe that God's Word has been revealed to selected individuals throughout history, but the Ten Gurus are of particular significance to them. The Ten Gurus are as follows.

- Guru Nanak (1469-1539)
- Guru Angad (1504-1552
- Guru Amar Das (1479-1574)
- Guru Ram Das (1534-1581)
- Guru Arjan Dev (1563-1606)
- Guru Hargobind (1595-1644)
- Guru Har Rai (1630-1661)
- Guru Har Krishan (1656-1664)
- Guru Tegh Bahadur (1621-1675)
- Guru Gobind Singh (1666-1708)

Sikhs believe that the Ten Gurus were already fully enlightened and liberated before they were reborn as gurus. They were chosen by God to re-enter the cycle of rebirth as gurus, and their lives are viewed as perfect and unaffected by the consequences of karma. The gurus were both spiritual and temporal leaders in their Sikh communities: they offered spiritual guidance as well as solving disputes and making decisions within the Sikh community.

The Ten Gurus are greatly respected, but never worshipped; their role is to point back to God and to teach God's Word.

Teachings

In the story, Rees and Sara learn that the gurus lead Sikhs to God, which is the most important journey of all. On this journey, Sikhs learn to put God and not themselves at the centre of their lives. This is helped by key Sikh practices such as reciting God's name (Nam Simran), serving others (seva), and living in a supportive Sikh community (sangat) which encourages humility and God-centredness.

Sikhism teaches that it is possible to go only so far relying on one's own efforts. Only when God bestows grace on a person will the ideal of God-centredness be fully realised. Who receives grace is decided by God, and is bestowed according to God's own reasons. A person may need more time or another rebirth, perhaps. However, a person does have the choice of accepting God's grace or rejecting it.

The bestowing of grace enables a person to become a Jivan mukt – one who lives as one with God. At death, karma has no effect so the soul does not re-enter the cycle of rebirth. This is the Sikh ideal.

Guru Granth Sahib

Before his death, Guru Gobind Singh appointed the Guru Granth Sahib (a sacred book) as the next leader and guide for the Sikh community. The book is treated with the same respect as a human guru (see chapter 1) and it performs a similar role: it points back to God and reveals God's Word as it was uttered by the preceding gurus. Like a human guru, the Guru Granth Sahib also performs a role in the everyday life of the community when it is consulted for guidance and decision-making.

At significant moments in a community or individual's life, the Guru Granth Sahib is consulted. The book is opened at random and a reading is taken from the top left-hand page. The meaning of the text is considered and applied to the relevant issue. This is called hukam (God's guidance or command).

Traditionally, when Sikhs name their children, the Guru Granth Sahib is also consulted, following a similar process. However, on this occasion, the first letter of the first word provides the initial for the child's name.

The importance of the Guru Granth Sahib is illustrated by its presence at all ceremonies.

Activities

Goals in life

This activity supports and develops the worksheets 'Make a picture frame' and 'Guides in life'.

In Sikhism, the goal in life is to journey towards God, Waheguru, and to become one with Waheguru. The practices described in the story book play a part in helping Sikhs reach their goal. Sikhs are helped on this journey by Waheguru's work through the Ten Gurus and the Guru Granth Sahib. They are also helped by living in a supportive Sikh community (sangat).

Having goals in life is very important. Goals give meaning and direction to our lives, which can help to make us happier, more fulfilled people.

- What is one of your goals in life?
- What steps do you need to take to get there?
- Who could help on your journey to your goal?

Draw a step-ladder with a picture of yourself at the bottom of the ladder and one of your goals at the top. On the rungs of the ladder write the steps you need to take to reach your goal. Beside the picture of yourself, write down those who could help you to reach your goal.

Share some of the pupils' ladders with the class. Select different types of goal to present to the class – for example, some goals are more short term while others are more long term, and some are more practical while others are more abstract. One type of goal is not better than another, just different because people are different. It is helpful though for pupils to be aware of and consider a wide range of possible goals.

As a class, constructively help to develop two parts of the ladders presented: the steps that need to be taken and those who could help in the journey towards the goal.

As a teacher, you could also choose to share one of your goals with the class, the steps you need to take to achieve the goal, and the people who could help you on your journey. Teaching point: having goals and working to achieve them is a part of the whole journey of life.

Create a timeline

Create a timeline to show the chronological order of the Ten Gurus. Place the timeline within an outline drawing of an open Guru Granth Sahib. This illustrates pictorially that the Guru Granth Sahib is the guide for Sikhs today and it contains Waheguru's word as it was uttered by the Ten Gurus. (It is important to be aware that the Guru Granth Sahib also contains some material written by non-Sikhs, but this activity focuses on the line of Sikh gurus specifically.)

To extend this activity, use books or the internet to research further the lives of the Ten Gurus. A number of the Ten Gurus are famous for various historical developments in Sikhism such as founding Sikhism, developing the script used in the Guru Granth Sahib, compiling the Guru Granth Sahib, and creating the Khalsa. Identify the contributions of various gurus and add them to the time line. The BBC Religion and Ethics site (www.bbc.co.uk/religion/religions/sikhism) is a useful source of information.

Chapter 4 Caring for the world

When Rees and Sara visit the planetarium and view the wonders of the universe, they begin to ask questions about its origins and the significance of human life. Their friends, Sanjit and Yasmin, share with them some Sikh answers to these questions.

Sikh beliefs about creation

According to the teachings of the Guru Granth Sahib, before creation there was nothing apart from God. There were no divisions, just the one eternal God. Then, God willed the universe into being, and the universe came from God – the galaxies, solar systems, and worlds. With creation, divisions appeared – for example, divisions relating to race, social status, and gender. These divisions have led to suffering because they have been used to justify unfair and unjust behaviour.

However, Sikhism teaches that the divisions are illusionary and are based on ignorance. When ignorance is replaced with enlightenment, the real unity of creation is recognised – all living things have God within them, and this unites them. All living things also have an ultimate common goal – living according to God's will (being God-centred) and becoming one with God. The Guru Granth Sahib teaches that just as the universe was created from God, so it will return to God.

The role of human beings

A human rebirth is very special, because human beings are able to make conscious decisions and become God-centred. Human beings are able to understand the interconnectedness of the universe and their own position within it.

Different religious traditions are often described as having either negative or positive views on living in this world. Negative views are often marked by escapist ideals, where worldly things are seen as a hindrance to attaining a spiritual ideal which lies outside the world. Positive views often see living in the world as an integral part of realising a spiritual ideal which is very much connected to the world. Sikhism has a positive view of the world because everything has come from God and everything will return to God. The path to liberation of the soul and unity with God can happen only through living in the world.

Belief in practice

These beliefs mean that correct relationships with other people and nature are central to Sikh practice. For example, the following practices are promoted:

- a simple lifestyle with careful use of resources;
- sharing resources and service to others without discrimination in the gurdwara and in the community;
- hard work and an ethical means of earning a living;
- giving generously to charity.

Also, there are many examples online of Sikhs being involved in environmental projects and charities, such as those explored by the children in the story, for example, Khalsa Aid (www.khalsaaid.org/).

Interconnectedness of action

In Sikhism living things are also connected to one another through their actions and the effect that their actions have on others. In the story, this is illustrated by a stone being thrown into a lake (an action) and one ripple leading to another, then another. Positive actions have positive effects on ourselves, others, and the environment. Negative actions have negative effects on ourselves, others, and the environment. Each action has very wide-ranging effects if it is fully mapped out. In this respect, Sikhism has much in common with both Hinduism and Buddhism.

Understanding the essential unity and purpose of all living things as well as understanding the powerful knock-on effect of all actions, provides the belief system which underpins Sikh practice.

Activities

How I wonder what you are

In the story book, the children visit a planetarium where they marvel at the wonders of the universe. As a homework activity, ask pupils to spend at least 15 minutes outside (or looking out of a window) watching the sky on a clear night. To keep parents happy, do this activity when night falls early.

Ask pupils to think about and record responses to the following questions:

- What different things can you see?
- What do you feel as you watch the night sky?
- Are there any questions that you would like answered, as you watch the night sky?

Back in school, invite pupils to feed back some of their responses. Link the activity to the story book – when Rees and Sara were in the planetarium, they saw many different things which produced both feelings and questions. There are different ways of answering those questions, and their friends, Sanjit and Yasmin, provide answers from a Sikh perspective. These answers give meaning and purpose to their lives.

What we do affects others

Think about the ripples created by the stone thrown into the lake. Select an action such as dropping a piece of plastic on the ground. Together draw up a concept map or spider diagram of different possible effects, such as an animal choking on it, someone else having to pick it up, becoming water-logged after rain and dirtying the shoes of someone who steps on it. Discuss the variety of possible harmful or annoying effects from one simple action. (Some computer software automatically creates concept maps and would be a useful tool in this activity.)

Next look at a positive action such as inviting a newcomer to play with you and map all the possible results of it, such as making a new friend for yourself, making another person happy, learning new games, being invited to a birthday party. Encourage the children to be creative and to think outside of everyday answers.

Work in small groups to think of other actions, both positive and negative, and to map all possible results.

Each group could feed back one action and its results to the class. Examine the actions in terms of the Sikh belief that the world is special and we should look after it.

Reflect on current practice

Often schools set up programmes, such as recycling paper, and continue to carry them through without educating new pupils as to the reason why. It can be helpful from time to time to consider our practices, think of why we do them, and reaffirm our actions.

Walk around the school looking for the many good things that you do. Also take note of where your practice could be improved, such as better positions for waste paper baskets or recycling boxes. Make a list of all your good practices and discuss the reasons for them. Be sure that you know the reasons for your commitment.

Chapter 5 The Sikh kitchen

Vegetarianism

Many, but not all, Sikhs are vegetarian, although there is no obligation to be vegetarian in Sikhism. Eating meat or not is left to personal choice. Vegetarian and non-vegetarian Sikhs will each have their own arguments to support their position. Whatever stance is taken on eating meat, a number of basic attitudes to food are promoted. For example, moderation should be practised in all things and the waste of resources is discouraged. Also, zealousness for a particular type of diet should be avoided because people can become attached to external rituals at the expense of developing inner qualities.

However, in the langar (the kitchen), only vegetarian food is made and served. This is because the langar must be able to provide food for everyone, and vegetarian food meets all needs.

The langar

An important part of every gurdwara is the langar (kitchen and dining area) which provides free food to all, without discrimination. The langar can be traced back to the first guru, Guru Nanak. Right from the beginning of Sikhism, inequalities within traditional Indian society were condemned. The Hindu Caste system can be explored further in chapter 3 of the teachers' notes for *Exploring Hinduism*.

Sitting together and sharing food together is an effective way of putting into practice Sikh beliefs about equality.

The langar is also an important place for Sikhs to practise seva (service). As the story book illustrates, members of the Sikh community take turns doing jobs in the gurdwara, for example, cleaning, cooking, and washing up. Again, this reinforces the Sikh belief in equality because no one's status in society prevents service to others. God is present in every living thing.

Practising seva (service) to others is also a way of worshipping God. Focusing on the needs of others, rather than the self, trains a person to become less self-centred (manmukh) and more God-centred (gurmukh). Becoming God-centred is an essential part in the Sikh spiritual journey leading to union with God.

Activities

Practising equality

In the lesson directly before a religious education lesson, inform the class that you would like to conduct an experiment and you want their views on the experiment after it has been conducted.

Randomly divide pupils into groups and organise the desks to create clear segregation between the groups. Each group is given a different colour or shape to represent the group. Members of each group are given a sticker with the relevant label on it to stick on their school uniforms. The groups have to follow some basic rules. Different groups must not:

- talk to one another in the class room;
- share things with other groups (such as pencils, rubbers, rulers etc.).

Continue with the lesson, keeping to these rules. Towards the end of the lesson, inform pupils that you would like to extend this experiment to two other areas, and different groups should not:

- play together at break times;
- sit next to one another at lunch time.

In the RE lesson, which should follow directly after this lesson, read chapter 5 from the *Exploring Sikhism* story book. Ask pupils to feed back their views on the divisions created in their class. Link this to the divisions cited in the story book and the Sikh belief in equality for all. Sikhs show equality in their religious practices by taking it in turns to do basic jobs in the gurdwara, eating together, and sharing karah prashad together.

Put the desks and pupils back in their original places, removing their labels. Make some karah prashad (following the worksheet 'Make karah prashad') and share it among the class.

NB colours or shapes are used because they do not reinforce any conventional stereotype and the activity intentionally takes place over a short period of time.

Keywords

Baisakhi Sikh festival, marking the beginning of the new year and the founding of the Khalsa

chauri fan waved over the Guru Granth Sahib as a sign of respect

Five Ks the five symbols displayed by an initiated Sikh, each starting with K

granthi a person who looks after and reads from the Guru Granth Sahib

gurdwara Sikh place of worship, which houses the Guru Granth Sahib

gurmukh the ideal of being God-centred

guru religious teacher and guide

Guru Granth Sahib most important sacred book in Sikhism, also known as the Adi Granth

hukam God's guidance or command which comes from interpretation of the Guru Granth Sahib

Kachera one of the Five Ks: white shorts

Kangha one of the Five Ks: comb for keeping uncut hair tidy

Kara one of the Five Ks: bracelet

karma action: there is positive action (karma) and negative action (karma)

Kaur a title given to all Sikh females, meaning 'princess'

Kesh one of the Five Ks: uncut hair

Khalsa community of Sikhs who have undergone the initiation ceremony

khanda main symbol associated with Sikhism

Kirpan one of the Five Ks: sword

kirtan singing hymns to worship God

langar kitchen and dining area in a gurdwara

manmukh self-centred (in opposition to the ideal of being God-centred or gurmukh)

Nam Simran reciting God's name

seva serving others

Singh a title given to all Sikh males, meaning 'lion'

Waheguru one of the Sikh names for God, meaning 'Wonderful Lord'

Write a story

Imagine you have visited a gurdwara with a Sikh friend. Write a story about it, giving details of all the places you visited and the things you saw there. The pictures and descriptions below will help you.

flag

The Nishan Sahib (flag) flies over the gurdwara. It is a triangle of yellow cloth with a khanda.

shoe rack

As a sign of respect, dirty shoes are left near the entrance to the gurdwara.

wash room

Before worship, people wash their hands and cover their heads with scarves or caps.

ragis

Musicians sit on a low stage next to the takht. They might play tabla (= drums) and the baja (= harmonium).

takht (= throne)

The Guru Granth Sahib rests on a special platform, covered by a canopy. People bow or kneel in front of it when they enter the worship hall.

golak

In front of the takht is a long box on which people place offerings of food or money.

diwan hall

The worship hall may be decorated with tinsel or small lights. People sit on the carpet to learn and worship. Men and boys sit on one side; women and girls sit on the other.

kitchen & dining room

Sikhs take turns to prepare food and serve it to visitors to the gurdwara. They all eat together to show they are equal.

canopied bed

At the end of the day the Guru Granth Sahib is put to rest in a special room in a canopied bed. It is shown the same respect as a human guru would receive.

Make a Khanda

The Khanda is the Sikh emblem. Its name comes from the double-edged sword at its centre. It is found inside and outside of the gurdwara. It may be a picture on the flag or a model made out of brass or a wooden plaque. It is made from three separate symbols which teach the Sikh belief in God.

1. The ***Khanda*** is a special double-edged sword. It stands for God's power.
2. The ***Chakra*** is a circle with no beginning or end, just as Sikhs believe that there is one God with no beginning or end.
3. The ***Kirpans*** are two swords, to show both spiritual and earthly power. They remind the Sikhs that sometimes they need to fight for what is right.

You will need

pencil
construction card
glue
compass or template
cutting knife or scissors
foil

What to do

1. Draw the three separate parts of the Khanda on construction card. Use a compass or template to form the circle.
2. Cut out the sections and cover them with foil.
3. Glue the three sections together. (Most glues will not hold foil together well, so before gluing, you will need to remove small sections of foil where the parts touch. Glue straight onto the cardboard.)

Baisakhi Day

Read this story and fill in the missing words.

Sikhism was ___________ in about the year 1500 by Guru Nanak. Although he was brought up as a Hindu, he had a close Muslim friend and so he ___________ a lot about both religions. The Hindus and Muslims constantly ___________ about religion, and Nanak wished there was a simpler way to worship God. When he was about 30, he had a special experience that caused him to ___________ that God is everywhere and in every human heart, not just in special religious actions. He began to teach this.

Sikhs did not have an easy time. In the year 1699, two hundred years after Sikhism had been started, the Sikhs had been ___________ for over forty years because the Emperor of India did not ___________ their beliefs. Some Sikhs had been executed. Other Sikhs had begun to hide their beliefs. One man believed that it was time for Sikhs to ___________ courage and to be proud of their faith, even to ___________ for it if that was necessary.

When the Sikhs came together to ___________ the festival of Baisakhi Day, Guru Gobind Singh stood up and asked 'Will anyone here die for me? Who will prove their faith and ___________ me their head?' The crowd was silent, frightened at the thought. Finally one brave Sikh ___________ forward and was taken into the tent. A few minutes later Guru Gobind Singh walked out of the tent alone, his sword dripping with blood. He ___________ for more Sikhs ready to die for their faith. One by one, four more men walked into the tent. After each entrance the guru walked out with a dripping sword.

Many Sikhs left, horrified, ___________ their guru had gone mad. Those who stayed ___________, amazed, as the five Sikhs walked out of the tent dressed in pure white. They were alive! It had been a test of their courage and commitment to their faith. These five men ___________ the first members of the Khalsa. They ___________ a special uniform so that everyone would know they were Sikhs. They would be prepared to offer their lives to defend freedom and justice for all.

Since that day Sikhs no longer ___________ their faith. Men and women still ___________ the Khalsa and wear the special uniform, the five Ks, to proudly show that they are Sikhs and are prepared to ___________ for their faith. Baisakhi Day is a special time to ___________ this.

Words to use

accept	argued	asked	became	believe
celebrate	die	fight	hide	join
learnt	offer	remember	show	started
stepped	suffering	thinking	watched	wore

Dress Amrit Singh

Amrit Singh is a warrior of the Panj Pyare. On Baisakhi Day in each town or village, five men dress up in a special uniform to remind the people of the first five members of the Khalsa, who were prepared to give their lives for their guru.

What to do

1. Photocopy this page on thin card.
2. Colour Amrit, his clothes and the five Ks. Cut them out.
3. Dress Amrit as a warrior of the Panj Pyare.
4. Bend the support on the dotted lines to make him stand up.

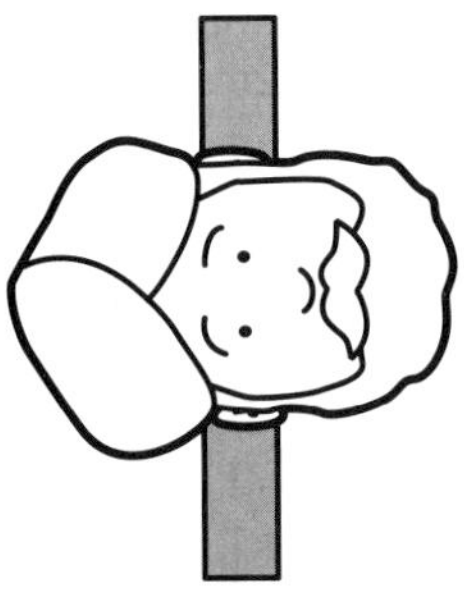

Kesh

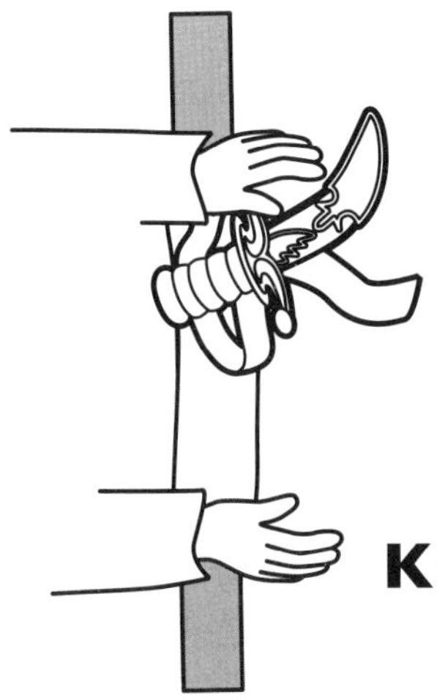

Kirpan

Kachera

Colour the robes and turban bright yellow. Colour the sashes blue.

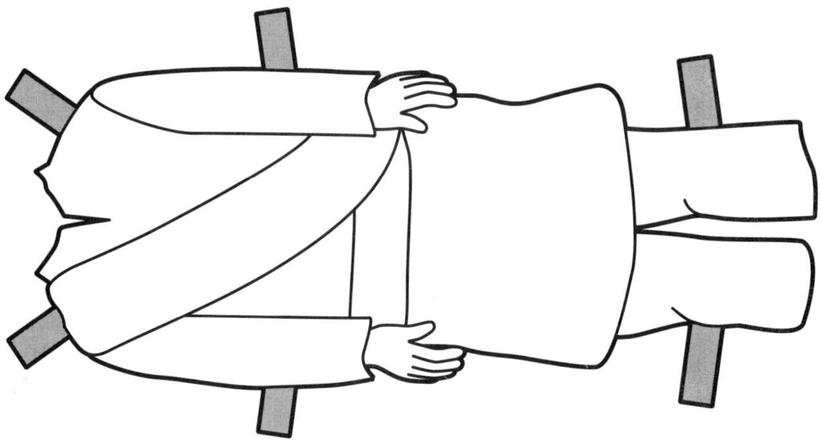

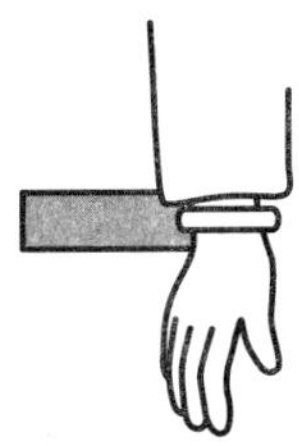

Kara

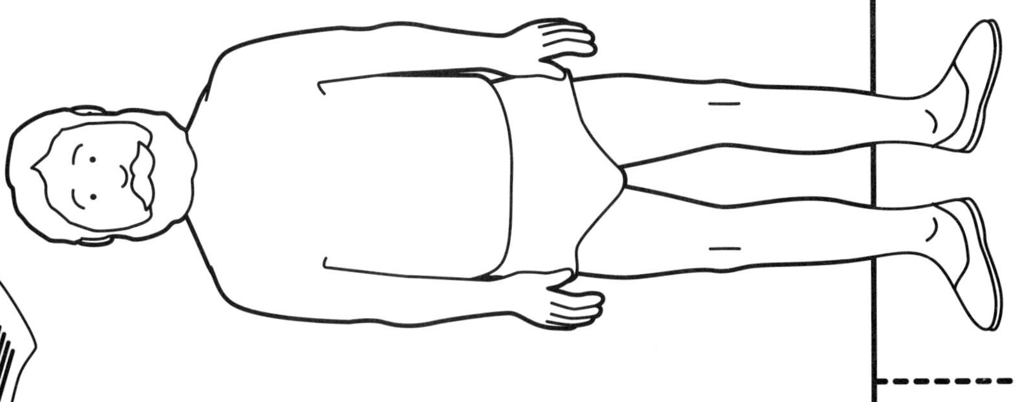

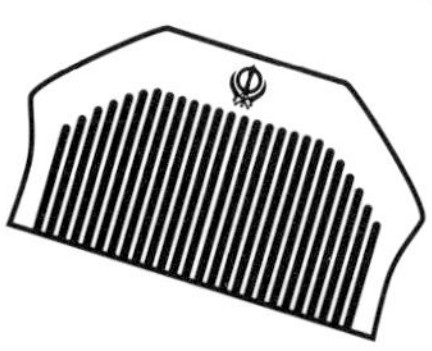

Kangha

Make a picture frame

Sikhs consider the ten gurus to be very important to them as their guides in life. Often they display pictures of the gurus in the gurdwara or in their homes.

Who is important to you? Who do you look to as a guide to how to live? Find a photo or draw a picture of that person and display it in a special picture frame.

You will need

- construction card
- craft knife
- decoration
- scissors
- glue

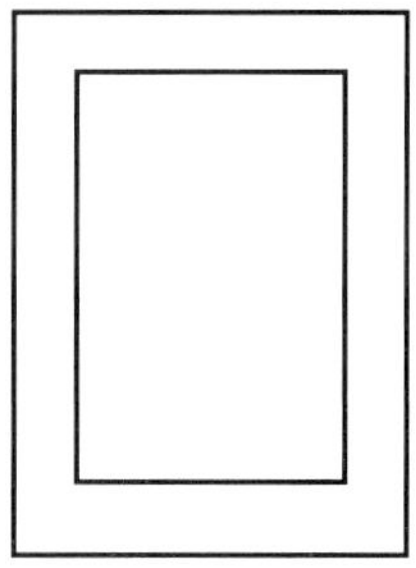

What to do

1. Cut out a frame from cardboard. Choose a size and shape to match your picture. The opening needs to be slightly smaller than your picture.

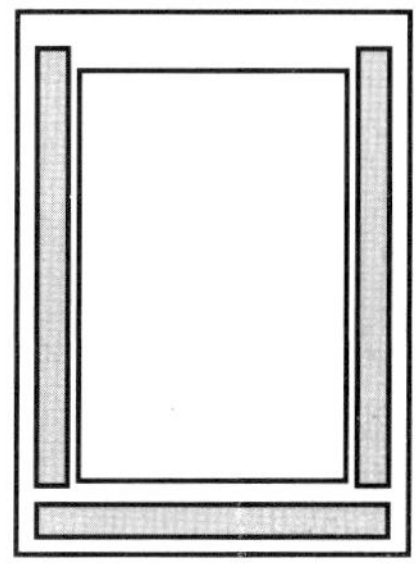

2. Glue strips of card to three sides on the back of the frame. These are spacers to allow room for your picture to fit. One side is left open for inserting the picture.

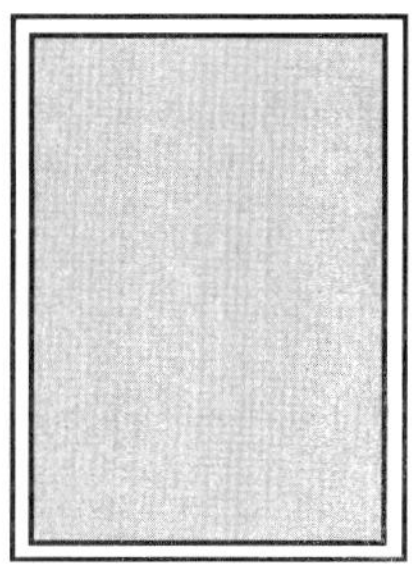

3. Cut a piece of card for the back of the frame. Glue this to the three spacers. (If your frame shows signs of warping from the glue, leave it to dry overnight in a plastic bag underneath heavy books.)

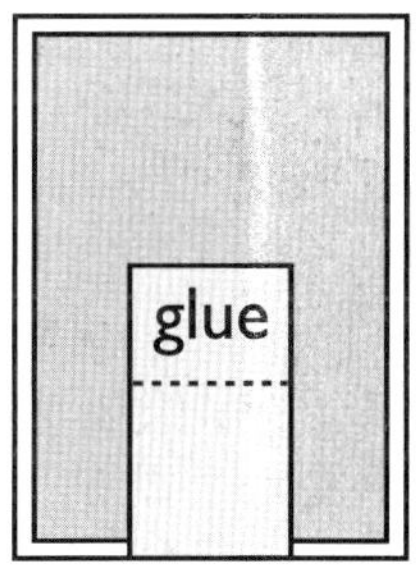

4. Make a stand for the frame. Cut out a rectangle of heavy card. Fold it one-third of the way down. Glue this fold to the back of the frame.

5. Decorate the frame. You could paint it or cover it with strips of foil. For a 2-D effect, decorate it with strips of foil of a different colour after your base colour is on. For a 3-D effect, dip string in PVA glue and arrange it decoratively on the frame, or glue on pasta shapes before painting. (If you want the frame spray-painted with gold or silver, it is best for an adult to do this outside, because of the fumes.)

Guides in life

Sikhs have gurus who guide them on their journey towards God, Waheguru. Ten gurus are human guides. The last guru is a book guide called the Guru Granth Sahib. Whenever Sikhs need help and guidance on how to live, they ask the Guru Granth Sahib.

We have many guides in life, too. Read what the children below say about their guides in life. Cut out the boxes and arrange them in order of importance to you. Discuss your choice in a small group. Complete the empty box with information about your own guide in life.

Ryan's guide in life is a pop star.
My favourite pop star has an exciting life. He has a great voice and lots of money. All the clothes, cars and parties must be fun!

Catrin's guide in life is a friend who is very ill.
My friend is very brave. She is always smiling and happy. She shows me that people can be brave even when things are difficult.

Peter's guide in life is a club leader.
My karate club leader is always doing sponsored bike rides and marathons to raise money for different charities. He uses his skills to help other people.

Gareth's guide in life is a religious leader in his place of worship.
My vicar helps me to understand God better and how to live my life in a way that makes God happy.

Sara's guide in life is a family member.
My grandmother always has time for me. She tells me stories and listens to me. She is very wise because she has been alive for a long time.

Caron's guide in life is a teacher.
My teacher knows a lot about all kinds of subjects. She can answer almost every difficult question. If she does not know the answer, she knows where to look to find it.

Tomos' guide in life is a sports star.
My favourite sports star practises hard to be one of the best in his sport. It must feel good to win a medal in a competition!

My guide in life is ____________

____

____

____

____

Care for the world

Why?

Sikhs believe that it is important to look after the world because it belongs to Waheguru. Discuss with your friends why you think it is important to look after the world. Write four reasons below.

1. ______________________________

____

2. ______________________________

____

3. ______________________________

____

4. ______________________________

____

How?

Sanjit and Yasmin mentioned many ways that Sikhs care for the world. Write these below and add in any other ways that you can think of.

______________________ ______________________

______________________ ______________________

______________________ ______________________

______________________ ______________________

What can you do?

1. Choose one way of caring for the world.
2. Design and make a poster about it.
3. Display your poster around the school or at home.
4. Plan how to do it. You may need to discuss it with your family or talk to your friends about doing what the poster says.

Save water

Turn off dripping taps.

Ripples in the world

If we throw a stone into a lake we make circles of ripples that spread outwards. Everything we do is like this. Our actions affect the people around us. Our actions affect the world we live in.

Draw yourself in the smallest circle. Write or draw on the ripples the things you can do to make a difference for good to the people or places mentioned.

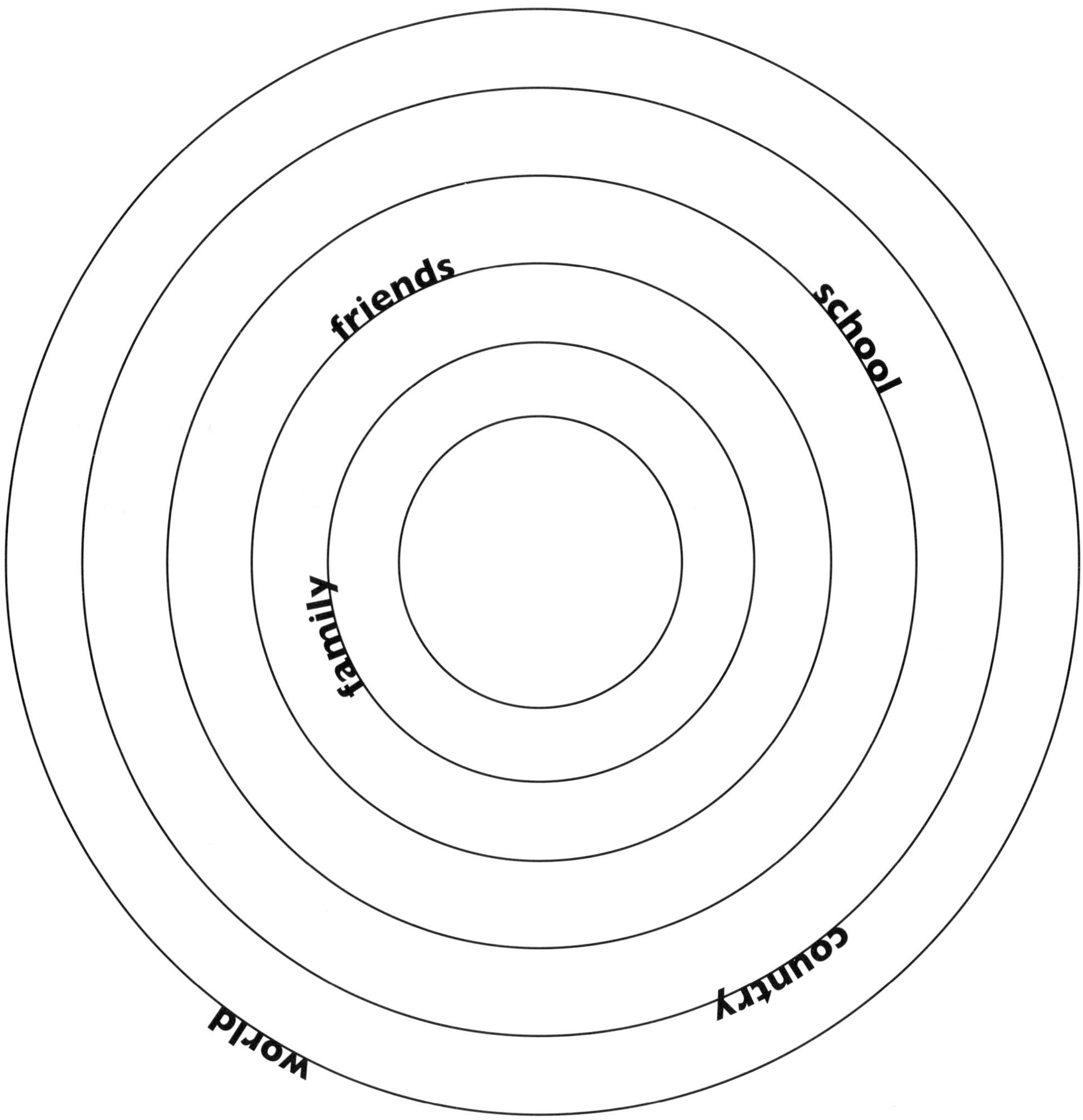

Write a poem

The Guru Granth Sahib (the holy book of the Sikhs) contains many hymns or poems written by the gurus. Here is one poem from the Guru Granth Sahib about the wonders of the world that God created.

Humans, trees, holy places
Coasts, clouds, fields
Islands, continents, universes
Spheres and solar systems
Life-forms - egg-born, womb-born,
earth-born, sweat-born
Only God knows their existence
In oceans, mountains, everywhere
Nanak says God created them
And God takes care of them all.

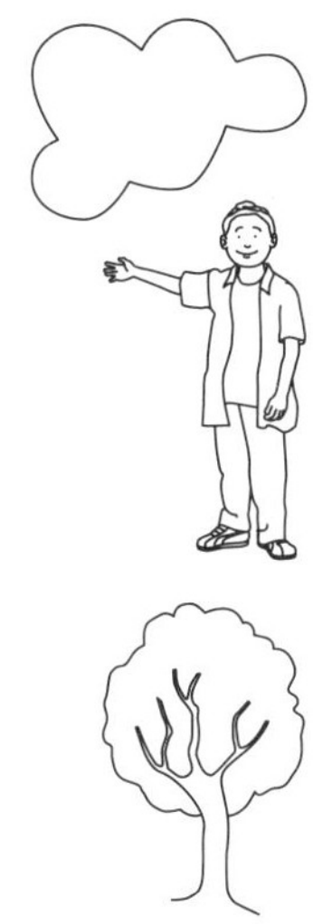

What to do

1. Write your own poem about the wonders of this world. Use this page to begin your first draft.
2. Copy your poem onto best paper and decorate it with a border of things you have written about.

My poem - *first draft*

Make karah prashad

Karah prashad means holy sweet. This is shared with everyone at the end of Sikh services. It is a sign that all are equal.

You will need

- 1 cup sugar
- 1 cup semolina
- 1 cup unsalted butter
- ½ cup water

What to do

1. Melt the butter in a saucepan over a low heat.
2. Add the semolina, stirring carefully. Keep stirring while it cooks for a few minutes until it is golden brown.
3. Mix in the sugar and water. Keep stirring it over a low heat until it is thick.
4. Leave it to cool.
5. Share it with other people. Remember that karah prashad is a sweet to share, not to eat alone.

Plan a role play

Imagine the visit of Rees and Sara, or two other children, to the kitchen and dining room of a gurdwara. What would they see? What would people be doing? Set up a role play of the scene.

One way to start

1. Work out all the jobs that are needed in the kitchen and dining room to keep it running.
2. Give these jobs to children in your group or class. Work out the actions needed. Other children can act out eating in the dining room.
3. Decide which part of the classroom or hall will be which part of the kitchen and dining room.
4. Plan your role play, perhaps with 'Aled and Sian' asking people what they are doing and why they are doing it.

Our play

roles	actors	location

My dictionary

You will meet many new words in *Exploring Sikhism*. Some of these will be English words and some will be Punjabi words. Keep a record of them, along with their meanings.

gurdwara	the place where Sikhs go to learn about Waheguru and to worship; it means 'Guru's door'
Waheguru	the Sikh name for God; it means 'Wonderful Lord'
guru	teacher and guide; a guru teaches about Waheguru and shows how Waheguru wants people to live
________	________________________
________	________________________
________	________________________
________	________________________
________	________________________
________	________________________
________	________________________
________	________________________
________	________________________
________	________________________
________	________________________
________	________________________
________	________________________

Write an article

Use the computer to write your own article about the Sikh gurdwara. Include headings, borders and pictures. These reminders will help you in your planning.

The gurdwara

Begin with your heading. Experiment to find the style you like best. Try WordArt or look at different fonts on the computer. Do you want it bold, italic, centred, coloured, large or small? Try out different combinations.

Diwan hall

Plan your article. You might find it easier to write about three or four different parts of the gurdwara, with a heading for each. You could choose the wash room, the diwan hall, the kitchen and the bed for the Guru Granth Sahib.

Think about the layout of your article. You could have it all across the page or you could choose to put part of it in two columns. Do you want each section of writing to have a picture next to it or underneath it? Experiment with different layouts.

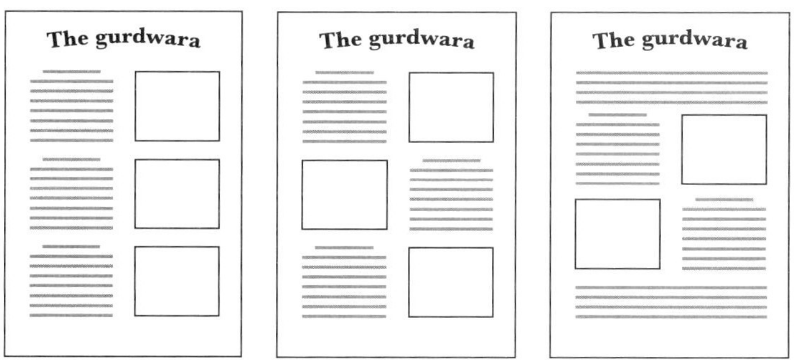

Your article will look best with a combination of writing and pictures. Find a picture in Clip Art or on the internet, or draw your own and scan it into your computer.

You might want to add some important information or a comment that you want to stand out. Put it in a border. You could give the address of the gurdwara closest to your home, or write how many gurdwaras there are in Wales or in the United Kingdom. If you know someone who worships at a gurdwara, ask for a personal comment. Find some interesting information to make your article more personal or more exciting.

Find the places

Find the places that Aled and Sian visited in the story.

Aunty Hafwen lives in the 
She lives at (2 , 8).

Sanjit and Yasmin live in the 
They live at (__ , __).

The gurdwara is the 
It is at (__ , __).

The cinema is the 
It is at (__ , __).

The planetarium is the 
It is at (__ , __).

The bottle and paper bank is the 
It is at (__ , __).

Draw the park. 
It is at (5 , 9).

Draw the bus to send them home. 
It is at (9 , 1).

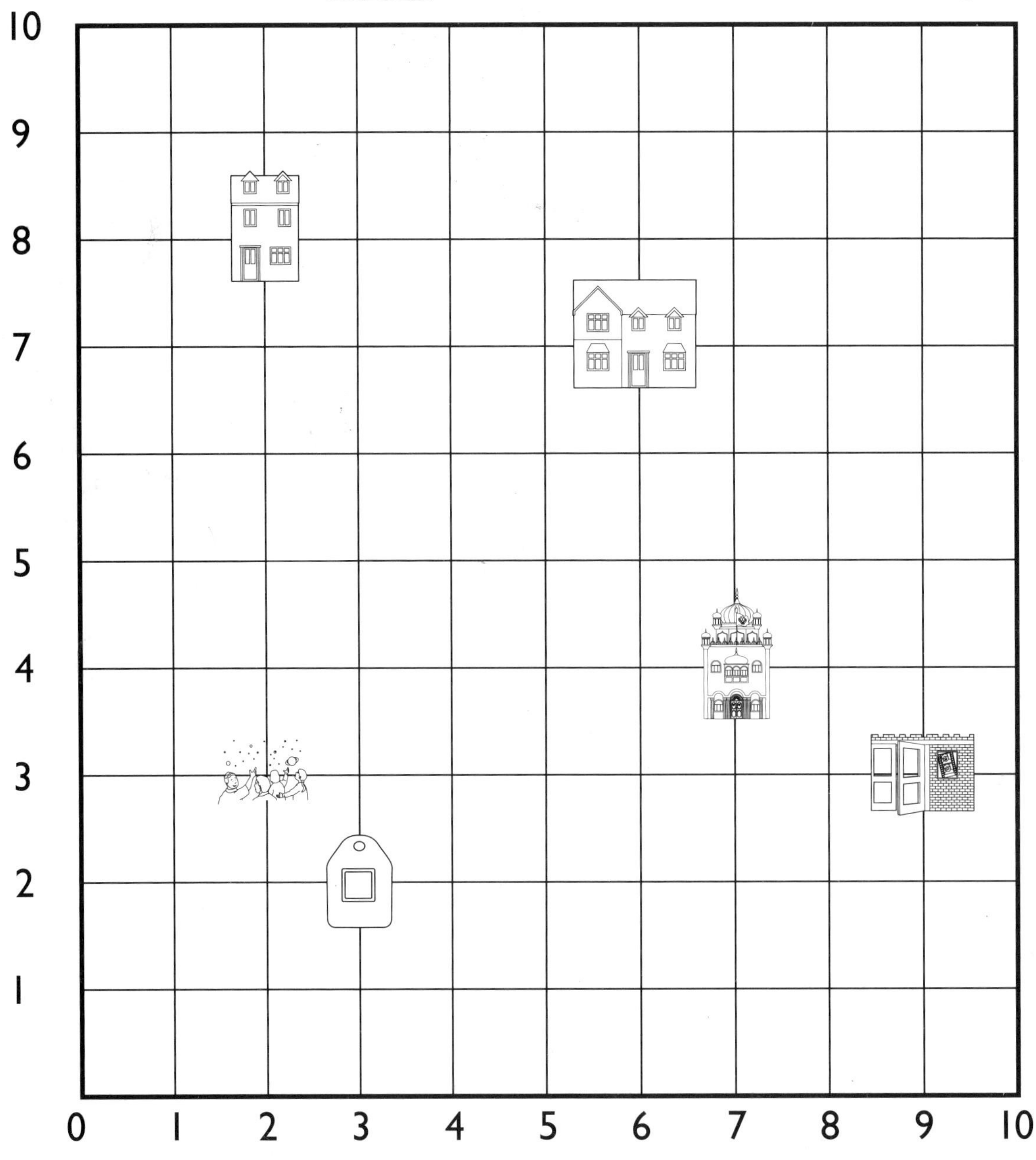